To the FMM Sisters,

With gratitude for your lovely
hospitality

The Silent Book

Bernadette T Wallis

2017

Limerick

The Silent Book

A Deaf Family and the Disappearing Australian-Irish Sign Language

For Hudson
Great grandson of Don and Kathleen

Bernadette T Wallis

First published 2016 in Melbourne, Victoria, Australia

Cataloguing-in-Publication is available from the National Library of Australia
http://catalogue.nla.gov.au

Wallis, Bernadette T

The Silent Book
A Deaf Family and the Disappearing Australian-Irish Sign Language

ISBN 978-0-646-95494-3

Proceeds of this book will go to
The John Wallis Foundation

www.missionarysisters.org.au
www.johnwallisfoundation.org.au

Cover Design: The Wonga pigeon, the Waratah and dragonfly are from two Aboriginal Dreamtime stories. The Australian-Irish signed alphabet letters, 'D' and 'K' for Donald and Kathleen signed by Bernadette Rebbechi. Special thanks to Michael Rebbechi for his creative design.

Poems: All of the poems are from the private collection of Bernadette T Wallis.

Photos: Photos are from Family collections, the archives of the Christian Brothers, the Dominican Sisters, the Missionary Sisters of Service and where specifically indicated for individual photos.

CONTENTS

FOREWORD

It is an honour for me to write this Foreword for Bernadette. Over a number of generations, members of her family have been friends with members of my family. While I alas never met her parents Don and Kathleen Wallis, I knew her aunt Marie Fulton (Wallis) and uncle Charlie Wallis, who were actually pioneers of their own community in Melbourne. Her aunt Valerie still lives in Melbourne. I would like to acknowledge these people in this Foreword.

I really appreciate how Bernadette has highlighted two hidden aspects of Australian history. She has wondered about the Indigenous history of the land on which this written history has taken place, and she has also written a personal history of a language and cultural community of which very little has been written. It is my hope that others including myself will be able to build on this work, in recording the history of the Australian-Irish Deaf community.

Australian-Irish Sign Language (AISL) arrived in Australia in 1875 with the arrival of Sister Mary Gabriel Hogan, a Deaf nun in Newcastle, along with five hearing nuns. She brought with her the Irish Sign Language, which flourished in a minority Sign language community in Australia. Australia is in the unique position of having two Sign languages, the majority Sign language, and AISL, the minority Sign language. A community flourished with the establishment of schools for Deaf children in the Catholic education system in Newcastle and Castle Hill, Sydney, and later at Portsea, Victoria. Catholic Deaf clubs were established in the major cities and until the Dominican Sisters and Christian Brothers decided to stop using AISL in schools in the early 1950s, this Sign language community flourished.

My doctoral studies were on the contact between AISL and Auslan. AISL in Australia has been the subject of oppression on a number of fronts. Its use is now restricted to conversations between school friends, family members and spouses. It is no longer used as a Sign language of instruction in Catholic schools, and has not been for many years. AISL is also no longer used in the religious domain by hearing priests or chaplains who now use Auslan. The use of AISL was actively discouraged in Australian Deaf Clubs. This linguistic and cultural oppression parallels that of spoken language minority communities. The Dominican Sisters and Christian Brothers published the last dictionary of the language in 1942. There are, however, wonderful stories of the older Brothers and Sisters using AISL with Deaf staff and students behind closed doors after the decision to stop signing in schools. Everyone loves a subversive story about Sign language use!

While the history of the schools, the teachers and pupils has been well documented and more is required to be done, the actual language documentation of AISL is now taking place. For the history of the AISL community, its characters and its activities being recorded, Bernadette's memoirs are a wonderful starting point and it is my hope that this will continue.

At the time of writing this Foreword I have just returned to London after four weeks in Australia, during which I had the opportunity to drive from Melbourne to Sydney (via Albury) and from Sydney to Melbourne (via Wagga Wagga and Corowa). It struck me how different the Australian bush and country is from Ireland, and particularly how different the climate is. I can only reflect on how very brave Sister Mary Gabriel Hogan was to come to such a hostile and different place to found a new Deaf community.

I commend this book to you, and I thank Bernadette very much for her most valuable work. I know that her parents would be very proud of her. I know that her sisters, aunts, uncles, cousins and Deaf friends are all very proud of her too.

Robert Adam, BEd., BA., M.App Ling
London, February 2016

Silent Sound

Can you watch a raging sea crashing
    against the rocks and hear silence?

Can you stand on the railway platform
    and through the tunnel
    hear the silent roar of the train speeding
    as the wind presses against your body?

Can you bodily hear music
    through the timber dance floor of the old church hall
    or the organ strongly played in the parquetry-floored chapel?

Can you hear as you sit to watch the silent television
    the passing by of the rubbish truck
    through the vibrations in the arms of the redwood chair?

Can you walk slowly along the beach
    and in the silence visually hear
    the ebb and flow of waves that never stop?

Can your tiny baby's eyes tell you in the silence
    that she can hear the dog bark outside
    or that someone rang the doorbell?

Can you smell the silent tractor in the evening air
    and know your husband returns home
    before your children can hear it?

Can you feel around your child's fingers and hands
    in the silent darkness
    and know the thoughts being conveyed to you?

Can you hear the silence of hands wildly clapping you
    as you receive your trophies in life?

Heightened senses bring fullness
Consciousness beyond all telling.

Bernadette T. Wallis

INTRODUCTION

I acknowledge the traditional and original peoples of the land in Australia and I pay my deep respect to them, especially those where my grandmothers and grandfathers and my parents lived, and where I also lived in Australia.

Throughout this book, themes of the Indigenous peoples with two Dreamtime stories and of flowing rivers are featured. Rivers flow and connect peoples and stories. They are the lifeblood, the veins of this body of land Australia, where human endeavours flourish interdependent with the Land itself – where my ancestors drew life and nourishment.

The book tells the story of my mother and father as Deaf people in the context of their lives in Victoria, their schooling in New South Wales in the 1920s and their adult lives. I bring to the fore the rural environment that surrounded their lives as children in their families and as adults in rural Australia.

When I started writing the book out of an urge to tell my parents' story, there was more. It became a passion when I realised the importance of recording the history of their language, Australian-Irish Sign Language, and how and why it came into Australia.

Australian-Irish Sign Language was introduced into Australia in the nineteenth century through Sister Gabriel Hogan, a Dominican religious sister who was deaf herself. She was appointed to teach Deaf children, so a school was eventually established in Waratah, NSW. As the population in Australia was increasing, and so too the Catholic population, there was an increase in the number of Deaf children.

Protestant based Denominational schools for Deaf children had also begun in Sydney and Melbourne, using British Sign Language. The Catholic community was strongly committed to providing a Catholic education for its children, including for its Deaf children. Since the community was largely Irish-born or of Irish descent and many of its teachers educated in Ireland, it was inevitable that in the Catholic system Deaf children would be educated through Irish Sign Language. (This is aside from any question of technical or expressive preference for AISL.)

Since greater numbers of Deaf children attended the Denominational schools, their Deaf language became the dominant language in Australia, which later became known as Auslan, Australian Sign Language. The Australian-Irish Sign Language ceased being taught in 1953. So, like many Indigenous languages, it is fast disappearing from consciousness.

As I visited the buildings of the residential schools where my parents were educated, I readily recalled the stories they had told of the settings, their friends and teachers. I was helped significantly through the archival material of the Dominican Sisters, the Christian Brothers and the Waratah section in the University of Newcastle, where much of the material from the Deaf School at Waratah is held. I had discussions with Sisters, Brothers and many significant people from the Deaf community. For many years I worked in a Catholic organisation, the John Pierce Centre for pastoral ministry with the Deaf community in Melbourne Victoria. This gave me a greater understanding and experience of the Deaf world and the children of Deaf parents, especially hearing children in these families, who were like myself. I have researched some historical developments of the education of Deaf children in Spain, France and Ireland. These historical developments provide the backdrop to the Australian story.

Dividing the book into three parts presents the story thus: Part I is about the first part of my parents' lives up until they leave school; Part II picks up the story that leads them into adulthood and family life in the world of the twentieth century. Part III, through my discovery of my Deaf heritage, enlightens the reader as to the story of Australian-Irish Sign Language and the journey of the language through the Catholic education system in Australia. I also briefly include some aspects of the story of the Catholic Deaf Associations in Victoria, especially in relation to my family's story. Some people are mentioned at specific times of change. Part I and Part II are written in the present tense giving some immediacy to the story. In Part III, I settled for the use of past tense as I explain my story of discovery of a wonderful heritage.

I have not attempted to give a full history of the intricate and complex global Deaf story – nor of the Deaf story in Australia, including Auslan, Australian Sign Language. The focus is on my parents in the Catholic setting and their language – Australian-Irish Sign Language and its journey. I believe, however, that this narrow focus illuminates a larger picture.

Not being a professional linguist in Sign languages or Australian-Irish Sign Language, I have not attempted to write from that perspective; but you will occasionally read of the complex movement of fingers, hands and body as I describe in writing the elements of a visual living language. I hope this book is a valuable source of education for the Deaf community as well as the general community.

TERMINOLOGY

Castle Hill

Sometimes the St Gabriel's School for Deaf Boys at Castle Hill was referred to as *Castle Hill*, but it is more commonly identified in the Deaf community as *St Gabriel's*. Thus, I have used *St Gabriel's* throughout this book to identify the school.

Coda

Children of Deaf Adults (Coda) is an organisation that brings together hearing adults who have Deaf parent(s). Although it is also open to Deaf adults with Deaf parents, they are in the minority.

Combined Method

In education, this refers to both the use of Sign Language and teaching lip reading and speech training for children who have some hearing and where it assists with their communication skills.

Deaf Community

I use upper case 'D' when identifying the community that identifies itself with this title which is primarily made up of Deaf people, partially Deaf people and those associated with the community who may not be deaf, e.g. parents/families of Deaf children, children of Deaf parents, teachers and interpreters.

Deaf Person

I made the decision to use upper case 'D' when referring to a person who is deaf or partially deaf and who further identifies herself/himself with the Deaf community. This is common practice in the Deaf community.

Hearing People

This term refers to people who can hear and who are not deaf. This term is in common usage in the Deaf community.

Home Signs

'Home signs' are signs designed in the intimacy of ordinary family life where there is a Deaf child.

Kathleen

Sometimes in this book Kathleen is called Girlie or Aunty Kath especially in stories that relate to her siblings and nieces and nephews.

Oralism

In education, this refers to using lip reading and speech with no use of Sign Language.

Sign Languages

A number of different Sign Languages are referred to in this book e.g. Irish Sign Language, Australian-Irish Sign Language, French Sign Language, American Sign Language, British Sign Language and the dominant Sign language in Australia – Auslan (Australian Sign Language). Because Auslan is strongly based on British Sign Language and because Australian Sign Language was not named as Auslan until 1986, I have sometimes used the phrase *based on British Sign* or used *Auslan* referring to the dominant Sign language in Australia and depending on the context. The common terminology in the past was the *Two-handed Sign Language* (based on the fingerspelling in British Sign Language) and the *One-handed Sign Language* (based on the fingerspelling in Irish Sign Language.)

Waratah

Waratah is a suburb of Newcastle situated five kilometres from the city centre. However, throughout this book I have used it to identify the Dominican school for Deaf children at Waratah, which had a number of titles throughout its history. The Deaf community identifies the school with the sign for *Waratah*.

FAMILY TREE

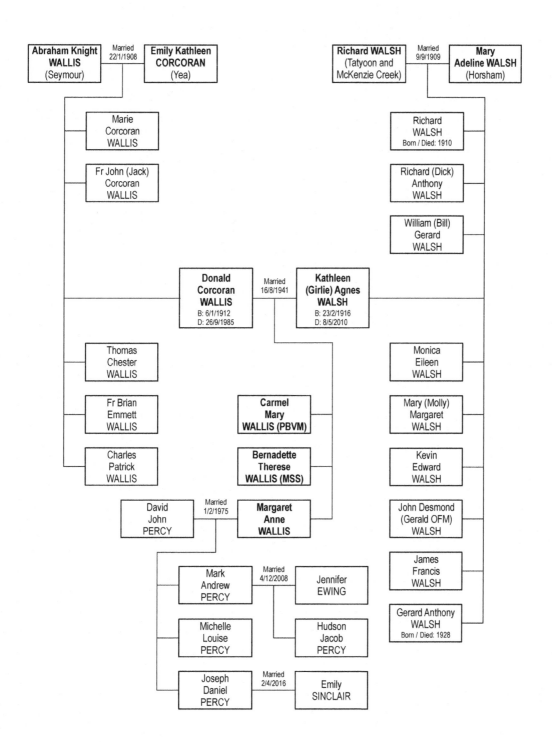

Abraham Knight **WALLIS** (Seymour) — Married 22/1/1908 — Emily Kathleen **CORCORAN** (Yea)

Marie Corcoran WALLIS

Fr John (Jack) Corcoran WALLIS

Richard **WALSH** (Tatyoon and McKenzie Creek) — Married 9/9/1909 — **Mary Adeline WALSH** (Horsham)

Richard WALSH Born / Died: 1910

Richard (Dick) Anthony WALSH

William (Bill) Gerard WALSH

Donald Corcoran WALLIS B: 6/1/1912 D: 26/9/1985 — Married 16/8/1941 — **Kathleen (Girlie) Agnes WALSH** B: 23/2/1916 D: 8/5/2010

Thomas Chester WALLIS

Monica Eileen WALSH

Fr Brian Emmett WALLIS

Carmel Mary WALLIS (PBVM)

Mary (Molly) Margaret WALSH

Charles Patrick WALLIS

Bernadette Therese WALLIS (MSS)

Kevin Edward WALSH

David John PERCY — Married 1/2/1975 — **Margaret Anne WALLIS**

John Desmond (Gerald OFM) WALSH

Mark Andrew PERCY — Married 4/12/2008 — Jennifer EWING

James Francis WALSH

Michelle Louise PERCY

Hudson Jacob PERCY

Gerard Anthony WALSH Born / Died: 1928

Joseph Daniel PERCY — Married 2/4/2016 — Emily SINCLAIR

REGIONAL MAP

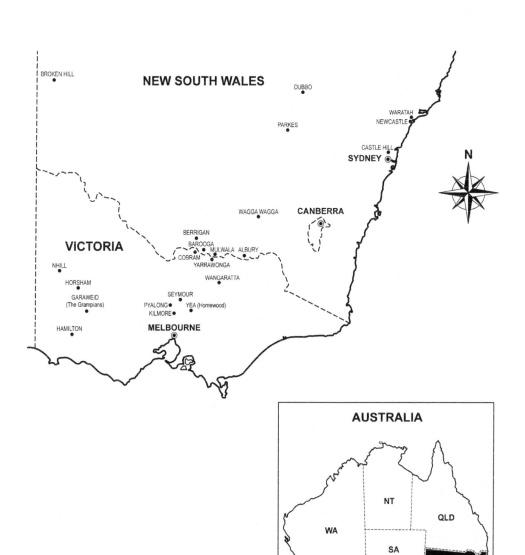

BROKEN HILL

NEW SOUTH WALES

DUBBO

WARATAH
NEWCASTLE

PARKES

CASTLE HILL
SYDNEY

N

WAGGA WAGGA

CANBERRA

BERRIGAN
BAROOGA
VICTORIA   MULWALA ALBURY
COBRAM
NHILL   YARRAWONGA

HORSHAM   WANGARATTA
GARAWEID   SEYMOUR
(The Grampians)   PYALONG   YEA (Homewood)
                  KILMORE
HAMILTON
MELBOURNE

AUSTRALIA

NT
QLD
WA

SA

NSW
VIC

TAS

PART I

Chapters 1 – 7

THE CHILDHOOD STORY

CHAPTER 1

MEETING AT THE MURRAY

Near the River

On the bush floor

In the undergrowth

Two Wonga pigeons

Seal their silent love

Forever

It is early 1936. The strong young tailor, Donald Corcoran Wallis, propels himself with one arm as he swims from the Victorian into the New South Wales side across the treacherous Murray River. His other arm is raised high protecting his self-tailored suit – keeping it dry. He emerges from the river as the ever-present dragonflies flit further downstream.

This is *Pangerang* Country where various Aboriginal tribes lived in concert with kookaburras, goannas, river gums, extensive wetlands and big skies. People of the district routinely find tools and artefacts that show the previous existence of many Aboriginal communities along the Murray River.

On the NSW side of the river, Don dresses in his suit and makes his way along a rough track around the river wetlands and through the trees to the dirt road. He looks at the rough mud map again to guide him to his destination. The homestead which he seeks cannot be seen at first but with blind faith he walks further on along the road and up the slope. The homestead, *Carlyle*, appears and he prepares himself for his first encounter with the occupants of the household – and more especially with a young woman whom he plans to visit.

As he approaches on this sunny morning, the homestead dogs bark and dance around excitedly alerting everyone's attention to the approaching stranger – everyone but the young woman. Two eager boys emerge from the house to discover the young man walking down the driveway. They engage with him and quickly realise that their twenty-year old sister should be summoned. After all she is the object of this venture – she is the reason he has travelled this significant distance from the Goulburn River at Seymour on a well-used and non-geared bike.

The tall handsome twenty-five-year old man is silent. He points towards himself and introduces himself to the young girl with his hands and fingers. He forms them into the hand shape of a 'D' that transitions quickly to an 'O' hand shape to pointing two fingers, the index and middle fingers, outwards forming an 'N' – D-O-N, Don. He has introduced himself with the sign name and identifier used by his Deaf friends and the community. She nods and smiles and raises her hand – the tips of her middle finger and her thumb touch one another with her other fingers stretched out. It forms a 'K', her palm turns upwards and the backs of the hands bump together twice. In pointing to herself she identifies herself as Kathleen Agnes Walsh. Just as Don includes the letter 'D' from the Australian-Irish Sign Language in his identifier, Kathleen uses the letter 'K' as part of her identifier.[1]

The exchange between Don and Kathleen is initially tentative but soon eyes dance, and arms, hands and fingers glide about. Both communicate in Australian-Irish Sign Language, the *One-handed* Sign Language. School stories are exchanged and mutual acquaintances are discovered – there is common ground.

They explore the farm – they walk together through the sheds and the dairy. Facing one another to communicate, they pause at the stables housing the teams of Clydesdale horses so important to life on the farm. Kathleen is proud as she shows Don the impressive new sheep yards and explains the nearby newly dug Mulwala canal that will flow from the Murray River through the countryside. She tells him about life on the Walsh farm and how, as well as helping her father, she spends hours in the dairy separating cream and making butter.

Don shares his rural life experiences, his love of horses, of hunting rabbits and of chasing foxes. He also shares about his life as a tailor in the city of Melbourne. They slowly walk back to the house, stopping often so they can turn to face each other again, so they can communicate – there are many questions between them.

Kathleen's mother, Mary Adeline, stands on the verandah and watches in silent amazement at the sparkle between her daughter and the visitor. She watches the ease in their communication. Her father, Richard, leans on the fence and puffs on his pipe. Feigning indifference, he furtively watches his daughter interact with the young man. He unsuccessfully attempts to disguise a grin that reflects the joy in his heart. The siblings keep a respectful distance – even they realise that this is not an occasion to insert themselves between the visitor and their sister. The family finds it easy to extend hospitality to this stranger, who communicates so effortlessly with their daughter. Don stays on this side of the river for the night as he shares the evening with the family – it is too late this night to swim across the river to his camp.

---

[1] It is the prerogative of the Deaf community to give a Sign name to a person as their identifier.

So how has this visit come about? Don's mother, Emma, aware of the social challenge for her son to find a suitable girl as a life partner who can communicate with him, has been on a matchmaking venture. At Deaf functions she constantly scans the gathering for a potential matchmaking opportunity. In Sydney she strikes gold when she ever so briefly meets Kathleen at the Deaf school reunion she attends with her daughter Marie. She bides her time and carefully puts to Don the inviting challenge that is almost a command:

Don, you must go and visit a young girl that I met at the Waratah reunion. She lives in the country across the Murray between Mulwala and Barooga. She has no Deaf people nearby. Her family sign but there is no-one she can communicate fluently with. Her social life is really limited – she needs Deaf people in her life. Go and see her!

Don's response is to obey. On his return journey to Melbourne where he works, Don stops overnight in Seymour where Emma runs Wallis' Café on the Hume Highway. He reports to his mother on his visit – she smiles – Don is very happy to repeat the pastoral visit – again and again. The friendship develops. Don and Kathleen both understand the travails of travel from their school years and it is not long before Kathleen becomes very familiar

ST. GABRIEL'S SCHOOL FOR DEAF BOYS, Castle Hill, N.S.W.

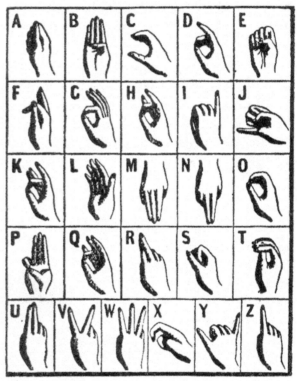

THE MANUAL ALPHABET (Single Hand)

with the route to Seymour and on to Melbourne. Don, in turn, finds the best bike route to the Murray.

They cultivate their friendship in the face of the tyranny of distance. Finding telegrams too expensive, surface mail and actually writing letters too painstaking and too slow, and personal telephone calls pointless, nothing takes the place of face-to-face interaction. And how do they organise such meetings between them? Family members, especially their mothers, become more and more active as messengers. While expensive and far from ubiquitous in *Pangerang* Country, the telephone is required. Kathleen and her mother go to town and squeeze into the red telephone box in the street to make the long distance telephone calls necessary to arrange meetings between the young friends. Emma at her end with Don speaks to Mary Adeline and between the mothers they translate messages to and from their young adult children – until a clear and satisfactory arrangement is negotiated for them to meet the next time.[2]

It is not long before the mothers of both Don and Kathleen meet. They share the story of discovering that their children were deaf. They discuss their common understanding of the parenting of Deaf children. More particularly, they discuss the future for Kathleen and Don.

Don's mother is a creative and forthright business woman while Kathleen's mother is family oriented, kind, hospitable and reserved. It is not as easy for their fathers to meet. They are caught up in the ongoing tasks of farm work and travel is slow.

While Don is frustrated that his father, Abraham, never learns to sign, he knows the kind eyes that focus on him. Kathleen loves her father and while he does not sign formally, they interact and communicate very well in their own way. A hard life on the land takes its toll on both of the fathers. Abe is already in his seventies and Richard struggles with a large family to provide for. Both of them will die within eight years of this first meeting between Don and Kathleen.

* * *

An important joyful occasion is reported in *The Argus Newspaper* in Melbourne on Saturday, 24 August 1940: *The engagement is announced of Kathleen Agnes, eldest daughter of Mr. and Mrs. R. Walsh, Carlyle, Mt. Gwynne, Mulwala (NSW), to Donald Corcoran, second son of Mr. and Mrs. A. K. Wallis, Wirrabong, Homewood.*

St Joseph's Church, Barooga NSW

Kathleen is now wearing a diamond engagement ring, which Don has proudly chosen for her. On 16 August 1941, five years after they meet, Kathleen Agnes Walsh and Donald Corcoran Wallis marry in St Joseph's Church on the hill at Barooga on the NSW side of the Murray River. Kathleen looks stunning dressed in her sister's bridal gown with some adjustments to make it appear unique as though it

---

[2] Mail was only delivered to *Carlyle* homestead once a week, so by the time a letter made its way from Melbourne, upwards of two weeks could have passed.

is designed especially for her. The handsomely attired and very nervous Don stands near the altar at the front of the Church, while he awaits the bride's graceful entrance.

Neither Don nor the bride can hear the organ played from the back of the Church. To the joy of the captivated extended family crowd, Kathleen walks elegantly down the aisle on her loving father's arm and shyly smiles stealing a glance towards her gentle and lady-like mother for encouragement. She focuses her eyes on the young man whom she loves with all her heart. As her veil is lifted from her face Don looks directly towards her with pride.

Don's sister Marie and brother Chester, and Kathleen's sister Molly and her brother Bill are the bridesmaids and groomsmen. As they settle into their positions, kneeling at the front of the little Church, Molly makes sure Kathleen's gown flows softly over her shoes and then takes the flower posy, so her sister's hands are free for receiving the ring, signing her vows and writing her signature on the marriage documentation.

Kathleen turns her gaze and looks up at the priest celebrant, Jack – Don's brother. He faces her and smiles an assuring *Yes, all is well*. She will be good for Don, he thinks – a wonderful companion and practical supporter. He ineptly communicates in Sign but well enough to set the couple at ease. He will say the prayers and readings, and guide them through the ceremony – there is no interpreter. Kathleen and Don know that the heart of the marriage ceremony is their consent to one another, the promise they make to each other to live together all their lives. Jack, who is well used to Deaf people, has already practised with the young couple and Don has had a good talk with his mother, Emma, about the wedding and his future with Kathleen. The serious Jack, in his role as priest, signs first of all looking to Don and pointing towards him:

Do you take Kathleen Agnes Walsh for your lawful wife, to have and to hold, from this day forward, for better, for worse, for richer, for poorer, in sickness and in health, until death do you part? Don nods his head up and down with a *Yes* and fingerspells the English, *I d-o*.

Kathleen does the same, as Jack signs to her: *Do you take Donald Corcoran Wallis for your lawful husband…* Neither of them clearly comprehends the English construct, but they do know its meaning. Kathleen's heart skips a beat as she visualises the life she is committing to – a life shared with Don, working together, eating together, raising children together and communicating together in good times and bad times. She holds her hand over her heart as a symbol of love for him and moves her hands up to lay her head on them and looks to the soil beneath her – until we die, we will stay together. *Yes, I do!*

Jack smiles at the silent couple and looks to Chester for the wedding ring, which he blesses. With the heightened intensity, Don places the ring on Kathleen's slender finger, then he signs: *Ring…I give you…my love…I show you.*

Kathleen looks at the ring and as they lock eyes, she responds: *Thank you*. Her eyes well up with tears that want to burst and roll slowly down her cheeks, smudging them as they increase speed. For a fleeting moment Don is unsure how to respond to the emotion and nods with the question, *OK?* As they walk out of the Church together, plenty of confetti is thrown over them, littering the grounds and publicising that a wedding has taken place here this morning.

For the wedding breakfast, they all return for the feast at *Carlyle* homestead, the place where Don and Kathleen first met.

For their honeymoon, they follow the popular trend and travel by train to the Victorian tourist town of Marysville in the mountains. They walk to Stephenson's Falls in the visual magic of the silent waterfall with its white spray, where two dragonflies flit about in tandem.

So Don and Kathleen's wedding unites two of Victoria's Irish pioneering families, one from the Wimmera, western Victoria that moved to Mt Gwynne on the Murray and the other from the Goulburn Valley, north-east Victoria.

---

i The verses at the beginning of each chapter in Parts I & II are based on the Aboriginal story of the Wonga Pigeon, the Hawk and the Waratah.
http://www.janesoceania.com/australia_aboriginal_dreamtime/index1.htm
Michael J Connolly *Munda-gutta Kulliwari* Dreamtime Kullilla-Art www.dreamtime.auz.net

CHAPTER 2

AT THE WINDING WANNON AND WIMMERA RIVERS

Charcoal coloured on their backs

White above their beaks

The Wonga Pigeons

Pick and peck

As they bob their heads

Up and down.

With Mt Napier to the south, and the Grampians mountain range or *Garaweid*[1] to the north-east, Hamilton is near the border of three traditional Aboriginal tribal territories. To the south is Gunditjmara Country, to the north-east stretches Tjapwurong Country, and Bunganditj Country [i] reaches out to the west. To the north, north-west and north-east of *Garaweid* are the townships of Natimuk, Horsham, Nhill, Dunkeld and Ararat and others in western Victoria. In this region known as the Wimmera, Irish pioneers settle, as do Kathleen's ancestors.

* * *

In the early morning on Christmas Day 1880, the birds are singing ahead of a hot summer's day at Tatyoon south of Ararat. Richard Walsh and his siblings wake in anticipation: the routine on Christmas Day is always different. But today Christmas Day becomes different, forever. Everyone is hushed, people are crying. Six-year-old Richard sits outside under the tree and hugs his favourite dog tightly. He hears whispers from the older members in the family, *Mother is dead.* Life is changed. Richard and his family move to McKenzie Creek immediately south of Horsham and become known as the *McKenzie Creek Walshes from County Kilkenny.*

---

[1] Garaweid is the name known by the traditional Aboriginal tribes.

In 1896 at Natimuk west of Horsham, ten-year-old Mary Adeline Walsh walks inside the modest mud-brick house wiping her copious tears with the sleeve of her jacket. Her two-year-old sister, 'Leen (Kathleen Matilda) runs to her and puts her arms around her, while her brothers look on with a mournful stir in their hearts. The have just learned that their mother has died. Little Mary Adeline becomes the key to life at home, as in ladylike fashion she attempts to keep house and develop the small garden in the flat dry country that surrounds their home. The family lives simply on the land, their Irish-born father working on Vectis property west of Horsham. Their maternal grandparents are nearby supports. Mary Adeline's family become known as the *County Mayo Walshes*.

* * *

In 1906 the two Walsh families unite when Richard and Mary Adeline marry in the Catholic Church in Horsham, a Church built with a significant donation of five hundred pounds from Mary Adeline's father. They plan to have children of course, five or maybe six, they expect. Life presents them with ten children. Baby Richard 1 is born – soon after, their firstborn dies and they bury him in the Horsham cemetery. Two more boys are born – Richard 2, known as Dick, and William, known as Bill. The births of the boys brings joy and happiness to the young mother, but during these years Mary Adeline also grieves her grandparents' deaths and then her father's death.

In mid-1915, Mary Adeline realises she is in the first trimester of her fourth pregnancy. Her grandmother who has been a mid-wife in the fledgling-Irish community for many years will not be there for her this time. With her husband often away working as an agent for stock, she calls on her young sister 'Leen for support. Carrying buckets of hot water from the fire place to the washing tub, she pauses awhile and holds her aching head and rubs her slightly painful joints, then returns to stoke the fire with more wood. She asks herself, *well why shouldn't I feel tired and achy at the end of the day. I work hard.* She rubs her sore eyes. Maybe I have hayfever. She notices a slight rash on her arm and dismisses it easily. It's gone in a few days. She rests more but that is not unusual for her at this stage of her pregnancy.

Unaware that she is mid-course of the viral illness, rubella, otherwise known as German measles, she feels her symptoms seem explainable and anyway rubella is not readily diagnosed in this pre-immunisation era. Mary Adeline is unaware of congenital rubella syndrome and its possible severe and permanent consequences for the baby she carries ranging from blindness, a heart defect, intellectual disability, pre-natal death – to deafness.

On 23 February 1916 in Gunditjmara Country, Richard and Mary Adeline's baby is born in the middle of the summer heat in Hamilton where St Riddell's Creek, a tributary of the Wannon River, runs through the town. As Mary Adeline holds her first baby girl in her arms in their home on the outskirts of the town, she thinks of her grandmother and misses her presence. Turning gratefully to her sister she says: *'Leen, we are naming this baby Kathleen Agnes after you and will you be her godmother?*

Do they hear the traditional dreaming story that the Aboriginal grandmothers tell as they catch dragonflies to test the hearing of young babies?

When babies are born in the dry season this is also the time of the birth of the dragonfly, which hums and buzzes around the air, excited about the birth of the new season. The grandmothers catch the dragonflies to test babies' hearing, making them buzz near the babies' ears. When a baby responds, we know that they have good hearing. If not, the old ladies bring the dragonfly closer so the baby can feel the vibration and sounds of its wings, then they sing to the spirits and the dragonfly: We all must look after this child together to help her to grow and be able to communicate. So, if you see a dragonfly buzzing around a baby, it is just looking and checking the baby's response because that's what they do. In the past everyone worked together – dragonflies, grandmothers and the spirits.[ii]

St Mary's Catholic Church, Hamilton Victoria

The dragonflies hover over the creeks and rivers as the family gathers in Catholic Irish tradition in St Mary's Church in Hamilton for Kathleen's baptism. The baby is not blind and does not have a heart defect. Neither does she have an intellectual disability. Richard and Mary Adeline listen to the prayers through the baptism ceremony, while Kathleen is proclaimed as a child of God in the gathered faith community. Besides the help of her godmother, all who are present expect to support the parents in the care and growth of this child. But no one knows that the baby girl is profoundly deaf. All are called upon to look after this baby – dragonflies, grandmothers and the spirits.

* * *

11

Entering life as a colourful and malleable child Kathleen is vulnerable to a world with daunting challenges that will weave a silver glistening thread throughout her life. The land and farm life are the backdrop to her early world and form her intimacy with the natural environment.

She is two years old when her parents move the family to Nhill, north-west of Horsham on the Wimmera River. Along the Wimmera River are five Aboriginal tribes of the Wotjobaluk, Wergaia, Jupagalk, Jaadwa and Jadawadjali people who lived and cared for the vast lands for thousands of years before white people claimed the land for growing grain crops and farming.

Setting up their home again, Richard makes improvements to the house with a big verandah around the side and front giving space and protection from the elements. Intently watching her father dig a deep cellar off the kitchen, Kathleen learns that this part of the house is for big people, not little girls who want to explore by climbing into the hole in the ground. She also learns this is where food-stuffs are kept cool in the harsh heat of the summer.

As she is the first girl, Kathleen's two older brothers, Dick and Bill, call her *Girlie*. She never hears her siblings call her by name. The boys look at her face-to-face and point to her, saying, *You – Girlie*. She learns the mouth shape for important words. She is very lively, quick to learn and curious about everything. Without realising it, they establish their own method of communicating with her using gestures and signs that she understands.

Her very slight hearing in her left ear helps her in the identification of vibrations. Feeling the vibration of a clap of thunder Kathleen looks up to read the body language of anyone else in the room – *has someone else noticed something different? She runs to look for herself – what was the sound, that thing causing vibrations through my body?* She develops her peripheral vision to a higher degree, so she notices everything and everyone. With strong intuition, she reads people and their non-verbal messages and often she *just knows*. Her strong sense of smell informs her, as well. Smelling his cigarette, she runs to the door to meet her father before anyone else knows he is home. Still no one realises she is deaf.

She is pro-active in her natural communications, naturally learning Deaf visual expression. *Who can mistake it?* She lets them know very clearly if she is happy, sad or mad. She shows them why as well. She drags her father outside to show him whatever it is that frightens her or that she wants him to know about – the snake that she sees or when she perceives that the cat scratches her when she picks up the kittens. Rivalry among her siblings is familiar to her and especially when more children take their place in the family. No one messes with her things or teases her without a showdown, as she points and gesticulates towards the offending people or things and tells her side of the story. Everyone knows why she is upset.

As Kathleen grows, so her ways of communication develop within the family. She uses *home* signs and gestures and her family respond for often-used words, such as thirsty, toilet, smelly, pray, cows, sheep, dogs, cats, horse-riding and comics. She makes raw sounds and articulates words that family members recognise – but not people outside the family. Her essential concepts include sugar, bed, drink, baby and dinner, Mum, Dad and the names for her siblings, Dick, Bill, Monica, Molly, then Kevin, John and Jim. This is the basis for her later understanding and development of language.

* * *

Kathleen is six years old. Her two brothers, Dick and Bill, contract the mumps and are confined to bed in the sleep-out with comics to amuse them. Warning Kathleen not to go near the boys and attempting to explain with very strong visual *home* signs and gestures about catching the mumps, Kathleen's mother also describes the consequences. *You too will have a swollen face and neck and feel sick, if you venture into the sleep-out!*

While her mother is in the garden Kathleen succumbs to temptation. Guiltily, she runs to the banned area and steals the Ginger Meggs comics. The next day she has the mumps. Yes, she knows she is naughty but her access to story through pictures and especially the animation of the Ginger Meggs comics makes the temptation too much to resist. She does not yet read or know English words so the visual depiction of story helps her to understand the flow of life in the stories, and her imagination is given both direction and free rein.

The family attends Sunday Mass, the fulfilment of their religious practice and a social event when Catholic families, mostly of Irish descent, gather to pray. Before and after Mass they gather in gender groups to exchange news – the men stand around under the pepper tree or the gum tree, while the women group together too. Meanwhile the children play around the Church yard, and the horses tied up to the fence, wait patiently in idle postures.

When the family arrives in the horse and sulky for the regular Sunday Mass, Kathleen enters the Church and immediately gravitates to the long timber seat in the fifth row on the right-hand side. It is their family's place. The same people sit in the pews behind them and in front of them each week. The children jostle around to find their position. Kathleen sits beside her mother, who wants to keep her calm and quiet, especially during the sermon. She sits Kathleen on her lap and lets her Rosary beads drop slowly into the palms of the little girl's sensitive hands. It tickles her. She likes the sensation. In turn she pours the beads back into her mother's hands. They repeat the process. It focuses her and she is quiet while Mass is celebrated.

It is in the early 1920s. Kathleen feels at home. On the wall she looks at the familiar Stations of the Cross, various statues and candles, as well as the flowers that adorn the Church. She joins her hands, genuflects and makes a sign of the cross on her body. She imitates her parents as she puts her head down for a brief moment, but quickly lifts her eyes to observe the world around her. Mass is in Latin – Kathleen does not hear any of it. She observes the priest and the male altar servers. She notices every movement and every action of the Mass, including how the priest holds up the chalice and host. She notices the water, wine, bread in the form of hosts, the washing of the priest's fingers, the way the priest holds his hands and how he makes signs of the cross and genuflects on his knee. As communion is given out, she notices how the people kneel and receive the host on their tongues.

One afternoon Kathleen is in a serious creative play mood. She sets up an old fruit box upside down as an altar, finds her mother's crocheted doilies and places them on top. She opens the cupboard and brings out a goblet and a cake plate, a piece of bread and raspberry cordial for wine. For candles she finds some straight sticks, places them vertically between the slats on her wooden box and gathers a few geraniums from the garden. In her mother's wardrobe, she finds a white petticoat that flows over her. All is set. She assembles her younger siblings in front of her, pretends to form words with her mouth and lips and proceeds with the ritual gestures, including a number of signs of the cross. She imitates the distribution of communion as well. She imagines that she stands before her siblings as a priest leader.

She sees respect and reverence when her parents go into the Church – they stop talking to one another, they look more serious, they join their hands and bow their heads. Kathleen understands the feel of different spaces and situations, as she watches the faces and body language of people – and interactions between people.

Her mother enters the playroom – horror! With a fear of God and fear of the Irish priest, her mother believes such play is sacrilegious. She wags her finger with a harsh expression on her face. Kathleen is mystified. *How could I be naughty this time?* She observes what happens on a Sunday in the Church. She mirrors the priest and carries out the holy event at home. *Is this not holy play?* Not that she has words to tell anyone. *Is this not a good thing to do?* She puzzles over the strong reaction of her mother. She is not *stupid*. She is a child who lives in awareness.

Kathleen initially goes to school at Nhill but the teachers have neither the skills nor the time she needs – and maybe the will. Bored, she is disruptive and unmanageable – she is a nuisance. Different and loveable, but at the same time, frustration flourishes within her. It is accepted that, in her difference, she will stay at home on the farm, where she is active and loved. *Does no one dare to say Girlie is deaf?* Her difference amounts to deafness. Some suspect she is deaf but no one is really convinced.

* * *

Kathleen accompanies her father on the farm to the dairy, down to the horse stables and over to their sheep yards, where local sheep sales take place. She rides with him on horse-back and she learns how to milk the cows. She likes her father's softness with the animals and marvels how he coaxes them to come to him in the middle of the paddock. She travels with him on what seems a day's journey, by horse and buggy, through the isolated Little Desert to visit relatives on the other side at Goroka near Natimuk.

With no formal language, she has no concept of aunts and uncles and cousins, or extended family. To her, they are people who accept or do not accept her, and are friendly or not friendly to her, a wild child and a charming child. She experiences the loss of not knowing they are clan and how they have a special place in the life history of her family.

Kathleen learns the practice of give and take in the family. In a supportive environment she takes responsibility for the younger children. Nursing young Molly on her knee as they travel to town in the horse and buggy, she takes for granted her role in the family. As the family grows she cares for the younger boys, Kevin, John and Jim – taking them for walks through the paddocks to see the animals or down the road to collect the mail or just to play. This gives her mother a break. When they are older she takes them to school and meets them on their way home. Totally immersed in family life, her siblings are her friends and she plays and laughs with them – and learns from them.

Suddenly her mother becomes ill. Her father is unable to cope at home with the children, so arranges for the boys to be cared for elsewhere and takes the three girls on the train to Portland to stay at the boarding school with the Good Samaritan Sisters. Kathleen has no idea what this is about or why it is happening. Her father cannot explain the situation to her – they do not have enough language between them. He turns to Monica and Molly with encouraging words and reassures them he will be back soon. Anxious and distressed, she is completely at a loss when her father leaves on the train without them – and she feels responsible for the two younger girls.

Monica and Molly are absorbed into the classroom with the other children. Because of the many other demands, the nuns cannot cater for Kathleen, who is still filled with unexplained questions. Kathleen cannot settle in the contained environment of the classroom, or understand Maths, English, reading or spelling, so she wanders around the school grounds and garden. She observes nature, the birds, trees and flowers and watches for who comes and goes to try to make sense of life. She does know she has to be a good girl. Every night in the dormitory, she comforts her two homesick sisters till they return home to the farm again. She cannot explain to her mother what the experience was like for her. Her mother in return wants to say, *I am sorry. I was ill and could not look after you. I trusted that you could comfort the girls.* Kathleen holds on to this indelible and painful memory.

As the children grow and become more competent and independent in the house and around the farm, Kathleen's role in the family changes. She is not needed in the same way. Kathleen begins to feel that she is missing out. She doesn't know how to read a book, write words or figures and why they do these things. During family conversations she is at a loss as to know what is going on. She soon receives the message that she is not as good as others and, more, that she is not good enough. Catching a glance of a serious conversation going on at the table, she looks questioningly. *What? Tell me.* She feels excluded. Another time from across the room she sees her sisters laughing. She is curious to know. *What? Tell me. Include me.* She resists exclusion from the family and demands a sense of belonging. She is deaf in a hearing family and hearing environment.

* * *

Still unsure if something is *wrong* with Kathleen and unaware that she is profoundly deaf even at seven years old, Richard and Mary anguish over their daughter. She is different – after all she cannot *speak properly* – she makes sounds – and sometimes her behavior is both noisy and disruptive. They worry and talk together – she doesn't seem to comprehend our instructions and she doesn't seem to recognise that she is making a noise. *What is wrong? Is she not quite right?* The reality is that Kathleen's natural alertness, intuition and willingness to participate means that she still unintentionally deceives them regarding really being deaf. For them as hearing people who have no understanding of a possible language and culture, *deaf* is bad, a tragedy, unthinkable.

They talk with relatives – they talk with friends. They talk to their doctor, a doctor who is highly regarded in the country town – he doubts that she is deaf too and gives them hope, a false hope when he believes he can *treat* the little girl – medically. In their utter dilemma they hand over their trust to him. After all, he is the educated one and they suppose he knows everything. Just now they want confirmation of their intuitive anxiety – something is wrong. They want something to change her and give their loved daughter *a better chance in life!*

Richard and Mary Adeline prepare to drive the horse and buggy. *Put good and clean clothes on*, her mother gestures to Kathleen, indicating they are going into town. The older boys hear their parents talking softly with some consternation. They know their parents worry about their Girlie. Bill is curious and wants to know why they are going to town. No straight answer is given to him. After seeing the older children going off to school and a neighbour come to look after the younger children, Kathleen quickly dresses and turns to her mother to plait her hair. She likes going to town with them.

Kathleen follows her parents into the doctor's surgery as she has done before when the children have been sick. The doctor looks at her and attempts to talk to her; he still does not believe she is deaf. She looks to her mother, who smiles soothingly towards her, as though everything is normal but it is not. *Is there a lie?* As her parents converse with the doctor in her presence, she watches them intently. *What is going on?* No words, just thoughts. She trusts in her parents; she is always at their side. *Is this about her?* Her parents are her connection to the world, to everything that goes on about her. She does not dare to close her eyes. If she closes her eyes, she loses contact and knowledge of what is reality around her – and safety.

What is happening? As quick as lightning she turns to the doctor and back to her parents. Her eyes go back and forth, back and forth, as if following the conversation that is taking place in front of her – and yet she does not hear or know what they say. She does understand that it is a serious conversation – a conversation about her and in front of her. *Is this about me?* She also surmises, *they think I am stupid – and I know I am ok! Where are the dragonflies?*

They make the decision that the doctor will treat her with the aim to try to make her *talk properly*. How will he carry this out? How does he approach her? Is she sitting up or lying down? Do they gesticulate to her about what to do? No one can really explain what is going to happen. *So what happens?* The doctor gives her *shock treatment*, an experiment that does not work.[iii]

On their return home young Bill, who is close and protective of his sister Girlie, resumes his stark questioning to his mother and father. *What did they do? Did they hurt her?* He knows something serious has happened to his little sister; he knows they call it *shock treatment* and she still cannot *talk properly*. The doctor, the expert, is wrong. Bill carries the burden of the secret deep inside his heart – *Girlie had shock treatment.* He will shed tears. He will tell one day. He will blurt it to a daughter in the next generation. Girlie's daughter! *Did you know your mother had shock treatment? She was seven. They tried to make her talk. They did not believe she was deaf.* Bill knows too – *she is not stupid, she is deaf, that's all!*

---

[i] Aboriginal names often have other spellings.

[ii] Ngumumma story, The Dragonfly by Norma Chidanpee Benger. *www.healthinfonet.ecu.ed.au/other-health-cNgumumma*. Used with permission.

[iii] It is not clear what type of shock treatment took place. It was different from the technological advances in such treatment that takes place in the twenty-first century. However, it was a grave event and left an indelible impression on Bill, who carried the secret till a few years before he died.

CHAPTER 3

ON MOLLISON'S, MUDDY AND DAIRY CREEKS FLOWING INTO THE GOULBURN

Speckled beneath

Like an Aboriginal painting

The Wonga Pigeons

Stay close and near

As they watch and learn

And monotonously coo.

With the mountains of the Great Dividing Range as a backdrop to the rolling hills and rock boulders of the rural area of Seymour and Yea, north-east of Melbourne, many creeks flow through the valleys, including Muddy Creek, Strath Creek, King Parrot Creek, Carver Creek, Spring Creek and Dairy Creek. After diverting through the crevices and descending into valleys, the creeks lead into the Goulburn River, known as *Warring* by the Taungurung tribe. It rises and falls with flood and drought in summer and winter. It is a river that gives life and causes death. It carries stories of Don. Three playful dragonflies dart up and down and around about from one side of the river to the other.

South east of Seymour and sixty miles north of Melbourne, Mt William, also known as Wilimee Moorring meaning *axe place* in the Woiwurrung language[i], stands tall. It forms a craggy plateau that is silhouetted against the sky and seen across grazing land from Kilmore and Pyalong. Surrounding lakes give a sense of peace and tranquility. This mountain is a place of great cultural significance for Aboriginal peoples, because of the quarry, where Aboriginal peoples for thousands of years made the axe or hatchet from the stone, and where they traded with distant Aboriginal tribes until the 1800s. The Woiwurrung, including the Wirundjeri peoples, roamed the creeks, rivers and lands in this area. At Pyalong, Mollison's Creek flows into the Cameron Creek at Sugarloaf into Sunday Creek, and eventually into the great Goulburn River.

* * *

In 1908 after their marriage, Abraham from Seymour and Emily known as Emma from Yea settle initially in the Yea district and then in Pyalong, where Abraham, a man of good standing in the community, purchases the property *Ardsley*[ii]. Great drought in this part of Australia follows.

In the household at Pyalong a new mystery unfolds. Maria, Emma's mother, worries about her granddaughter Mary known as Marie. Something is different. With further promptings from Maria, Abe and Emma discover that Marie, their first child and only daughter, is profoundly deaf. She is three years of age and runs away when she is called by them. As family members insistently shout to her to stop or to return, she continues to run down the road. She does not acknowledge their calls in any way. Marie recognises things and displays a fascination for everything around her. Seeing her facial brightness and curiosity, they know she is intelligent. Her parents are bewildered. Even though she shows signs of an intelligent mind, she does not say words or develop spoken language; she is different from other children. Awareness dawns on Emma.

Marie needs extra attention and management, extra watchfulness and care. Physically, she is healthy and is growing according to normal childhood patterns of physical development. A pretty girl, she plays and explores outside but her play is in silence, except for occasional vocal sounds. For her, there are no parameters or boundaries; all is possible in her mind. She takes no notice of any directions given to her and requires face-to-face communication with *home* signs, gesticulations and gestures that may make sense to a Deaf child.

At the final realisation of Marie's deafness, the twenty-three-year old mother, Emma, is stunned and devastated. As Abe sits at the old familiar table he puts his face into his hands and weeps inwardly. He cannot articulate his feelings.

Emma is slightly relieved to know the diagnosis, because she already knows something is different about this child. Abe is twenty years older than Emma and glad to have offspring. His focus is to provide for the family and he occupies himself with the land, farm life and the activities of the local community. They both come from large families, expect a number of children and therefore know the importance of work in order to survive. They now question themselves as to why they have a Deaf child but there is no explanation.

As a competent woman, Emma doubts herself and questions her mothering skills. How do you bring up a Deaf child and how do you discipline such a child? Abe and Emma have never encountered a child or adult who is deaf from birth. They do not know anyone who is both deaf and educated.

Emma's faith finds her at prayer on her knees amid her tears. She prays many rosaries, beads fingered pleadingly through the night. As she kneels in the little Church at Yea on Sundays, she bargains with God for John her next child: *My son if he hears, I will give him back to you as a priest.* She pleads for a child who can hear her voice and the sounds of the animals, the horses neighing, the turkeys gobbling and birds singing, the rain on the roof at night and the trickling of water in the creeks. She wants a child who calls her the tender spoken word *Mother* and whom she can prepare for the priesthood.

As Abe and Emma journey through their grief their conversation with one another shows their determination and hope for their daughter that she grows and develops as a happy person and one who is responsible for her own life.

* * *

The first three children have Emma's surname, Corcoran, as their second name. After discovering Marie's deafness, Abe and Emma look for an indication that shows if John is deaf. Do they play the game of clapping behind his head to see if he responds? Does the dragonfly buzz and hum, so the baby feels the vibration and sounds of its wings? Does Grandmother, Maria, sing to the spirits and the dragonfly in her prayer and sheer hope that the baby hears? Emma's prayers have been answered. He speaks and vocalises understandable English words and develops spoken language. Emma confides in her mother about her relief to have a son who hears and who might be a priest one day.

The next baby arrives in the summer heat. As fires burn from

St Patrick's Church, Kilmore Victoria

Gippsland in the East to Garaweid, the Grampians, in the west of Victoria in 1912, Donald Corcoran Wallis is born on 6 January and baptized two weeks later at St Patrick's Church, Kilmore. His aunt, Elizabeth Ryan, is his godmother. With the baby in their arms Abe and Emma travel home to Pyalong in a horse pair open carriage, skillfully driven by Abe – a journey of ten miles.

When Emma first breast-feeds Don, she perhaps does not give a thought to the possibility of him being deaf. Given that John is not deaf, who would have thought it might happen again? Before too long, she quickly notices the signals that indicate he is different from John and the signals that he is similar to Marie. Which of the tests does she apply? Clapping behind his head? Dropping a saucepan? Slamming the door? Shouting or screaming? Do his eyes follow her more intently around the room than did John's at that age?

When Abe comes home at night, how does she share her terror and her realisation that another child is deaf, that Don is deaf? Devastated, she asks the question, *God how can this happen again? Why?* Abe sits in the familiar chair at the kitchen table and again puts his heavy head into his hands with utter disbelief – he is heartbroken. Morning dawns and he looks at his son with intent and with new eyes. He waits to make eye contact and searches for answers. *Why is this little boy deaf too?* As the dragonflies buzz and hum in the native bushes between the creek and the house, Grandmother Maria is nearby to support and they once again strive to fill their hearts with courage.

Emma and Abe know Don is deaf much sooner than they knew about Marie's deafness. With a clear diagnosis at this early stage, they already have experience of how to be with a Deaf child and how to parent him. They know the importance of having eye contact when they communicate with him and they gently guide his head, so his eyes look at them face-to-face. He quickly learns the smile of approval and the scowl of disapproval; he sees mouths open, move and close again and when his mother holds him close and whispers, he feels her warm breath while their eyes meet. The *home* signs she uses with Marie, she now uses with Don at an earlier age. He receives the basis for language and social interaction.

When Don is two years old, what *home* sign do they have for *geese* that roam around the yards and are kept to sell for Christmas dinner? Among the hazards of life on a farm are geese that attack. Four-year old Jack[1] hears the commotion and runs outside to see his mother rush into the wild gaggle of geese to rescue Don. Don does not hear the vehement sound of geese that interpret their young as under attack by a child who runs around with such energy and playfulness. He is oblivious to the warning sounds of danger, so that his mother is forever watchful and her maternal instinct forces her to rush to his rescue. Don is saved from the frenzy of the geese and she holds him closely in her arms. Jack, the older brother, watches on and perceives that he too, must be aware that his siblings are deaf and that like his mother, is required to protect them when they do not know danger.

Gentle discussions take place between Abe and Emma and between Emma and her mother. *Why do we have Deaf children?* They ask one another if there are Deaf members in their families, like grandparents, great aunts or great uncles, cousins? No, this is a new experience as there are no members in their families who are known to be deaf. Abe and Emma wonder and ask unanswered questions. *Is it because of me or us carrying a recessive gene and passing it on to our children?* Medical science

---

[1] John becomes known as Jack in the family.

does not come into their consciousness. Yes, the children are congenitally and profoundly deaf from birth. They later learn that Non-syndromic neurosensory autosomal recessive deafness is the most common form of genetic deafness.[iii] Deafness is the only symptom confirming nonsyndromic deafness.[2]

* * *

Just prior to her marriage, Emma suffered personal tragedy with the death of a younger brother and a younger sister in Yea. She now has three children and two of them are deaf. Added to this, with the tough times of the World War I era, the family is touched by danger when fire destroys their home at Pyalong in 1915. Although all are safe, Emma feels great distress at the loss of her few treasures and wedding photos. After the fire and having nothing, Abe sells the *Ardsley* property and buys *Wirrabong* down Dairy Creek Road at Homewood, a few miles from Yea. Abe and Emma and their family settle in the earthen floor home, where they are poor and dress poorly using string for laces in their boots.

In subsequent years, three more boys are born, Thomas Chester, known as Chester, Brian Emmett and Charles Patrick. Abe and Emma receive another surprise when Charles Patrick is born profoundly deaf too. Emma cries with the realisation that she has Deaf children and questions again, *What have we done wrong? How can this be?* In the sequence of the family, Marie is deaf, John is hearing, Don is deaf, Chester is hearing, Brian is hearing and Charlie is deaf. It seems that each alternate child is deaf, except for Brian. *Should I be deaf and not my brother, Charlie?* Brian always carries this thought with a sense of guilt and responsibility. He is angry that his younger brother is deaf and carries sadness that he never reconciles.

* * *

After completing a course by correspondence on lolly-making, Emma goes to town and sells the lollies that she makes during the week. Sundays see them travel in a horse and buggy to Sunday Mass where they also meet friends and relatives. Emma regularly visits her neighbours and towards the end of the day, walks down the road where she meets her great friend, Mrs McCarthy, her closest neighbour. She confides in her friend and they chat together, as they exchange their news and make arrangements for the next few days.[iv] Emma engages with the community and is generous with her involvement in functions. Don observes her interactions and learns the importance of communication with people, especially neighbours.

---

[2] With more research in recent years a form of recessive gene that has been discovered is Connexion 26, which is responsible for approximately 20% of all genetic childhood deafness.

Horses dominate the animal life on the farm and they are invaluable for transport and work. Both Abe and Emma ride. Emma rides side-saddle most elegantly and drives a pair of horses with skill. Abe clears land in the district using a team of bullocks and horses, something he has done from his early teenage years. *You never see a Wallis with a bad horse*, says a local of Seymour[v]. Don observes Jack with no bridle or saddle riding Bonnie up the dirt road to and from the local Homewood school. Soon Don climbs on Bonnie too, galloping across the paddocks beginning his affinity with horses.

While at home, Emma is aware that her hearing son, Jack, is lonely because his two Deaf siblings on either side of him are away at school, and that he chats more with her, as he lives in a carefree environment. He also takes to heart his parents' concern and anxiety about the Deaf children in the family. Abe and Emma worry about finance. *How will they manage their children's special education?*

* * *

Around Yea is Taungurung Country. At the Goulburn River Aboriginal people gathered in previous centuries. Here children play joyfully and people reflect as they fish, bathe or draw water for the camp or house. The river welcomes Don and trains him to understand the various messages of the currents: where to be carried and where to swim against the flow, what areas are safe and where the undercurrents lurk. Don learns that water can be a friend or foe as he learns to read and understand the Goulburn, his playground. His brother, Jack, earlier drags Don from the dam nearby when he nearly drowns but Don is unafraid and bounces back being at ease in the water.

In their playground they find gold nuggets flowing down from gold mining upstream. Don finds a discarded tobacco tin where he stores his riches. From year to year, while he is away at school, he places it safely for when he returns home. He takes it with him into his adult life, so he can show the next generation, his children. The tin survives his moves from place to place.

Don, on a lonesome day, roams the hills of *Wirrabong* and beyond the property bounds. As he goes bush, he sees the cowslips and finds the delicate purple orchids. Having set the traps for rabbits for a meal for the family in the evening, he sits on the grass entranced by the silent wedge-tailed eagle that flies high overhead. Its solitary presence captures him as he follows it with his eyes – he is enthralled as the eagle, as eagles have done for thousands of years, catches the thermals and seemingly floats in stillness as it looks down on prey down in the valleys. He senses the mighty eagle as it watches over him too.

While he is lonely and resilient at the same time, he easily entertains himself in his quest for knowledge. With his active mind and body, Don wants to know where the eagles nest and bring up their young. He decides to investigate. He climbs the hills and as he comes closer, the eagle circles overhead with a wildness that Don has not seen before. He is close to the eagle's territory. In fact, he is too close for the eagle's comfort and suddenly Don has to duck down as the eagle attempts to attack. He puts his hands up to protect his head as the eagle thrusts its talons and a burning pain sears Don's left hand. He holds his bloodied hand close to his chest as he makes a quick descent. His concerned mother is quick to remind him that he is fortunate. While he is left with a scar that proves his adventure, he understands it is important for a Deaf person to have the use of fingers and hands for clearer communication.

Don and Charlie and their Deaf friends enjoy visual humour enormously – they grasp its special nuances in a way that is unique to Deaf people. They see in comic body motion, including eye movements, facial expression or the slightest shift of shoulders, arm or leg, subtle meanings and messages that hearing people can easily miss. Sitting in the theatre as Deaf people, they are not disadvantaged as the silent Charlie Chaplin movies are shown. It is one of the few situations where they are fully able to partake of mainstream entertainment.

They especially enjoy their own heightened awareness of the visual cues giving even more enjoyment. It is no wonder that Don and Charlie roll in laughter as they watch a familiar expression of visual comedy that touches the funny bone of Deaf people. Charlie Chaplin, an English comic actor and film-maker, lived close to the school for Deaf children in London in his early childhood, giving him firsthand knowledge of life without spoken words. At the age of nineteen, entering into the film industry world of Los Angeles, he met a Deaf entertainer and artist, Redmond Granville,[3] from whom he learned Sign language, deaf communication techniques and the silent world. Comfortable in that silent world, Charlie Chaplin included Redmond in his movies – an inspiration for the young boys Don and Charlie.

Abe worries while he advocates for his children's education – he wants the best for them. He ponders on their lives constantly recognising that he is unable to communicate in depth with them or to mentor them as a father. He does not learn Sign and he misses much involvement in their lives. Is he self-conscious with his hands not able to shape signs clearly? Or is it that his hands have aged and twisted with arthritis and the toil of the land thereby testing any possible agility with hand movements for Sign language. His mind does not connect with his hands in a way to communicate or express himself.

---

[3] Charlie Chaplin establishes a life-long friendship with the Deaf actor, Redmond Granville.

Don, Marie and Charlie do not have any recognisable speech. Their sounds do not resemble spoken words. Don's laughter is beautiful and sounds as if it comes from deep in the earth beneath him and through his feet and body into the space around him – it is infectious and joyous. He enjoys humour and a good story when he and Charlie meet with friends in social settings and in friendship.

And they are totally deaf – really deaf. They have no hearing. Odd and indeed strange it is when people refer to them as hard-of-hearing, hearing-impaired or with a hearing impairment.

They are deaf. Of themselves, they sign the English word *deaf* and they plant two fingers across their ears followed by two fingers across their lips and fingerspell D-E-A-F to make sure people receive their message. *Did they not learn from the vibrations of the three dragonflies?*

---

[i] http://en.wikipedia.org/wiki/Mount_William_stone_axe_quarry.

[ii] *The Kilmore Free Press* 14 December 1911

[iii] *http://www.ncbi.nlm.nih.gov/pubmed/9285800*: Non-syndromic neurosensory autosomal recessive deafness (NSRD) is the most common form of genetic hearing loss.

[iv] Presentation by Anthony McCarthy, Yea, held in Wallis Centre Archives, Hobart, Tasmania.

[v] *Personality Profile – Chester Wallis* by Bronwyn Wheatley, Kilmore Free Press, 6 Nov. 1991, p.15

Meanderings

Aunty Marie, my Dad and Uncle Charlie

Live in a silent land

Enriching and nourishing them

In their human experience
  Of play,
  Learning,
  Work and relationships.

Their silent land is fully alive
  With sights and movements

Emotions flowing with thoughts
  And currents of ideas

Entering silent rivers of the mind and heart

Meandering towards the open silent sea
  Of human life.

They know silence

Filled with sounds of communication
  Hope,
  Love
  and dreams.

A resilient and sustaining silent land,

The experience of our Deaf family.

Bernadette T. Wallis

CHAPTER 4

TO MT GWYNNE ON THE MURRAY
BETWEEN BAROOGA AND MULWALA

The Wonga Pigeon

Lifts her head

Expands her heart

And continues to

Pick and peck

On the floor of the bush.

Many of the towns derive their names from Aboriginal folklore. Nhill is said to mean *the home of the spirits.* The Aborigines believed that the mists rising from the waters early in the morning were the spirits of their ancestors.[i] The Wimmera River with red gums and tea trees marks the eastern boundary of Little Desert Park where the wildflowers and ground orchids flourish in season in the sandy soil. In the nearby wetlands the bird life is prolific inviting the migratory birds to pause awhile on their journey.

In Nhill, Richard and Mary Adeline struggle with the question of how to educate their intelligent Deaf daughter. Kathleen is ten years of age. She experiences difficulty fitting into regular school. But, although, she cannot read, St Patrick's Sunday School awards her with a book, *King of the Golden City* by Mother Mary Loyola: *Presented to Kathie Walsh for good conduct. Parish priest N.J. Daly. Christmas 1925.* Someone recognises her goodness.

The local parish priest speaks with Richard and Mary and informs them of the Catholic school for Deaf girls at Waratah near Newcastle in NSW. He shows them the advertisement in the Catholic newspaper, *The Advocate* that also has an article encouraging parents of Deaf children, even pleading with them to send the children to Waratah for a good Catholic education, even if they cannot afford the fee. This is attractive, but the idea needs to be weighed up.

Richard and Mary Adeline think hard about it. They love their daughter. *Can they love her enough to let her go?* The Waratah School is far, far away from their home at Nhill, which is in a remote part of western Victoria. The logistics of travel seem too difficult. The educational opportunities for Richard and Mary Adeline's other children are already of concern too. Do they make the hard decision? There is no reason not to move to a new location to make Kathleen's attendance at the school at Waratah a practical possibility.

Richard and Mary Adeline are resigned to their decision to move – they see it as being for the greater good of all their children and their education, and particularly for Kathleen's Deaf education. With considerable and necessary haste in their momentous decision, they buy the property *Carlyle* at Mt Gwynne situated between Barooga and Mulwala on the NSW side of the Murray. On the Victorian side are Cobram and Yarrawonga. Importantly it is close enough to the railway line between Melbourne and Sydney to facilitate Kathleen's travels to Waratah.

Now they tell the children. Richard calls the boys and with few words he explains the plan. Mary Adeline gently tells the little girls, Monica and Molly, then takes ten-year old Girlie aside and attempts to explain to her in pictures and theatre, that they will leave the familiar home, farm and town of Nhill to go to another house, which is a long, long way away. She waves her arms in a long easterly direction. Her older brothers turn to Girlie and continue to visually explain with gestures as she looks to them questioningly.

It is the end of the year 1926 when the family prepares for the imminent journey east. While everyone finds the idea of the move a big rift – aunts, uncles and cousins – they know that distance will take its toll on what is their close family connection. Girlie enjoys and trusts her fourteen-year-old cousin Dick because he accepts her in her difference and looks out for her. She will miss him. He is also fond of his uncle Richard and all his cousins and is sad and grieves deeply in silence. The strength of good, shared childhood experiences will colour their memories forever. They farewell one another as they hold their emotions in check.

Girlie watches with intrigue and amazement as they put all their belongings in wooden boxes and heavy steel trunks and load them onto the dray with a few other goods and some food and water. As the older boys, Dick and Bill, look ahead with the excitement of newness and adventure, the four Clydesdale horses are harnessed in readiness to pull the dray. Two extra horses are prepared – one with the sulky and the other on a halter that will follow along beside.

With fourteen-year-old Dick holding the reins, Mary Adeline cradles baby Jim as she climbs into the sulky with eight-year-old Monica, four-year-old Kevin and two-year-old John. As Girlie watches over six-year-old Molly, they climb onto the dray just behind their father and find a comfortable niche for the journey. Bill sits beside his father with the dog. Richard takes the old leathered reins and they slowly draw away from their former home that had the cellar, down the sandy track and onto the dirt road for the journey eastwards.

After they snake their way through the flat countryside and finally stop towards evening on the side of the road, the horses are taken out of their harness for a feed of chaff and solid rest, while the family eats bread, corn beef or salted mutton and fruit that Mary Adeline has packed. Overnight, on hessian bags, they shelter under the dray and with blankets they lie close to one another to feel safe and secure in the open air under the Southern Cross. In the darkness and the silence, while others chatter, Girlie watches the moon look towards her, and the stars in the night sky draw her through the darkness into a place of nowhere, somewhere – in the middle of Victoria. She wonders what this journey is all about and what is in store for the morrow.

They travel more than four hundred kilometres. Each morning they rise early and their journey resumes. How many days does it take? Is it eight or ten? They finally reach the crossing of the Murray at the twin towns Cobram and Barooga and approach their new home. It is late in the day when they finally arrive at *Carlyle*. Furniture comes with the purchase of the house on the property, so the homestead is ready for them to move in with their own few goods. Girlie climbs down from the dray and enters their new home. She begins a new chapter in her life.

* * *

Backyard *Carlyle* homestead Mt Gwynne Victoria, circa 1930

As they settle, the surrounding place names become familiar to Girlie and her family – Mulwala, Yarrawonga, Mt Gwynne, Barooga and Berrigan. Thousands of people from the *Pangerang* tribe previously lived along the Murray River including at the twin towns, Mulwala and Yarrawonga. Mulwala means *big lagoon* or *big back water*. Yarra means *water running over rocks* and *wonga* is from the many Wonga pigeons nearby. Barooga means *my home*.

Pangerang/Baranga Country reaches east along the river towards Howlong and north from the river to Berrigan. The river was important to *Pangerang* peoples – they knew how to live with its seasonal variations – its winter floods and summer trickles – and they lived in harmony with the river even when drought caused it to stop flowing and dry up and the dragonflies disappeared. Early white settlement marked the beginning of the end for the flourishing of the *Pangerang* tribe.

By 1870 the last corroboree took place and by 1888 Gunyuk, *Black Swan*, the last member of the *Pangerang*, had died.[1] The ancient history of this Country became silent.

Girlie explores her surroundings including the wetlands, where she is drawn to observe the variety of bird life. She experiences a silent environment and her spirit rests, even though a cacophony of birdcalls surrounds her. The Wonga pigeons on the floor of the bush and the black swans on the water catch her attention and just like the *Pangerang* children in this area before her, she watches and learns.

An Aboriginal Dreamtime[ii] story tells of the Wonga Pigeon and the Waratah. The Wonga pigeons always stay together in pairs on the floor of the bush. One Wonga pigeon goes missing and the other Wonga pigeon flies high into the tree to find her mate and is attacked by Hawk who claws and takes her higher to its feeding place. The Wonga pigeon struggles to be free. She is unable to fly, her breast is wounded and she lands bleeding and broken in the waratah bushes. As she falls and lands onto the white waratah flower, her blood drips and changes it to red. As she jumps from waratah to waratah, she continues to bleed and that's the origin of the beautiful red waratah flower today. It is a story that will link Kathleen's fascination with the Wonga pigeon to the red waratah flower and her new school at Waratah.

* * *

---

[1] Gunyuk, is remembered by her English name, Mary Jane Milawa.

The school at Waratah is yet unknown to Girlie – she is yet to understand that it is the place of her formal learning. Mary Adeline anguishes as she asks herself: *How do I now explain to my Deaf daughter with yet no formal language that school for her is far away from home? How do I tell her that at this school she will learn differently and be educated by the Dominican Sisters?* And she can't explain it to her. She continues with her anguishing questions. *How can we live without her – she has always been with us day in and day out? How can we part with her?* This is our ultimate love and hope for her.

In 1927 with the following questions, the Dominican Sisters from the school at Waratah request some basic information for enrolment of Girlie, who graduates from Girlie to Kathleen:

Name of Parents or Guardians

Address

Occupation

Child's Name

Date of Birth

Q.1 – Does the child appear to be of sound intellect?

Q.2 – Is the child both deaf and dumb?

Q.3 – If not deaf, what is the cause of the inability to speak?

Q.4 – Does the child take intelligent notice of people and objects?

Q.5 – Does the child make signs to express its wants or ideas?

Q.6 – Does the child appear to be like other children in all respects, except the inability to hear and speak?[iii]

Mary and Richard look at the questions and answer them easily with a *Yes*, except for question three. What is the cause of the inability to speak? They leave it blank. The next issue is the cost of Kathleen's education.

For the purpose of raising needed money Richard buys a young prized Clydesdale stallion and quickly builds rapport with the stallion from which he will receive a fee as it sires the mares in the district. He plans to use the money to cover the cost of school fees, including accommodation for the year. Richard is pleased with the purchase and with his financial plan.

Richard becomes known as experienced with horses, sheep and cattle. Within the first week his neighbour requests that the new stallion serve his mare and he wants the stallion taken to his yards, rather than his mare brought to the stallion. Richard is reluctant but the neighbour is persistent. While Richard knows the stallion is flighty and is not yet settled into the surrounds, he hesitates and then gives in. Handling the stallion on a halter with the skill of a gentle horseman, Richard drives his own horse and sulky down the track to his neighbour's stables. With a halter on, the stallion canters alongside with its white mane and tail flowing, already confident with Richard.

During the night a noisy, threatening thunderstorm with deathly lightning forms. The stallion panics. It is killed when it attempts to jump the lightning electrified wire fence. Richard is devastated and heartbroken. He has lost his new thoroughbred stallion – and a source of income.

They cannot see how to make payments to the Dominican Sisters for Kathleen's board and lodging and the fees for education. The Sisters hear of their predicament and insist that they still bring her to their school, even though they cannot make any payment for fees for that year. Because of the incident, Kathleen begins school in April, well into the school year of 1927.

As her mother packs a metal trunk with new clothes made for her daughter, her heart aches. She points to the clothes in the trunk and to Kathleen, as she indicates, *the clothes are for you!* Today is the culmination of plans made the year before when they sold their property at Nhill in the Wimmera and bought the farm, *Carlyle*, so as to be closer to the railway line at Benalla, still hours of travel away.

As Richard and Kathleen board the steam train, Kathleen feels safe with her father. They travel north to Albury, change to the wider railway gauge and then take another train to Sydney.

As the train chortles along, Kathleen stares out the window. Occasionally, she opens the window and feels the breeze on her face. Annoyingly, bits of soot from the coal-fuelled train get into her eyes. She closes the window and continues her gaze. One by one, they cross over creeks and rivers and she notices the water flows east and in the distance she wonders, without words, where it goes. She carries pictures in her mind of the creeks and rivers she knows and the creeks and rivers she has crossed. She falls asleep through the night.

With his eyes half closed her father sits quietly opposite her, and watches her intently when she is not looking at him. While she is excited at the prospect of a holiday, her father's heart breaks as he worries about the decision they made. She does not understand that at the end of this journey her formal education begins at the age of eleven.

The third segment of the journey is the train trip from Sydney to Newcastle at the mouth of the Hunter River and to Waratah. They cross over bigger rivers. Kathleen sees the rivers expand and flow to form into oceans, like she has never seen before. With this vision her mind is challenged to expand and enter into unknown realms of meaning as vast as oceans on horizons.

Richard and Kathleen arrive at Rosary Convent Waratah where the Dominican Sisters conduct the school for Deaf girls, known as the *Institute for the Deaf and Dumb*. No longer are Deaf boys educated here, as earlier in the history of Waratah. Earlier still, it had been known as the *Deaf and Dumb Asylum*; the concept of asylum indicating one who is given shelter or needs treatment or confinement.[2] They were places for individuals for whom society could not cope.[3] Was Kathleen not able to be coped with? And the word *dumb* in the name does not fit with this intelligent young girl.

After leaving his daughter on arrival that day, Richard stays in nearby accommodation, a pub where he has a beer and sits with his thoughts. *Has she settled? Will she be alright?* Returning to the school next morning he peeks into the window to see his cherished daughter with tears smudging her face. He feels the constriction in his heart. And she searches for her father and for reasons why he has left her and left her so vulnerable in the unfamiliarity of this place and in the strangeness of communication, arms and fingers flying about in what appears to be chaos. Confusion besets her and a sense of helplessness comes over her as he returns home to the family, knowing she thinks he has abandoned her.

* * *

School is a foreign world for Kathleen. She is student Girl Number 192 in the enrolment register at Waratah. Many times Kathleen has supervised her siblings on their way to a local school that could not manage her education because, as a Deaf child, she required a different method of teaching, as well as a different mode of communication. She now begins her understanding of a language, Australian-Irish Sign Language.

As the girls of all ages gather around Kathleen, they are curious to know who she is. *What is her name? Where is she from?* In an animated manner they sign to one another and then locate the sign name for Kathleen. They understand that it is their prerogative to give her a name, while she watches on, unable yet to respond to them. Will they give her a name that is descriptive, for example if she has long curls or a scar on her face, they may give her a sign name that surrounds the curls or the

---

[2] While such places were used for those with physical or mental needs, they were particularly used as a mental hospital, formerly termed a lunatic asylum.

[3] As much as the proceedings of recent inquiries into child abuse have found distressing instances of fault within Church based institutions, the reality is that it was Church organisations that often took up the challenge to care for children for specific reasons. The Dominican Sisters, as many religious orders did, came to Australia in the nineteenth and twentieth century and established social service structures and educational systems at a time of great poverty and educational dearth.

scar. Or the other alternative – can they form her name from one or two letters from her first name or last name? Kathleen – yes, they give her a 'K' shaped sign, her visual name in the Deaf community. They point to her and show the sign 'K' – again and again. She continues to watch the strangeness of signs – somehow they begin to make some sense to her.

Kathleen already understands that spoken words and signs have meaning, especially nouns that indicate a particular thing or a person but she is not conscious that this is an aspect of language. She learns many more nouns and her teacher gently guides her by showing her an article, pointing to a picture and giving it a sign. Then they show her how to spell the noun or the thing with the alphabet. *C-h-a-i-r, d-e-s-k, f-l-o-o-r, w-i-n-d-o-w*, hand, face, arms and legs. Suddenly her mind clicks in for her. Suddenly she realises – every thing – every animal, every bird, every place, every mood, every sense and every person has a name.

Adjectives come next together with colours and sizes and shapes. *Hard* chairs, *timber* desks, a *red* jumper, *black* shoes, *little* lambs, a *square* box! She signs the noun, *shoes*, and then gives it colour too. Her mind is enlightened, a world opens up to her and now she sees so many things – *so what is the sign for that and that and that?* The days are too short for learning, and the nights are too long in coming because she wants to lie in her bed and think about the day and the new signs – and think about her family and how she misses them.

Verbs and action are next. *How does someone present the picture of the little lambs? What are they doing?* They are *playing*. How do the hands move about to show *play* and *jump* and *frolic*? Now this is interesting. And the days and learning go on.

Personal pronouns are easy – *you* and *me*. Point to the other and to yourself. Then what about *us* and *them*? Then later she learns about *he* and *she*, *him* and *her*. Not so easy! This part is more difficult English. She not only learns to sign her own language, she learns written English, a second language.

She learns to sign words, read back other people signing to her, read and write English and do arithmetic, and she survives the humiliation and embarrassment of being in a class with the six and seven-year old children. Kathleen is a tall girl, pleasant and gentle.[iv] She longs to be with the older girls of her own age. In a drama production, she is dressed in a costume[v] as a maidservant, not knowing why or what she is supposed to be doing. All over her face she shows sulkiness and distress and sheer confusion. There are still gaps in her understanding and her heart anguishes as she carries loneliness and grief with her – especially being away from home during her early adolescent years.

Kathleen's teachers write to her parents and give them news of her progress. They also send letters with instructions for the family to also learn the Australian-Irish Sign Language and at least the *one-hand* alphabet. While on the farm with all its activities, Mary Adeline takes her practice of the signed alphabet very seriously, forever grateful to the Sisters for their foresight and attention to detail to improve family communication for when Kathleen returns home.

Determined to improve her signing and her understanding of a new language, Kathleen lies in bed at night with her hands under the blankets. She practises the alphabet and other signs, including her prayer signs. Soon, she is upgraded to the next class – and the next and next.

Sometimes Kathleen does not understand what the Sisters try to teach her. So she asks for help from the other Deaf girls. They explain things clearly to her, especially in mathematics and written English. The girls she chooses mainly have some hearing and are able to lip-read a little. Kathleen sees that the Sisters give them more time and thinks they are more favoured because they are brighter and easier to teach.

Later her mother questions her. Kathleen explains to her mother that because she is totally deaf, she finds that it is hard to understand some subjects. She further explains to her mother with some regret that she does not receive as much attention from the formal teachers as the others do now. But she also signs to her mother that the *clever* students and the teachers who are deaf can explain difficult concepts more easily to girls like her.

Upstairs in a special area, one of the girls shows Kathleen the telescope. This creates in her a passion for the stars and for all beyond the stars. Kathleen loves the night skies and everything beyond that forms mystery for her. Is this the *beyond* her mother points to at Church, when she tries to describe *Something – God?*

Kathleen learns the official sign for *God*, which points to the skies. She knows her mother looks up to the sky too, then closes her eyes to pray, as though there is something important about *up there* and *deep down inside behind our eyes and into our thoughts.*

She exclaims in sign at the array of tiny lights in the Milky Way and she makes story pictures in her mind of shapes that the stars make. At school she learns the story of

On Silver Days

My eyes are raised to the pale pink sky
Silhouetted graceful figures of birds in flight
Gliding, aligned in pristine sequence
Catch my breath and lift my fallen spirit
On silver days.

My slender fingers are raised in that sky
Formed in grace and shaped in flight
Rapturous meaning in native form
Catch my longing heart and lift my eyes
On silver days.

Bernadette T. Wallis

Bethlehem, the bright star and the Jesus nativity story, which makes sense of the crib she has seen at Christmas for years. She remembers the night under the Southern Cross when they sheltered under the dray as they crossed the State of Victoria from west to east.

As she kneels beside her bed that night, she closes her eyes, places her head into her hands and thinks of big skies, so big it is beyond thinking. The telescope takes her into another world of thousands of pictures beyond herself – and she finds solace there.

On some lonelier days at Waratah, she walks to the side at the back of the building and visits the large aviary. She drifts towards it and she observes the Little Corellas and remembers her Wonga pigeons and the black swans back home. In the process she thinks about signs and goes over her sign for *birds* and *flying*. At the aviary she rests her thoughts of home and lets herself feel the longing for loved ones. She notices the variety of migrating birds and their flight patterns in the sky and imagines they are also flying over *home* on the Murray River. She watches as they change places and support the weakest by allowing them to fall behind into their slipstream. For the moment she is in that slipstream herself. She imagines herself changing places as one of the weak ones who has fallen behind and needs the support of stronger ones.

* * *

After ten long months, her first year at the school is finished and Kathleen packs up her luggage for the Christmas holidays. The government supplies free rail concessions to and from school for the children, since Waratah is recognised as a national Institute. The long return trip is an exciting one not only for Kathleen but the other girls who come from further south as far as Melbourne and Tasmania. As they take the journey home over three and four segments, to Sydney, Albury and for Kathleen to Benalla, the mood is one of joy and expectation. Her knowledge has expanded to include information that she can now communicate in a more organised and skilled way.

As she gazes out the window of the slow-moving steam train she remembers the first trip with her father and the disillusionment at its end. As she crosses the same creeks and rivers flowing east, she realises that she returns different – different in a new way.

On arrival at the Benalla Railway Station after travelling more than seventy kilometres in the horse and gig, her father and three of the siblings wait in anticipation for her. The steam train pulls in with all its fuss – noise, steam and whistles. Kathleen alights. Deaf children still on board wave ferociously, signing good-byes and a happy Christmas. The family looks onto the scene in awe and amazement. They have never seen a Deaf group together and have never seen Deaf people communicate in a Sign language. They are Kathleen's friends. This is new. The initial awkwardness with her father and family is overcome by love and longing. Kathleen is new and yet the same loved Girlie.

The conversation with her well-loved and gentle father is one of reconciliation and many questions. She is comforted when he gesticulates to her that he came back the next day to see her through the window. He explains he saw her tears. He also gestures that he cried too with tears that rolled down his cheeks. She is glad they missed her and she is glad that the family did not really abandon her, as she was tempted to believe.

Her mother's letters are written directly to her now and not dependent on the Sisters translating the letters. Kathleen is excited to see the family, the farm and the animals again and to see her young siblings who have grown considerably. She proudly shows her sister, Monica, that she reads, as she holds an open book with a sense of achievement. Her sister Molly has set up an aviary and they can now share their stories of birds and they observe them and watch how they feed their young. Now she is older and with language she shares more and understands more.

As they pace the horses, the trip home to *Carlyle* cannot come quickly enough, but it becomes dark. *Where do they stay overnight?* Whatever – early in the morning they continue to cross over creeks and finally the river at Yarrawonga, where dragonflies lift themselves into flight and begin their morning fly-overs as the sun dawns. A few more kilometres – Kathleen's mother greets her at the gate. Kathleen receives the greatest surprise of all. Her mother signs to her with the Australian-Irish Sign alphabet. This is a poignant moment for her. The possibility of deeper communication with her mother now exists!

---

[i] http://littledesertlodge.com.au/media/uploads/Koorie-History.pdf.

[ii] http://www.janesoceania.com/australia_aboriginal_dreamtime/index1.htm.

[iii] From a thesis by J.A. Burke, *The History of Catholic Schooling for Deaf and Dumb Children in the Hunter Valley* 1974 held in Dominican Archives Strathfield NSW p.37.

[iv] From the *Diary of Agnes Lynch* 1930 held in the Waratah section of University of Newcastle *Archives.*

[v] The students in this photo were all named in the Waratah section of University of Newcastle *Archives,* except for Kathleen. No one recognised her. She is now identified for their records.

CHAPTER 5

FROM THE GOULBURN RIVER
TO WARATAH AND CASTLE HILL

The Wonga Pigeon

Jumps to a branch

Close to the ground

Preens its plume

In dappled sunlight

And glides down again.

Among the Taungurung tribe, there were the *dwellers on the mountains* and the *dwellers on the rivers*,[i] and of the tribe, the Warring-Illum Balug people lived on the Upper Goulburn River and the Yauung-Ilam-Baluk people lived around Yea. The main camp was at the junction of Muddy Creek, later re-named Yea River, and the East side of the Goulburn River. The children of the tribe would watch the dragonflies dart along in the shadows of the evening sunset.

Don's sister Marie is ready for formal education in a school. In their search for quality care and an education system for Marie, Abe and Emma are influenced by Catholic Church leaders who speak passionately about the national Catholic Deaf School conducted by the Dominican Sisters at Rosary Convent, Waratah. They are also motivated by their Catholic faith and the emphasis on Catholic education. It is the only Catholic school for Deaf children in Australia.

Emma has a strong Catholic Irish mind-set with a social conscience and a deep faith in God's providence that God will be with their daughter and take care of her through the Sisters. Taking six-year-old Marie with her, Emma leaves the small children, Jack and Don, at home under the care of her mother and Abe, while they begin the long train journey from down the road at Homewood. They catch the small steam train that runs from Alexandra through Yea and Homewood to Seymour. At Seymour they catch the train to Albury and then another one to Sydney and yet another to Newcastle. At Newcastle they board the small train to Broadmeadow near Waratah.

The driver from the school at Waratah meets them at Broadmeadow in his horse and cart. While he carefully transfers the luggage, Emma focuses on the horse.

She gives it a strong pat and leans her tired head against its neck for a brief moment, pausing to rest her mind before she climbs into the cart. She would like to take the reins too, but her mind is whirling and her heart sinks at the thought of the next step – leaving her daughter at the school and returning home without her. There are silent tears, inward tears – but just now she knows her daughter requires more than she can give.

Marie begins at Waratah just one year after the death of the foundress, Sister Gabriel Hogan, whose Irish influence remained as strong as was her life commitment to the use of Sign language as fundamental to the education of Deaf children. The Dominican Sisters at Waratah have been tutored under Sister Gabriel and are committed to her philosophies. They are women with great experience and knowledge of the life and needs of Deaf children and are ready to impart that experience and knowledge to parent and Deaf child alike.

Twenty-eight-year old Emma takes the opportunity to engage in a lengthy conversation with them, asking many questions regarding deafness in families and the education of Deaf children. *Why are her children deaf? With their experience do they know of other parents who have more than one child who is deaf?* Yes, it is true. There are families with more than one Deaf child. *Does the discussion happen about recessive genes? Does she draw a blank? What is the best way to help her children?*

In managing her daughter, she already develops *home* signs. The Sisters explain that Sign language is more than signs in themselves; it is a language. Emma tells them that she also has a two-year old son at home who is deaf. *How can she, as Marie and Don's mother, learn Sign as a language? Explain more please, how can I learn and what are the proper signs to communicate?* The Sisters tell Emma to learn as soon as possible, so that she can use it with her young son even before he goes to school.

The Sisters show Emma the Australian-Irish sign for Waratah – a hand sign of a 'W' in the Australian-Irish alphabet, the thumb holding the little finger down, allowing three fingers spread in an upright position, and moving her hand in the shape of a circle beside the right temple or ear. She shows her little daughter, who looks with interest and intrigue, not sure what to make of what is happening right now.

With Marie at her side, Emma meets other mothers and their Deaf children. Some are well experienced and know the routine of the school. She looks around and notices children signing to one another in such a fluent flow-like dance and with vibrancy that lights up the environment. Marie watches them intently. They are excited to see one another and give each other hugs, then they step back to leave a space between them in order to sign and communicate their stories about the Christmas holidays. She also sees some children draw back and resist. Tears run down their cheeks as they cling to their parents. They want to return home – they need coaxing and reassurance. Others are happy – this place is family for them.

At Waratah many of the teachers and staff who are Deaf ex-students who have stayed on after they finished their formal education, surround Emma and little Marie too. Emma gains an inkling of hope and the courage to entrust her daughter to the Sisters. She holds herself erect when she leaves her daughter in their hands not allowing any more tears to break through just now. She is strong, and both Abe and Emma want the best for their daughter. With the support of the Sisters Emma teaches herself to sign the Irish alphabet and other signs. In turn she teaches Don at home and continues to take on the responsibilities of bringing up her other young children with everyday tasks at home – and she is pregnant again.

Abe and Emma worry about their finances. *How will they manage their children's special education?* As time moves on questions of deafness subside into the background. Their lives are full with other interests and they have other concerns with family, work and the farm-life.

* * *

Marie comes home ten and a half months later for the long Christmas holidays and Emma acquires further skills in Sign language from her daughter. Marie signs to her brother Don, and teaches her brother Jack too. She feels strange to be home again and it is strange for her brothers. She misses her friends back at school, whom she lived with every day for twenty-four hours a day through the year and with whom she communicates well. On her return she travels on the train with her friends, this time under supervision of older Deaf people who care for her – and she has much to share with her school friends and teachers, who, with ease, flow with language through their bodies.

In 1918 during World War I, Don turns six and is ready for school at Waratah. Emma travels with the two children, Marie and Don and Deaf adult teachers who chaperone the children returning to Waratah for school. Marie signs to Don, *School…Big building…many big stone steps to climb.* She attempts to explain where they sleep at night and how each day they learn many things. She continues, *You will see birds in the aviary…and a telescope to see beyond the stars.* It is all beyond his imagination. He sleeps on the train through the long night. As Don arrives at Waratah he runs up the big stone steps that are just as his sister explained. Of course Miss Hanney is there and ready to meet the new children. It is not long before his mother leaves him with her. He stops and suddenly feels lost and lonely. His mother has gone – he is not very brave just now. Small and innocent, like a chick ousted from the shelter of its shell into a new vulnerable, yet protective space at Waratah, Don begins a new life and develops within a new family.

The Sisters and Deaf teachers nurture him from this early age and influence him considerably. Quizzically and warily he looks at the Sisters in their traditional religious dress, black veils and long white habits, wearing headgear that hides their

43

hair – only their faces can be seen. Everyone accepts them as normal – and they smile and laugh welcomingly so that gives him comfort. But it is very strange to him. Using Sign language as taught by his mother and sister, Don shyly communicates with the Sisters and teachers. While he misses his mother, the green hills and the rock boulders, the horses and the free spirit of home, the Waratah community sign to him in ways he comprehends and understands – they take over both parenting and teaching roles.

Don meets his first teacher, Sister Columba. She has a special gentle way with small children like him and becomes a significant person for him. She finds the key to his mind as she does with any Deaf child. She treats Don and other children as individuals and not as just another child in the institution. With her kind heart and depth of human empathy she enters into *all the joys and sorrows of the silent little ones*. She wins their confidence so completely that *they look at her as a true mother, guide and friend*.[ii]

As one of her *silent* children, Don approaches her with confidence. He *clings* to her. Her Sign language tells him that he is understood and renders to him what he needs. Nothing is too much trouble or too good to give to her children.[iii] She is firm when it comes to a principle that involves her Deaf children[iv], insisting on what is best for them. Waratah is family to Don for five years, providing a home away from home with such easy communication and loving care.

* * *

Don quickly learns the intricacies of Australian-Irish Sign Language – both to sign the language and to understand what others are signing about. For this facilitates true communication. Captivated, he watches the stories that are signed to him in class or in the playground or at dinner or wherever, and his mind is extended, whether they are stories with pathos and drama or stories with intrigue and humour. He thirsts for information in picture form that lifts his mind and forms the basis for his adult life's quest for knowledge. Learning and knowing solves mysteries that form in his mind from the gaps of information to which his deafness contributes. Knowledge also forms further questions for the life journey.

Even as a more introverted and serious child, Don expresses his passion for sport and wants to achieve and do well in everything. He becomes a good soccer player and while the boys are alert and watchful as they run the field, the umpire develops a unique method of controlling the game, waving arms and signing instructions on the field. Proudly holding the sign which indicates the year and grade of his team, Don, as team leader, feels the responsibility heavily, as he lines up with his Deaf soccer team for the group photo. The children keep very still for the cameraman for what seems like an eternity. Intently, Don watches the photographer under the black cloth with the camera and really wants to know how it all works. While he is tired of sitting and waiting, he also wishes to be a good little boy. The photographer comes back to the school to show the photo to the excited boys who are identified as *Rosary Convent Soccer Team*.

At the end of the year when Don returns home to Homewood, his little brothers wonder who he is. They puzzle over the bigger boy entering into their space and into their home. They had forgotten him as their brother – they cannot communicate with him. Not yet! Just six weeks later, Don disappears again from their lives – for another year of school.

* * *

Even though the girls dominate in number, the small Deaf boys form an integral part of the life of the school at Waratah. As they reach the age of fourteen it is evident that they require a different environment for their ongoing education. Adolescent boys are difficult to manage in the setting and numbers are increasing.[v] Don's parents and other parents realise the problem too. The Sisters cannot offer the boys a trade and nor can they provide them with strong male mentors. Sister Columba garners support from not only local bishops but also those outside of NSW as well. *Is she responsible for the exchange between Archbishop Daniel Mannix of Melbourne and thirteen-year old Gerald Turnley in 1921?*

From Victoria, Gerald is at school in Waratah and writes on behalf of all the boys asking for financial assistance so that a new school for Deaf boys will go ahead in Sydney. He tells the Archbishop of his desire to attend a Christian Brothers' school because he desperately wants to learn a trade. All the boys sign the letter, including Don, at nine years of age.

Institute for the Deaf and Dumb
Waratah, N.S.W.
August 16th, 1921

To Most Rev. Dr. Mannix,

May it please your Grace to read this letter from a deaf and dumb boy. I know you will not be displeased with me, because you said you would help 'the weak and oppressed.'

When the Brisbane Express passed through Waratah on Wednesday morning, 10th August, all the deaf mutes were on their balcony waving white, green, and yellow streamers, because they were so glad that your Grace had returned to Australia. Did you see them? I hope so. Sister asked me if I would like to write to your Grace about the Brothers. I said, 'Yes, but Sister must help me.'

I am in trouble, because I shall be fourteen soon, and I must leave the Nuns' school; but I am not half educated yet, so I want your Grace please to pray that the Christian Brothers from Ireland, promised by Dr. Kelly, will soon get the school for deaf mute boys in Sydney.

I want to go to the Brothers' school when it is built in Sydney, and to learn a trade, and always be a good Catholic.

The Christian Brothers are only waiting for money to begin the school. Will your Grace kindly help us by telling some rich people about the urgent needs of the deaf and dumb boys and then they will give money for our school?

The boys will all write their names for you; they all join in begging your Grace to help them. The deaf and dumb are 'weak and oppressed,' because so few understand their wants, or care to be troubled about them.

There are three other deaf and dumb boys here from Victoria, and six girls.

I hope your Grace will forgive me for writing so much, and we all hope you will hear our voices, which (though dumb) plead for pity to the kindest human Heart, also Divine, and also do they beg pity and help from those who represent Him.

I am, with deep respect,

Your Grace's affectionate little friend,

GERALD[vi]

It is not difficult to surmise that the Sisters helped formulate this letter written by Gerald. The Sisters are influential and know how to win the hearts of people and how to ask the pertinent question of one whose charter it is to care for the most vulnerable in society. Archbishop Mannix replies to thirteen-year old Gerald with a subtle message for the Sisters as to why they did not build in Melbourne!

Raheen
Kew
Victoria
19th September (1921)

My dear Gerald,

I was delighted to get your letter signed by all the boys. It is a beautiful letter and if you and the Sisters would allow me to publish it in the Catholic papers, I think it would enlist sympathy for the Deaf and Dumb boys. Of course, your name need not be published.

I am coming to Sydney next month and I hope to hear good news from the Christian Brothers and from the Archbishop about the new institution.

Will you tell all the boys I am very grateful to them for their kind thought of giving me a real Australian welcome on Wednesday 10th August as the train passed Waratah?

Tell the Sisters too that I am sorry they did not build their nice Convent down here in Victoria. It is such a long, long way to Waratah.
With every good wish and blessing for you and all the boys and girls and Sisters,

I am

My dear Gerald,

Sincerely yours,

+ D. Mannix[vii]

---

* * *

Finally, the Sisters inform the parents that all the boys will transfer from Waratah to the new school soon to be built for boys at Castle Hill under the management of the Christian Brothers.

On 26 April 1922, Brothers Joseph O'Farrell and Damian Allen arrive in Australia aboard the *SS Ormonde* to teach in an ancient and new land. Entering into picturesque Sydney Cove, they are filled with expectation, arriving just less than fifty years after Waratah is established. Brother Dominic O'Shea is already in Australia and joins them on the foundation staff for the first twelve months. After further training in Ireland, Brother Henry Esmonde arrives a few months later to join them in their earnest endeavour – their mission in Australia.

This new development excites the Deaf community who are expectant too as about fifty ex-students from Waratah gather to give the Brothers a warm welcome in full sign.

The Brothers plan to build an exact replicate design of St Joseph's School for the Deaf in Cabra, Ireland and use the same methods of teaching and the same order of day for the Australian Deaf boys in the school.[viii] The philosophy of the Brothers in their teaching of Deaf children in Australian-Irish Sign Language indicates men with educated minds and thorough training in Deaf education.

Initially, the Brothers with some of the boys move into the homestead – the mansion – as a temporary and very difficult arrangement. Known as *Southleigh*, the grand two-storey timber mansion with a grey slated roof stands on a gentle hill and can be seen for miles around. A rail siding not far from the front gate is called *Southleigh*, where the light steam train with two carriages runs between Westmead and Rogan's Hill. The railway line runs parallel to the gravel road into the village of Castle Hill.

Preparations are made and the first sod of ground is turned to build the School. On the 10 September 1922, Archbishop Michael Kelly of Sydney blesses the project and lays the foundation stone of the first building. He announces in a pastoral letter that the name of the school is to be St Gabriel's School for Deaf Boys and he places it under the patronage of St Gabriel the Archangel. In this way he connects the school to the story in the gospel of John the Baptist's father, Zachary, who was struck speechless during the pregnancy of his wife Elizabeth in her old age. Luke 1:18-23. Of course, the name also has overtones of Sister Gabriel Hogan, who introduced Deaf education through Irish Sign Language into the Catholic system in Australia.

Reports describe that on *the far-famed hill of Parramatta* is fast appearing the future Cabra of NSW and that *an army of tradesmen* are renovating the existing premises and erecting the new institution.[ix]

The Sisters prepare the young Waratah boys with explanations in Sign of the new school. Leaving the security and safety of the feminine environment of nurture and care, Don feels nervous. From the age of six, Waratah has been his home, where he lived for ten and a half months each year without returning to family, but at the age of eleven now, he will enjoy the freedom from bossy girls. Really he is eager at the new prospect of boys only at the school. *What will his new teachers look like? Can they sign and communicate like the Sisters and others at Waratah?*

Don soon learns the sign for St Gabriel's school, which is a 'G' from the Australian-Irish signed alphabet, where his thumb and index finger touch with three fingers softly spread and upright, then he lifts the hand with the 'G' sign and circles it twice at the side of the head, close to his ear. He notices that the position of his hand is the same as for Waratah, but with the 'W' and not the 'G' from the Signed alphabet.

∗ ∗ ∗

On 5 April 1923 Don shifts into the new St Gabriel's school with the other boys from Waratah. In the school register he is Student number 10. Open space surrounds them. He pauses as he stands and looks around at the three hundred and sixty degree view across the hills and valleys of the countryside. While shrubs and some trees are close around the mansion, the land is clear,

St Gabriel's School for Deaf Boys

where there had once been farming and grazing. With excited anticipation, Don establishes himself in the new setting with new teachers – they are all male. They wear long black habits with narrow white collars around the neck.

Don soon learns about the Brothers and their particular characteristics and background. Learning Sign language early in his teaching career, Brother Joseph O'Farrell, aged forty-five, comes as a first class teacher directly from St Joseph's School for Deaf Boys in Ireland.[x] A storyteller, he holds the boys' interest in class using fingerspelling and Sign language with grace and neatness in his movements. He is clear with the matter of his lessons guaranteeing the boys' attention.[xi] And while he is kind and considerate, welcoming and appreciative, his gifts are sometimes hidden behind his stern exterior and commanding presence.[xii] Don is conflicted in his loyalty with Brother O'Farrell. He dislikes the strictness but appreciates the quality of his teaching.

Appointed as Brother O'Farrell's co-worker, Brother Damian Allen, aged thirty, specialises as a teacher of the Deaf. He also had learnt Sign language at Cabra. With his impressive big movements in sign, he too is clear and fluent as he communicates and teaches the Deaf boys. His style makes it easy for them to understand and be understood. Cheerful and friendly, graceful and distinctive in his signing, he invites respect from the boys. A larger than life character, he is a man of action and activity, deeply religious with prayer as the mainspring of his life.[xiii] An energetic Brother Allen with his own flair for drama recognizes the boys' natural gifts for acting. He excels in working with them in presenting stage performances that include biblical or historical episodes. The huge casts give opportunities for as many Deaf boys as possible to participate.

Brother Henry Esmonde is the young one, aged twenty-two. His infectious smile is endearing and he develops his reputation as a storyteller. With eloquent signs, he sits on the desk with the Deaf students around him broadening their education as he relates historical stories. Winning the affection of his pupils, he keeps his teaching interesting. He has no discipline problems.[xiv] His impressive facial expressions and gestures leave no Deaf person in doubt as to his pleasure or displeasure, especially when it comes to *the violation of God's law*.[xv] He makes rapid progress in the highly specialised art of instructing the Deaf.[xvi] He is frustrated and angry when the boys appear to be smart or when they attempt to explain themselves out of a difficult situation. However, over the course of his time in Deaf education, he mellows and develops a more forgiving attitude.

Brother O'Shea is also qualified as a teacher of Deaf children from earlier days in Cabra. While he comes with experience of general teaching in Australia, experience of the Australian culture and with some knowledge of the local scene, he is of rigid character and finds it difficult in this fledgling school for Deaf boys where the conditions are still basic.

An older man, Brother James Martin Hayes, having come from County Cork in 1890, works on the farm – and plays cricket. With the help of other Brothers and the boys, including Don, he builds temporary workrooms of which they are very proud. Besides classrooms they require work spaces for the purpose of teaching trades, as well as making clothes, including sport wear, for the boys. They also build stables and improve the farm attached to the school. It eventually supplies all the vegetables, butter, milk, eggs and bacon required by the school. The boys take part in all of the activities on the premises and Don learns a variety of skills as well.

Brother Hayes is an authority on poultry raising; Don follows him with interest as he enters the fowl yard. He observes the chooks and their behaviour and collects the eggs, as he did at home. At least Don knows about geese from the time he was attacked as a small child. When the rooster crows in the early morning, Don and the boys are not disturbed. No noises disturb them. During their breaks from the classroom, the Brothers teach them in ordinary conversation about such noise as roosters' crowing, so they further understand the behaviour of chooks in the fowl yard and the annoyance of people who are awoken at dawn in the early hours of morning.

* * *

The well-educated Brothers communicate, discuss and sign with the boys every day. The Irish Sign Language used by the Brothers differs slightly from what has developed at Waratah. While the boys adjust to their signs and the Brothers learn signs from them, the Irish Sign Language that began at Waratah nearly fifty years earlier has already developed with the Australian influence and morphed, as a living language, into Australian-Irish Sign Language. It is no longer purely Irish Sign Language, but Australian-Irish Sign.[1]

The Brothers teach the *Combined Method*, as is the situation at Waratah. They have strong convictions in the way they teach and what they teach the boys. They believe that Deaf children are cut off from all communication through the ear and this can be addressed through the eye, a visual approach to communication. They proudly use a method in their teaching based on three principles:

Firstly, that they use the visual language of pictures and signs and gestures;
Secondly, that the *finger* alphabet and writing makes them acquainted with written language; and
Thirdly, in some cases, that articulation and reading of the lips help those who once heard but lost hearing when they were young.

The Brothers write articles in the Catholic paper, *The Advocate*, explaining that the Sign language is the most efficient and the easiest medium for communication with their Deaf students. They also advocate the *Combined Method*, where they teach Sign language, lip-reading and articulation of words for students with residual hearing who would benefit from it. Don – and later Charlie – is not in this category.

Each day, the Brothers teach to awaken and inform the minds of Deaf children as they give ideas and knowledge by means of the visual language. Believing that through sign the boys will learn about objects and people, they add words to give further knowledge. Initially the Brothers teach the children that words convey the same ideas to our minds that pictures and signs do to theirs; they then teach them to change signs for words until the written or printed character is as readily understood as the picture or sign. The Brothers know that the process takes a long time, as they repeat the process with every English word. They teach the names of

---

[1] The same happens in Auslan, Australian Sign Language that developed primarily from British Sign Language.

51

visible objects (nouns), of visible qualities (adjectives), and of visible actions (verbs), and through gradual teaching the boys acquire understanding. To master the syntax of the English language the Brothers work with the boys with perseverance and hard work.[xvii]

From Ireland, the Brothers bring *a perfect system of graded language charts* which are all hand-painted by an Irish Deaf artist; and *each picture is designed to teach a special part of the English language. The first chart introduces the child to scenes in the home and to scenes outside of it.* The Brothers note that at first the child *can only look at the objects and point out with a vacant stare at the teacher. He takes the little hand of the child and teaches him to make a natural sign to represent the various objects that interest him.*

Their patience is rewarded and they are uplifted when they see each boy brighten up as he discovers *he has now a name for things he saw so often at home, but could never express. He crosses his hands on his breast for his mother who fondly loves him, and imitates a man with a beard for his daddy. He places his hand on his knee to call the dog, and pats his left hand for pussy-cat. These words he learns to spell in the signs of the alphabet on fingers, and afterwards learns to write on his slate.*[xviii]

While the charts are Irish-European based, the Irish Brothers encounter differences and learn of Australian cultural concepts familiar to boys like Don. They find new signs for such words as kangaroo, emu, koala, Vegemite, for the different football codes, for the Melbourne Cup and for the place names for towns the boys know: Melbourne, Sydney, Seymour and the towns where each of the boys come from. The Brothers learn these signs from the older boys, who already have a language for such concepts from Waratah or other Deaf residential schools in Sydney and Melbourne.

The Brothers also encourage fingerspelling, which assists with place names and people's names, where there are no signs yet. Don is taught to discipline himself with fingerspelling of words and this in turn supports his English spelling and writing skills. Emma and Abraham are pleased when they see it assists him in his writing of English with pen and paper, so as to communicate with his father and people outside of the Deaf community. Don's English reading skills are enhanced and this enables him to acquire further information and extend his comprehension and understanding in his education. His parents see that these skills add to his work prospects.

In this process of education, the Brothers bridge *the chasm of mental darkness* by these steps, and the road to knowledge is open to the Deaf child. They are very clear that they expect that the students apply themselves to study and that teachers need to use their skills and ingenuity.[xix] Don expects this for himself. He puts his energy into whatever job he undertakes and he uses his talents to address obstacles and challenges in creative ways.

The Brothers appreciate the opportunity to share the Catholic faith through their teaching and practice. As the children learn their prayers in signs and advance in the visible language of signs, the Brothers give a more in-depth instruction and carefully prepare the children for the Sacraments, including First Communion. The Brothers work with senior pupils to further their knowledge of Christian Doctrine, Bible History, the History of Australia, English, Grammar, Geography, Arithmetic, and Drawing.[xx]

* * *

A new wing is built approximately two years after the laying of the foundation. More accommodation assists with the problem of the increase of both students and staff. From early morning to nightfall, the school is a place of routine and strong discipline. Don's education here is based on the thinking, principles and approach of the founding Brothers. Abe and Emma watch their growing son year by year. Don has the opportunity for further training, physically, socially, morally and especially for a trade that gives future possibilities of work. They know, too, that Don's brother, Charlie, will also have the same supportive opportunity.

Between 1925 and 1926, Mary Thomson, formerly Meehan, who is deaf and originally from Melbourne, is employed as the Matron. She is an important influence on the boys and adds a softer touch to the school. As an ex-student from Waratah, she signs and communicates easily with the boys. Her task is to care for them and more especially the junior boys and their personal needs, so she allays their fears and anxieties when homesickness and loneliness strike. She shows affection and sits in an armchair in the centre of the junior boys, who surround her.[xxi] One small boy sits on a wooden rocking horse; one is on a small tricycle and the other sits in front of Mary, as he cuddles closely the little well-loved dog at St Gabriel's. She loves her boys and guards them protectively.

* * *

As the majority of schools for Deaf children globally are residential schools with an institutional style of living, they are a breeding ground for the development of Sign language and Deaf culture. In Waratah and St Gabriel's, developments in Sign language occur according to the need, as in other Deaf groups and communities. Different signs can arise for the same meaning in different settings and with use is accepted as the local dialect.

Don sees this happening in his own family, as well as through other residential schools and local groups of Deaf people from various parts of Australia. The *home* sign that Don uses for the steam train, which passes by not far from his home at Homewood, is different from the official sign at his school. At a later stage using the official sign, he adds colour and further meaning to his own sign. The *home* signs that he and his Deaf friends make are witnessed by other Deaf children and sometimes add to their lexicon and can influence the official sign.

The Brother in charge instructs Don, *Go into the village and fetch items from the pharmacy. Don't be long.* Known as a competent horseman, Don is happy to complete this chore riding on the school horse. He takes the route into Castle Hill village along the railway line. He sees the light steam train coming down the railway line and sets up a race with the train. His aim is to cross the railway line in front of the train as it comes into the village – to his competitive glee. As he gallops beside the train, he and the horse are one. The train driver watches carefully and anxiously as he holds his breath – Don does it! He gently pulls up his horse after crossing the line and feels the thrill of his heart racing and the horse panting beneath him.

He is highly gestural as he signs to his mates and tells his story. They visualise the huge wheels of the steam train with shafts rotating and smoke billowing, the horse sweating, and a close shave to a tragedy where the train and horse may have collided. His adventurous story is then related to everyone with gusto, except the Brothers!

On his holiday home he repeats the story in full sign to his brothers. Charlie, as a four-year old, regularly visits the Seymour railway yards on his three-wheeler tricycle attracted by the visual movement of shunting trains. He is captivated by Don's animated story and cannot wait until he, too, can race the school horse along the railway line with the light steam train at Castle Hill.

* * *

The Brothers explain to the boys that to work satisfactorily in the world they must have good social graces and know how to behave in society. This also pleases Emma and Abe. The boys are exposed to many opportunities in the social arena, including the meeting and entertaining of many civic and Church dignitaries who visit St Gabriel's. Don is fourteen years of age when a visitor describes his experience thus: *the respectful manliness in the boys and the genuine love of the Brothers for the work and their little charges, are the idea and the secret of the success we witnessed. Comparing these smart and happy children with the dreadful state of the uneducated deaf and dumb, one can realise the great work for God and Country being done at St. Gabriel's.*[xxii]

The Brothers emphasise sport, which pleases Don who is a natural. They consider sport seriously and use it as a method firstly, of building the boys' confidence, secondly, of developing their physical skills and lastly, of maintaining a healthy mental state. In his gymnastic sport's wear in the Drill Class, Don displays his skill in the pyramids that are formed. As the boys stretch their bodies in the St Gabriel's Gymnastic group competition they win the Shield at the Castle Hill Agricultural Show in 1924.

The boys enjoy drama and entertaining and in the process learn their Australian European history. In 1926 at the St Gabriel's Christmas Benefit Concert in the Australian Hall, Sydney, young Don is in a costume of a colonial officer and one of his mates is Captain Cook in the Deaf boys' display of the British arriving on Australian soil.

While there is no swimming pool at St Gabriel's at the time, Don is content to swim in the creeks below in the valley that are similar to the creeks and rivers at home. While swimming in the summer, Don challenges himself swimming freestyle, butterfly and breast-stroke, as well as underwater for many meters with controlled breath. He surprises everyone wherever he emerges. The McCarthy boys down the road at home often join Don and Charlie in the Goulburn River. Don watches out for young Anthony as they play and swim and Anthony watches Don in awe as he swims across the river with a pea rifle held high in one hand,[xxiii] a skill Don develops. The dragonflies flee upstream to avoid the splash and wash of water.

St Gabriel's boys down by the river in the bush. Don at front on far right.
Centre: the older Brother Hayes, circa 1925

[i] *http://www.seymourhealth.org.au/*

[ii] Fr M. F. O'Reilly, From a *Talk at Requiem Mass for Sister Columba Dwyer*, 26 March 1924, Dominican Archives, Strathfield

[iii] *Waratah Report* 1923/1924:5-6

[iv] Fr M. F. O'Reilly, From a *Talk at Requiem Mass for Sister Columba Dwyer*, 26 March 1924, Dominican Archives, Strathfield

[v] On the occasion of the 75th Anniversary of St Gabriel's, Brian James Johnston researched and compiled *Memories of St. Gabriel's – 75th Anniversary Commemorative Book* printed by NSW Government Printing Service, 2000, p.5

[vi] Gerald Turnley Letter to Archbishop Daniel Mannix, published in Institution for the Deaf and Dumb Waratah, NSW Report, 1921-1922, p.52

[vii] Archbishop Daniel Mannix to Gerald Turnley, published in Institution for the Deaf and Dumb Waratah, NSW Report, 1921-1922, pp. 53-56

[viii] The Christian Brothers' Educational Record – Necrology pp.455-490

[ix] Catholic Press, 27 July 1922

[x] Necrology The Christian Brothers' Educational Record p.341

[xi] Ibid

[xii] Ibid p.342

[xiii] Ibid p.284

[xiv] Ibid p.110

[xv] Ibid

[xvi] Christian Brothers' Educational Record: Chronology p.107

[xvii] Christian Brothers' Educational Record, 1927 Article: *The Education of the Deaf and Dumb in Australia*

[xviii] Ibid p.146

[xix] Ibid p.145

[xx] Ibid p.146

[xxi] Ibid photo p.63

[xxii] Annals of St Gabriel's 1926, p.51

[xxiii] *Presentation* in Yea on the occasion of a Celebration of the 104th anniversary of the baptism of John Wallis by Anthony McCarthy. Held in Missionary Sisters of Service Archives.

CHAPTER 6

WARATAH ON THE HUNTER RIVER

Along new tracks

The Wonga Pigeons

Continue to pick and peck

Close by as they keep in sight

Stay safe

And never look up.

The Wonnarua Koori people with the Awabakal, Worimi, Wonnarua, Geawegal, Biripi and Darkinung tribes were inhabitants of the Hunter region of New South Wales. They cared for the land for thousands of generations.

Along the expansive and wide Hunter River (*Myan* in the local Aboriginal dialect),[i] the dragonflies are playful in the summer months as they prey among the mangroves for mosquitoes. They display their skill as they alight on a leaf or a branch that flows with the current, pause a moment and quickly lift and hover. In the wetlands the bluegums and paperbarks display their beauty and uniqueness. Beyond the wetlands the Waratah blooms, the bright red native flowering tree that thrives in sandy soils. The *red flowering tree* is stunning in its beauty among the dusky greens of the Australian bush. The name Waratah is given to a suburb in the town of Newcastle.

* * *

The adolescent fourteen year-old Kathleen is inspired by the story of Sister Gabriel Hogan who came to Australia from Ireland to found the school for Deaf children at Waratah. She learns that Sister Gabriel was described as the educator at Waratah and that Sister Columba Dwyer was described as the heart of Waratah. The third pioneer of Deaf education at Waratah was Miss Marianne Hanney, who had also watched over both Marie and Don from the tender age of six when they began school – and until they left Waratah. These pioneer teachers were a formidable trio of women educators.

Miss Hanney is still at Waratah when Kathleen arrives and they converse together about important things now – and about the story of the school. From experience she knows that Miss Hanney is kind and gentle, and she sees that Miss Hanney is respected as the soul of Waratah.

Sister Gabriel died in 1915 and Sister Columba died in 1924. Kathleen wants to know more about them. She learns more from Miss Hanney, who was *identified* with the School.[ii] Miss Hanney explains:

In 1875 Sister Gabriel, a young, smallish Deaf woman from Dublin, arrived in Australia and established the School for Deaf children using her own language, Irish Sign Language. She herself was deaf. She brought her gift of teaching to Australia and she believed that education was a priority for Deaf children.

As a brilliant educator, the approach that Sister Gabriel took to Deaf education was well defined. She fiercely defended Sign language as essential for Deaf people's free expression in communication. She firmly believed that education in Sign language created the opportunity for an expansive life education. She said Yes to the Combined Method in education, but believed that all Deaf children should be educated through expressive Sign language. She did not believe in giving excessive time to speech training for those profoundly deaf, but that time was precious. Too much time in speech lessons lessened time for education. Sister Gabriel understood Deaf education and the issues involved in living as a fulfilled Deaf person in a hearing world. Her philosophy of education matched her practice. She wanted what was the best for all the children. She loved them and taught that disability was not a handicap to becoming a person whose life had meaning.[iii] As an educator, she desired to give students a thorough and comprehensive education,[iv] so they could equal any other student in the national education system.

Kathleen has the great benefit from the solid legacy of Sister Gabriel Hogan. As a Deaf woman and as a person who excelled in the world of education, Sister Gabriel was a wondrous role model for all the students.

As the numbers of children increased, Sister Gabriel had set up a scheme to enable more teachers to be well trained as educators of Deaf children. She saw the need was dire. She initially trained two women – Sister Columba and Miss Hanney herself.

And who is Sister Columba Dwyer? Some of Kathleen's older friends signed stories about her, because their memory of her was fresh in their minds – she taught them when they first arrived as young children.

Sister Columba was very popular and a great leader. In 1885 after finishing her training as a Deaf educator, Sister Columba became the superior of Waratah. She believed it was time for growth and development as a national school as it was the only Catholic Institute for Deaf children in Australia. She invited eminent people from both church and civic circles to attend events at the school and she began to organise occasions for the children to go out into the public arena, even though the Sisters themselves did not go out with them. She showed the quality of the school and explained how it provided a good education for Deaf children. This attracted funds for the school, as well as the good will of the local and church community.

Her two brothers were the first Australian-born bishops and they helped the school by publicising its value of providing a Catholic education for Deaf children. While they learned some Sign language, she made sure they kept the school in view of the other bishops in Australia so they would support it.

In the classroom Sister Columba taught the little ones and introduced them to Sign language with understanding and skill. She was gentle and encouraging and influenced them as a mother and parent to them all. Everyone knew that she insisted that all Deaf children would be welcome in the school. When she died prematurely at the age of fifty-four, the Deaf community grieved her.

Kathleen is curious about Miss Hanney's story as well. Miss Hanney explains that she was born in 1869, became deaf at the age of seven while living at an orphanage and was then taken to Waratah where she naturally adopted the language as her own. A quick student and long term resident of the school, Miss Hanney stayed on to become a teacher and was the first of a growing group of Deaf ex-students who stayed on at Waratah for many years after they finished their schooling.

Kathleen notices how she interacts with the children – compassion oozes from her so Kathleen and the other children trust her – after all Miss Hanney is one of them. As a Deaf woman, she stands in solidarity with them. Her facial expressions are soft and genuine. Her bodily manner focuses totally on face-to-face communication. She does not deviate in distraction while she engages in an encounter with the other.

As a woman of faith, Miss Hanney conveys naturally in sign to Kathleen the importance of *God* in her life as she also did for Don. She makes the sign, as she points with the index finger above the head to the sky – her head and eyes rise in the same direction. Miss Hanney encourages prayer and conveys her strong sense of spirituality. She nurtures their faith and devotion to Mary and the saints. In graceful sign, she tells stories from the Gospels, as well as stories of the saints as people who can inspire them. She eloquently signs the story attributed to Saint Philomena, the name that Kathleen chooses for her Confirmation.

Miss Hanney explains to Kathleen about Jesus as friend, Mary as mother and Joseph as carer and protector. Kathleen prays to them to look after her and all the children of the world. She prays rhythmically. Her body prays in graceful sign, *Jesus, Mary and Joseph, have mercy on me.* In her heart she wants compassion bestowed on everyone.

The older Deaf women teach the children the familiar prayer of the Rosary and how to pray it in Australian-Irish Sign Language as a rhythmic prayer – the ten Hail Mary prayers and the Our Father prayer. When praying the Rosary without signing, they finger their beads and focus on images from the stories of Jesus and Mary that flow through their minds in picture form, as they come to know the mind of Jesus, the Christ, as a guide in their living.

Being in a Church is a visual experience with its stained-glass windows and statues, which show Jesus, Mary and the saints, as well as lit candles which carry with them images of the sacred. The students at Waratah live in the milieu of faith and its practices with Mass, the Sacraments, Benediction and celebration of feasts in the Church, so that it becomes part of their lives.

Kathleen is captured by sacred places – maybe a Church, a place of beauty, a canopy of eucalyptus in the mountains. In simple, gracious and gentle sign, Kathleen describes her experience of the sacred – the awareness begins in her mind, is apprehended in her heart and rests in her being. She experiences something greater than herself – that she belongs with all humanity and with all creation.

Older Deaf girls who come from other Deaf schools are welcomed to learn about their Catholic faith. Miss Hanney influences her students as she broadens her concerns beyond immediate issues to world issues, especially those involving children in different parts of the world. Through her influence, she imparts her compassionate traits and her graciousness to many of her students, who learn to attend to others beyond their own needs. As well, she inspires the desire to live as good people in the wider community.

* * *

Sister Martina Carrigan

For the next generation of educators, Sister Gabriel trained Sister Martina Carrigan and Sister Gonzales Arnold. Kathleen knows them. She sees how the young sisters learn Sign language and how, with daily use, it is embedded in their thought processes and teaching. The language is not an appendage for them. They are steeped in it, as it forms part of their everyday life.

Sister Gonzales is a local girl and develops a keen understanding of the mind of the Deaf child. She is sympathetic as she exerts great influence over the children.[v] Sister Martina makes her major contribution to Deaf education after Sisters Gabriel and Columba die and when she returns to Waratah. A gifted teacher, Sister Martina becomes her main teacher when Kathleen is fifteen years of age. Signing is second nature to Sister Martina. She is clear and graceful and she carefully spells each word distinctly with the palm of her hand towards the person so no one can mistake or miss a letter.[vi] She understands her pupils, communicates well and develops their potential.[vii]

She is innovative and begins changes in the way of educating Deaf girls – and she is strict. While she appears harsh and stern, Kathleen benefits from her even though she finds her sternness off-putting. In fact Kathleen dislikes her and shrugs her shoulder with a grimace as she pictures her in her mind.

During the holidays Kathleen sits with her mother and tells her that she is in trouble with Sister Martina. She looks at her mother and signs *I…only running upstairs on Sunday afternoon with girl friends.* The girls do not realise the racket that resounds through the timber-floored dormitory as they ascend the stairs and run through the room. Unfortunately for the girls, Sister Martina has visitors downstairs under the dormitory for a meeting and they look at one another, distracted by the excessive noise. The Sisters are embarrassed as they take responsibility for the girls, who should act with more decorum! Something small has grown out of all proportion in reality and in Kathleen's mind. It shows up her unrest as she expresses her distaste for the institutional life. Even so, Kathleen shows her mother with pride the book she receives from Sister Martina as an award at the end of the school year – for what, she does not know, but obviously an encouragement award.

Sister Martina aims to ensure the adolescent girls are lifted out of any kind of victim mentality or self-pity because they are deaf. She tells them that the best thing to do is to forget they might be in need of special treatment from hearing people and to forget their deafness.[viii] In other words get on with your life. This sounds hard and a shock to them, but she

Lift Heads High

Heads lifted high
Startling light liberates the dark space of the mind
Daring not to be defined by its inviting limits
Not confined by the velvet lie
Of self-pity and piteous benevolence.
Forget deafness
I am no nuisance to myself nor others
Ingeniously, see
The forbidden doubt of hope
That feels pleasure of defeat.

Lift heads high
Bring the sparkle of your hands into clear blazing light
Like high mountain springs
That seeps into every crevice forming rivulets
Revealing fresh notions
With the clarity of fired wisdom.

Highly lifted heads
With the courage to storm beyond boundaries
To hope that lives the joy of a life fulfilled.

Bernadette T. Wallis

continues with her strong message. Mix well with hearing people and do not be a nuisance to yourselves or others, she tells them.[ix] She seeks to instil in the girls a love of the niceties of life[x] and she challenges them to their limits so they can benefit from their education and live good lives. Some students love her, even when she is harsh – she keeps in touch with each one of her pupils, ever anxious about their *eternal welfare* and always interested in them and their lives.[xi]

Sister Martina becomes superior in 1932 after Kathleen leaves school and she instigates the change of name for the school, which becomes *the School for Deaf Girls*.

* * *

Under the influence of Sisters Gabriel and Columba and Miss Hanney, then Sisters Martina and Gonzales, the teachers of the next generation and those of the 1920s are trained at Waratah.

Sister Theophane Howlett comes to Waratah initially because she has some nursing training and has the skills to looks after the Sisters and the Deaf children.[xii] Her work develops into a teaching role. Sister Regis Mason also understands the mentality of her students and especially the students who rely totally on signing. She brings fun and humour[xiii] with her skilled capacity for Sign language.

Then there are the Deaf teachers, the ex-students besides Marianne Hanney who live at Waratah. Esther Hutchison and other younger Deaf women are significant teachers and mentors. Because Kathleen had come to Waratah later in her educational development and her understanding of language, Esther takes a special interest in her. The typically adolescent Kathleen looks up to Esther and dreams of being confident, strong, direct, happy and attractive like her. Deaf themselves, they comfort and encourage Kathleen. They know and love Deaf children and treat them as individuals and as part of their Deaf family.

Other ex-students who live at Waratah, including Maud Bruyn, Nellie Burke, Doreen Dendle, Dorothy O'Neill, Mary and Nellie Elligate, manage the sewing room and act as teachers to the younger girls in various types of needlework and crafts under the supervision of Sister Regis. The women make priests' vestments and Church altar cloths, as well as clothing for women and children.[xiv] When the *hemstitching* machine arrives, they rejoice in the progress with this modern equipment installed.[xv] They are paid for the items they make. Also some of the ex-students work in the institution in domestic roles.

The experience in the sewing room and their time at Waratah prepares the two Deaf sisters, Mary and Nellie Elligate, for their future life. They are much older than Kathleen. Having attended the Victorian School for Deaf Children at St Kilda they, at the age of fourteen and fifteen, attended further schooling at Waratah for the purpose of learning about their Catholic faith in the last years of their education. They stay on for a while – for a few years – before moving to Wodonga as seamstresses in the town. They also work for the Church – cleaning, cooking, making vestments and much more. They know the priests well in the diocese and communicate freely with them by pen and paper. Avid supporters of the Australian Rules football code, they are Essendon supporters and discuss such things with anyone they meet.[1] They leave after Kathleen's first year or two.

* * *

The Waratah community creates a centre for Deaf engagement in language and cultural development. Unwittingly, as they form their strong residential community, they contribute greatly to the education and sustained development of Australian-Irish Sign Language. In communication with one another, new signs are formed and with usage become part of the lexicon of the language. They naturally exchange ideas and discuss Sign language and dialects in different parts of Australia. In the community they converse about Sign names of cities and towns, different sports and developing medical and industrial technology signs as well as names of public personalities, including politicians. *What signs do they use for King George V, or the Australian Prime Minister, James Scullin, who was the first Australian Catholic Prime Minister, or Phar Lap who won the Melbourne Cup?*

To assist Kathleen and the other students with the understanding of history, the teachers use a visual way of presenting the material through drama, so plays include Mary Queen of Scots, The Emperor of Timbuktu, Henry VIII, St Patrick of Ireland and Roses of Dorothy and The Pharisee's Daughter. While she is a participant in some plays, Kathleen joins the audience for others and gains further understanding, filling out the many gaps in her general knowledge.

Excitedly, the costumes and props are prepared in the sewing room by the Sisters, students and the ex-students. They are lavish and add colour and vibrancy to a visual event that Deaf people greatly appreciate.

The syllabus for the older students in History includes the usual Ancient History, History of the Middle Ages and Modern History, as well as Sacred History, Australian History and Ancient Britain History, the Crusades, the History of Wars and much more.[xvi] Kathleen is still catching up in her language development, so does not have a full understanding of the matter in hand. The subject also includes biographical sketches with stories of Joan of Arc, St Thomas More, William Shakespeare, George Washington and the Irishman Daniel O'Connell who

---

[1] Between 1936 and 1948 at the railway station in Albury, Nellie and Mary met the Deaf children who were travelling to and from the Deaf schools at Waratah and St Gabriel's and supplied them with sandwiches and cakes. They enjoyed meeting the younger generation of the Deaf community. The children looked forward to this interlude at Albury where they changed trains on the long journey. Nellie and Mary were life-long friends of Kathleen and Don.

campaigned for Catholic emancipation in Britain in the early 19th century. As well, her teachers include the story of Abbe de L'Epee, the priest who is responsible for Deaf education in France.

While the Sisters are enclosed in the convent according to rules and regulations of Church Canon law and their constitutions, they find ways and means of maintaining contact with significant people to make sure the cause of Deaf children in their care is in the public eye.

As the children perform in concerts on special occasions, they are trained to entertain the many visitors at functions and celebrations. People of the district take a great interest in the involvements of the Sisters and the Deaf children. The Sisters believe in the importance of Deaf children being seen and known in the community and involve them in the community. This also helps to attract financial support to the Deaf Institute for its ongoing viability. And the people claim the national *charity*, the school for Deaf children at Waratah, as their own and recognise their responsibility to support it. They bring local produce and treats for the children. Doctors and dentists are generous and give free service for medical and dental needs. Funds are raised in diverse ways and by diverse people.

While the children are included in various public events and entertainment, some local people learn basic signs so they understand them in a general way – and mostly the Deaf children make themselves understood. The people transport Kathleen and her friends to fairs, the cinema and celebratory Church occasions. They assist with decorated floats for the Irish celebration of St Patrick's Day, when they depict St Patrick robed in the Bishop outfit with a mitre and crozier and *Erin* leaning on her harp with Irish maidens surrounding them. The children are excited when the Newcastle Rotary Club members take them out for *motor drives*. The children become bearers of information and report to the Sisters as to whom they meet and the content of conversations.

In 1928 the local Mayor arranges a special viewing platform for them, and Kathleen is excited to see at close range the world-famous Bert Hinkler, making world history in his aircraft as it lands onto the Newcastle racecourse.

The Waratah girls also play sport with other students from Catholic schools in the district. As the girls head out for picnics at the beach dressed in full uniform, Kathleen recoils. With her fair skin, the sticky warm weather, the sand and her inability to swim, for her the outing lacks its lustre.

In mid-year holidays, Kathleen, like other children, goes with some friends of the Sisters for the break. Home is too far away. The Sisters correspond with Kathleen's mother so that she knows her daughter will be cared for. Kathleen tells her mother she stayed with people south of Sydney, where she attended Mass at St Mary's Towers, Douglas Park, but she cannot tell them the names of the people who hosted her.

Through sharing stories of their families with one another, the girls gain a well-developed knowledge of Australian geography: they learn of cities and small rural towns, farming areas and isolated properties. Life-long friendships spanning the length and breadth of Australia are cemented. Kathleen keeps contact with Olive Minton, Gertie Kinsella, Dorothy O'Neill, Mary Cloonan, Eileen O'Hagen, Patricia Jackson and others.[2] They share a special bond, almost family-like, with shared stories of laughter and tears, hopes and dreams, and more especially, a shared language, the Australian-Irish Sign Language. The Catholic Deaf community of the future is strengthened through their friendship born at Waratah.

* * *

While Kathleen is still very attached to the way of life in her family of origin, she feels the pressure from her teachers to stay at Waratah. She feels pressure to live her life within the institution and to work in the sewing room or in other parts of the Deaf Institute as many of the other young Deaf women do.

A number of the students who stay at Waratah do not marry. The underlying, unspoken issue is the question of marriage – the inference is that Deaf people should not marry because they run the risk of giving birth to children who are deaf.[xvii] This erroneous belief filters in from the wider community and is influential in developing the idea that young Deaf girls should be kept secluded. An attitude of protectionism exists too, to save the girls from the *world of danger*. Forcible sterilisation is widely used in the USA in these 1930s.[xviii]

In her nature Kathleen is kind and compliant. Although she is limited in education, she has potential to be a good influence on students, a good worker with talents in crafts such as crocheting, fancywork and knitting, and to be very helpful at the Institute. It almost seems common sense to return to the place where she has friends, where she can work with free board and lodging, in the time of the Great Depression in Australia, and where she can communicate with others easily. If she returns to work at Waratah, she will be readily accepted and approved of as a good Deaf person. She recognises that this is a nice feeling for a Deaf person in a hearing world where often, Deaf people are not accepted. She also recognises, however, this would be the safe option and one that she may well resent.

Feeling overwhelmed, she finds it difficult to know what to do. In conflict with herself, she has different inklings running through her mind and she knows that beneath her exterior, her anger can easily be enkindled. She wants to follow her true

---

[2] Married names: Olive Anderson, Gertie Hennessy, Dorrie Lovett, Eileen McKay and Patricia Counsel

At Waratah, Kathleen with students and ex-students, circa 1931

desires and not become embittered as a Deaf person in later stages of her life.

She looks for confirmation of her thoughts and feelings on the issue that are important in her mind. She does not ask her teachers for advice, because she fears their expectations, that is to come back to Waratah after the Christmas holidays. For this special conversation, Kathleen turns to a young Sister in confidence and hopeful trust. *She will understand these things close to my heart. My true desire is to go home.* She really wants to leave and go home to the family at the end of the year, rather than stay on. *What decision will she make?*

The young Sister knows the thinking of the sisters who teach Kathleen, so she understands the dilemma, but trusts her own intuition. With a young wisdom and with a gentle smile, the Sister signs to her that of course it is your decision and whatever the others say – *it is really up to you.* She laughs lightly and encouragingly with Kathleen – and Kathleen knows a new freedom. She asserts her independence and she reaches another stage of her human development. In making this major decision in this defining moment regarding her future life, she develops into a strong and courageous young woman who believes in herself. When she arrives home for Christmas, her mother approves and respects her decision. Kathleen sends the return train ticket back to Waratah and goes outside to see a dragonfly settle briefly on the grapevine leaf near the water tank and then take off on its evening journey. She leaves school at sixteen at the end of 1931.

* * *

Just over four years later Kathleen attends the school reunion at Waratah. With some trepidation and certainly with anticipation, she walks with confidence up the grand stone steps at the entrance of Waratah. She meets Deaf friends, the Deaf teachers, the Sisters and revisits the schoolrooms, the dormitory and the aviary with the Little Corellas. She recollects the days she found a new understanding of language and life.

At this reunion, she meets other people as well; there is a fleeting encounter with Emma, Don's mother, who attends the reunion with her daughter, Marie. She does not realise that this fleeting encounter will mark the beginning of a new chapter in Kathleen's life.

---

[i] *http://www.maitland.nsw.gov.au/MCC/Public/UserFiles/File/Heritage/RiverWalkMCC_Dreaming.pdf*

[ii] The Magazine of the Catholic Deaf, *Past and Present*, Christmas Number 1939, p15

[iii] *Obituary of Ellen Hogan* (Sister Gabriel), 1915 Dominican Archives Strathmore

[iv] Sarah Fitzgerald, *Open Minds Open Hearts*, CCOD publication, Lidcombe, NSW 1999, p.61

[v] *Obituary Hannah Arnold* (Sister Gonzales) 1944 Dominican Archives, Strathmore

[vi] Ibid

[vii] On the occasion of Sister Martina's Golden Jubilee, an Article was written by Mona Brooks in the *Annals of Our Lady of the Sacred Heart* 2 January 1951

[viii] Ibid

[ix] Ibid

[x] Ibid

[xi] Tribute to Sister Martina by Brook, an ex-student of Waratah. It followed Sister Martina's death

[xii] *Obituary Mona May Howlett* (Sister Theophane), 1972 Dominican Archives, Strathmore

[xiii] *Obituary Gertrude Mason* (Sister Regis), 1977 Dominican Archives, Strathmore

[xiv] *History of Catholic Deaf Education in Australia 1875 – 1975* Dominican Sisters' private publication 1975, p.13

[xv] Ibid p.14

[xvi] *The Syllabus of History for the Deaf at Waratah*, Mother Columba Dwyer, 1918. Held at the Archives of the University of Newcastle

[xvii] Most Deaf parents, approximately 90%, have children with hearing.

[xviii] Austen, Sally & Crocker, Susan, Editors *Deafness in Mind – Working Psychologically with Deaf People across the Lifespan*, Whurr ex Publishers Ltd. London & Philadelphia 2004, p.10

CHAPTER 7

CASTLE HILL
UP FROM TOONGABBIE CREEK IN THE VALLEY

On new pathways,

The Wonga Pigeons

Continue to bob their heads

Jump from here to there

Take a glance upwards

And stay always nearby.

For thousands of centuries before the Deaf boys roam the bush and swim in the creeks, the Aboriginal people of *The Hills* Country were the Darug tribe, nomadic peoples with natural boundaries and with a number of large family groups. The Burramattagal clan was located in the Parramatta/North Rocks catchment of Hunts and Darling Mills Creeks; the Toongagal or Tuga Country was in the Toongabbie Creek catchment. Other groups lived around the Cattai Creek/Hawkesbury River catchment. Their language was the Darug language, the inland dialect.[i] In the Hills district were their sacred sites, gathering places and ceremonial spaces. To the south, the great Parramatta River with its many tributaries, including Toongabbie Creek wound through the valleys.

In this land of Aboriginal stories, Don is a young growing adolescent being educated and formed at St Gabriel's at Castle Hill, twenty miles north-west of Sydney. He explores the creeks and finds his own sacred sites where he sits quietly for a few moments and notices a number of dragonflies flitting in the breeze, here, there and back again. The Deaf boys love to picnic and explore the bush and swim.

* * *

The Brothers are aware that this is the first school for Catholic Deaf boys in Australasia.[ii] They also know it is *home* for the boys and a *long-nourished and dearly cherished project* of the Archbishop of Sydney, Michael Kelly, who is a great friend to St Gabriel's. This place on the hill is considered an ideal site with the *panorama embracing the richly cultivated olive, orange and citron groves, interspersed with lime and passion fruit and extends eastwards to the unrivalled harbor of Sydney, while the Blue Mountains shelter the fruit fields from every other direction.* A visitor exclaims: *One carries a life remembrance that breathes of heaven and the lucky inhabitant enjoys the calm and repose of the Garden of Eden.*[iii]

The religious Brothers at St Gabriel's are mostly young. Their youthful exuberant energy matches that of the boys – open to nourishing their spirits.

The Brothers include the boys in the wider Catholic community and in normal Church liturgies, rather than keeping them confined to the school situation. Don travels with other boys into Sydney for his confirmation at St Mary's Cathedral. They travel on the little steam train he loves. It is an important occasion with Archbishop Michael Kelly officiating. The Brothers interpret for the boys who are seated in the front where they see the action. They do not hear the Latin that is spoken or the choir that raises its hymns, but they see the procession and the movement of people on the altar. Don knows it is a special day for them to commit themselves to God. As the theology of the day describes, they become *soldiers for Christ* in their lives. The boys are *thoroughly instructed in their religion* – in a theology of the time.

Archbishop Daniel Mannix speaks highly of the faith of the Waratah and St Gabriel's students: *The pupils of these two schools are taught the great truths of their religion. When they assist at Mass in the school chapel, they do so as intelligent Catholics.*[iv] Don's mother, Emma, especially delights in this claim of the Archbishop.

The Brothers' awareness and understanding of Irish oppression determined them to raise the status of the poor with a standard of education. They subscribe to the common belief of this time that fear and control are important tools for effective educators. Their severity enforced a strict regime – the boys are kept fully occupied. In the classroom, at play or on the farm, the Brothers and boys are together for twenty-four hours a day and seven days a week. Challenged in their care and training of the boys, they discover the experience both demanding and rewarding. All the Brothers influence the boys, whether they are teachers or not.

Don sees a number of Brothers come and go from St Gabriel's. Brother Edward Foy from Charters Towers in Queensland is the cook and instructor of arts and crafts. He is young and energetic and is present for three years and returns later.

From Melbourne, Brother Francis Colman Kelly and Brother John Adrian Dean both return at different times although they are not teachers but serve at St Gabriel's for some years. Born in County Westmeath in 1879, Brother Ambrose Geoghegan arrives in 1929 aged fifty, having taught in other parts of Australia. Because he previously trained and taught in Ireland, he immediately signs fluently with the boys and knows Deaf ways. He works in the grounds and contributes to this Signing community.

Some of the Brothers work for short stints at St Gabriel's. Some of them come from the novitiate at Strathfield shortly after their training and profession. *Is this because of a visionary provincial superior, who looks to the sustainability of trained and skilled teachers of the Deaf for the future?* Or maybe it is to broaden their life experience and to give them the opportunity of being with Deaf children who are a special group to whom the Christian Brothers now commit themselves.

Between 1925 and 1932, six of the Australian-born Brothers, all in their twenties, who come to St Gabriel's stay for only one or two years. These men leave the Brothers, for whatever reason, to find other pathways in life. They have an invaluable experience learning something of the language and culture of the Deaf community.

Discipline is tough and life is simple. The boys are alert to what happens in their midst and attempt to make meaning of the daily comings and goings at the school. They observe the interactions between the different Brothers and their peers and learn to recognise the moods of each day. With their bright, quick eyes, the Deaf boys have a knowing beyond speech and sound. Yet, not all the pieces fall into place. Really, not everything makes sense in their day-to-day life. Don is reserved in nature and holds his thoughts and feelings close to his heart, while he puzzles over the missing pieces – the gaps in information.

* * *

After Don's sister Marie leaves school at Waratah and Jack enters Springwood seminary to train for the priesthood, Emma establishes *Wallis' Café* on the Hume Highway Seymour, and asks Marie to work with her. Marie excels as a pastry cook and people come from everywhere to buy her homemade pies. As an intelligent woman who engages, with interests in politics, religion, life in the town or on the land, or anything else, nothing pleases her more than to enter into discussion on paper. Whenever she has a willing customer who will sit with her and write, nothing else makes her happier.

Marie occasionally writes to Don. He receives regular letters from his mother who questions him about his schooling and his study. Letters from his father are less frequent. Don learns news of home – news of his younger brothers, news of the neighbours and news of his father's activities on the farm. He is fifteen and reciprocates by writing to his parents of the activities on the school farm. A few months after his brother Jack goes to Springwood – just across the valley from St Gabriel's – he writes a letter.

St Gabriel's School,

Castle Hill.

5.5.27

My dear Parents,

A few lines to let you know that I am well. I hope you are well as we. How are you and all at home? I would be glad to get a letter from you. I often think of you and Jack. I often look at the Blue Mountains and think of Jack. I wrote to Jack last week. I would like to write a letter to you often but I always neglect it. We can see Springwood from here.

We had a great day at Wirth's Circus. It was beautiful. The elephants, lions, dogs, horses and bears and clowns were wonderfully clever. They rode bikes, danced, counted and played clever tricks. We are all delighted. I would like to see it again.

Eight dentists and a doctor will be here all day next Sunday. They will examine our teeth and pull and fill them.

One of the pigs has 5 new bonhams today. They are all black. Br. Connor says another will have 8 bonhams tomorrow or next Sunday. We are fond of the little bonhams. They are very funny. Our two pups can run and play now.

We have a new Chevrolet motor car here. I think we will often get a drive in it. I think Fred and I will go to Springwood next holidays.

Well Mother, I have no more news at present but will write again. I thank you and Father for sending 10/- today. I had written this letter to you when Br. Allen gave the 10/- to me. I was surprised to get it. Write soon.

Good-bye for the present,

I remain,

Your loving Son,

Don

Don is captivated by the birth of the piglets on the school farm. He does not realise that the Irish Brothers still use Irish words from their native language, such words as *bonhams* (banbhs) for piglets. Not surprising are the school colours – green and white, a touch of the Irish.

Don's mother is pleased that the boys have their dental needs attended to – by Messrs. F. G. Barber, L. Bell

St Gabriel's School for Deaf Boys. Br M A Geoghegan at the front door of the old Southleigh mansion, circa 1927

and Solomon G. Daniels, J. Pennell, and Crawford who make quarterly visits to St Gabriel's offering their services.[v] Dr F T Allen from Stanmore offers medical services.[vi]

Don and Jack write to one another and Don enjoys a visit to Jack – he enjoys getting out and about. As they walk down the footpath, they sign to one another of the family news and of what is happening in their lives. Jack's mates are most impressed when they see him signing to his brother so question him later with the usual questions. *How did you learn to sign? How come your brother is deaf?*

As Jack struggles financially at the seminary to pay for books and other requirements and depends on his parents, he tells his mother in a letter at the end of the first year, that the students put on a concert and raised three pounds for St Gabriel's at Castle Hill. In the second year at Springwood he tells his father in a letter: *I won ten shillings in a raffle but promised before I got it to give it to charity... Another student added to it and we are going to raffle a leather bag for Waratah. We hope to get three pounds. It will be something towards their funds.*[vii]

In 1929 Jack moves on to the seminary at Manly, a ferry-ride from downtown Sydney, so visits are a little less frequent. When Jack is to be ordained as a deacon, Don, due to an easy mix-up in communication turns up unannounced and is present for the ceremony, which is normally an internal affair. Nevertheless they welcome him and point him to the seat in the front row so he can see the proceedings. Don revels in the royal treatment that he receives and especially with the special breakfast that follows – he loves food.

When his young brother Charlie arrives at St Gabriel's at the age of six, Don takes him on the ferry to visit Jack, who he hardly knows because of the age gap and having been away from home for some years. Jack makes sure they meet his fellow seminarians. They now know Don and greet him warmly. Such meetings provide the seminarians in this era with the opportunity to put a personal face on the Deaf community. They learn first-hand of the national Catholic Deaf schools and their role in educating a minority group of Australians who are deaf and use Sign language. They read the special Deaf magazine produced by the Sisters at Waratah and the many articles in the Catholic papers. The custom develops that all seminarians before their ordination go to Castle Hill and learn how to be with Deaf people in their ministry.

* * *

In the summer school holidays, the Wallis family sits around the table for meals. Hands fly and stories are told. Information is shared and the discussions are intense. Food gets cold as eating pauses while eyes focus on hands and facial expression. They laugh and tease one another and tell more stories. It is difficult to eat and sign at the one time! It is frustrating for their mother Emma as she coaxes then and sternly insists they eat first – then they can converse! She knows that her insistence does not always work.

More conversation takes place between the Deaf siblings themselves than between the hearing members and the Deaf siblings. Don, Marie and Charlie engage fully in their complex Australian-Irish Sign Language in a way that is not quite possible when signing with their hearing brothers, Jack, Chester and Brian. With them they need to slow their signing and engage more simply and deliberately, as their comprehension of the language is limited – enough to have basic conversations. The hearing brothers, however, feel at ease with Deaf people and know to make broad gesticulations and gestures if they are not understood.

Don, Marie and Charlie do not have any recognisable speech. They make sounds that do not resemble spoken words. Sounds emanate or erupt when angry, in sheer frustration or in surprised fright, or in fun and joy. The family and close friends understand the various emotions or meanings of their sounds – but sometimes need to be in sight, as they can carry temporary questions until they clarify what the sounds indicate. Don can sound harsh sometimes when he does not mean to be.

In signing conversation he makes sounds of a deep murmur or grunt that is familiar to immediate family or people used to Deaf people. His sound of laughter is infectious, loud and joyous. It comes from the deep earth beneath him and it is as though it comes up through his feet and body. He enjoys humour and a good story when he and Charlie meet with friends in social settings and in friendship.

Don is a teenager when the new radiogram is brought into the household at Homewood. His parents, Emma and Abe, are pleased with the purchase, a new phenomenon for this country area. As music emanates to the delight of the hearing members of the family, Marie and Don walk outside and into the space of the paddocks to reconcile the deep realisation that the pleasure others receive from this musical contraption was not to be theirs. Music for profoundly Deaf people is not heard through their ears. Although sound or rhythm is felt through vibrations, such as timber floors, the music is not appreciated in the same way. While loss and grief enter Marie's and Don's lives, it is also a time of sadness for the hearing members of the family, who see them upset and unable to join in the excitement in the same way. Although they seem to be victims of deafness, these times strengthen them in facing their reality.

While their three children attend the residential Catholic Deaf schools, Abe and Emma read and re-read anything in the media that relates to deafness. They are immediately moved as their eagle eyes gravitate towards an article that may enlighten their minds or ease their hearts. Their hearts are heavy. They miss their children, not seeing them for so long while they are at school.

* * *

It is a time of expansion for St Gabriel's and the school's building program has created significant debt. Brothers Allen, Paul Nunan and Avellino O'Connell are appointed to carry out the fundraising programs for St Gabriel's. They travel nationally to raise awareness of the need for Deaf education. Brother Allen with his rare charisma gathers significant numbers of people to work with him and he forms committees in many places to raise funds. Fund-raising events include cabarets, dances and raffles. Brother Nunan, who came to Australia as a child from County Cork in 1873, strongly believes in the right of every Deaf child to be educated and speaks strongly to this point. With Brother O'Connell, originally from Hay in NSW, the two Brothers involve themselves in the adult Catholic Deaf community by way of support and friendship.

Brother Allen revels in the train trips to Melbourne to supervise the Victorian boys going home for the school holidays and stays there until returning with the boys for the new school year. He takes the opportunity to meet the parents of Deaf children from the school including Abe and Emma. He gives talks to the parents of Deaf children at various centres encouraging them to send their children to St Gabriel's for their education and for a qualification in a *useful calling or trade*. He reminds parents that with education the boys can *gain good wages and can settle down in life, independent, self-supporting and happy.*[viii] He meets with and encourages the ex-students in their organisation as a Catholic Deaf Association in Victoria.

* * *

Meanwhile, in temporary workshops at St Gabriel's, the Brothers produce clothing required for the boys and for themselves. Don's friends train in trades for boot making, woodwork, metalwork and carpentry. In the same workshops, Don takes up tailoring with encouragement from his mother, who is sure this will give him a good job.

Who are his teachers in this trade? An Irish Deaf man Patrick Joseph Corr,[ix] referred to as a *deaf and dumb tailor* at the age of twenty in the 1901 Census of Ireland, comes from Ireland to Australia in 1912 with his two brothers where they land in Brisbane, Queensland – and where Patrick works as a

Tailoring at St Gabriel's 1931. James Healy (tailoring foreman) Jack Beath, Pat Coolahan, Des O'Reilly and Don Wallis

tailor. As an educated Deaf man who reads and writes he has surely attended St Joseph's in Cabra. *Did the Brothers know he was in Australia? Had they been in touch with him?* He certainly knows they were coming. He and his wife and small child move south and are there at the celebration to welcome the new Brothers to Sydney.[x]

Seeing St Gabriel's built, the experienced tailor is pleased to take on the tailoring education of the Deaf boys and begin teaching the trade right from the establishment of St Gabriel's. Patrick, a very good teacher and exacting in his work, is a great companion and mentor for Don and the older boys at the school. He also coaches in football. At St Gabriel's he and his wife Helen are in a community that understands them – they are Irish and they can communicate easily and freely.

Patrick with the Irish Brothers make visual picture stories of their home country and their travel to Australia as they communicate with the boys. With their hands, arms and facial expression, they describe the high seas with boats that heave and rock incessantly for weeks at a time with storms, thunder and lightning on endless oceans of water. How the boys would have watched as they engaged with interest and fascination, broadening their understanding of the world! On the other hand, how Patrick and the Brothers would have missed their country and told stories of their families as they explained the politics of Ireland – how different their country was from Australia.

Another tailor, James Healy, an older hearing man, is later added as tailor foreman. As Don develops the skill of tailoring, they see his determination to excel in the art. Very proud of his work, Don makes his own three-piece business suit by the age of fifteen. He develops a sophisticated understanding of fabrics and a good sense of dress. Don thanks his tutors for their encouragement and their insistence on good work. They, in turn, sign to their young student: *Proud of you! Always keen to improve and perfect your work in the tailoring trade.* At the ages of seventeen and eighteen, Don stays on at the school for further tuition and work experience.

Many of the Redemptorist priests are well known to the Deaf community because of their monastery that was established near Waratah, where they regularly celebrate Mass or Benediction and other devotions at the School. Becoming well acquainted with them, they are good friends of the Deaf community and some of them learn to sign. In 1924 when the Redemptorists build a monastery at nearby Pennant Hills for training their students, they are pleased to connect with the Deaf school at St Gabriel's, a few suburbs away.

Given the official task of making the religious habits for the young men who join the order, Don travels to the monastery by train or sometimes on his bike. There he gets his instructions. Don communicates by pen and his notebook, as he asks for the details and as he focuses on the task. He takes measurements of each of the men and is given the fabric for the job. He drafts the garment, cuts the fabric and makes the black clerical habits. He carries out his time-consuming tailoring work thriving on even the most painstaking chore of sewing by hand every buttonhole. He approaches his work with immeasurable preciseness and also with great pride and a strong sense of equality – he can do this work better than most!

The young men, who are in training, are new to the experience of communicating with the young professional tailors, who are deaf. They are intrigued and enjoy their friendly interactions. Each time Don visits them for fittings, he teaches them more signs and encourages them to practise the alphabet. He and other Deaf tailors give them a good basis for an understanding of Deaf people and their culture and they develop good relationships with them. The young Redemptorists learn that besides a ministry to people in the parishes, there is also the ministry of pastoral care in the Deaf community.[xi]

* * *

An endearing twist of interconnection between Don and Kathleen happens with the young Redemptorist student, Herbert Myers. Don patiently and enthusiastically teaches him Sign language. After his ordination Father Myers is appointed to Mayfield near Waratah and connects with the Waratah community. They welcome him with joy and especially with his basic Sign language. With constant interaction at Waratah, he improves his signing and is another person with whom Deaf people communicate easily. He is constantly aware and interested in Deaf people. His work on Redemptorist mission teams takes him on travels to different parishes in NSW to conduct weeklong missions. The grapevine in the Deaf community is very effective and he soon has a list of names of those who live in isolated rural areas. He watches out for them and commits to visiting them.

It is not long before he is in the Riverina in a parish that includes the township of Berrigan. Kathleen is twenty, young and, yes, she is isolated from her school friends, so she is on his list of Deaf people to visit. She is amazed and surprised when Father Myers contacts her parents at *Carlyle* homestead and invites her to meet him at Berrigan. She does not know him and she is excited because he signs. She is pleased, as she travels in the horse and gig with her parents and pulls up at the presbytery to see him. He has news of Waratah: the nuns, her friends and the Deaf community. He also attends to her spiritual needs and they converse at length in Australian-Irish Sign Language.

Kathleen's face lights up cheekily as she tells her mother of her gossip session with the young Father Myers. Remarkably and coincidentally, Don teaches him the language in which Father Myers communicates with Kathleen, the young woman, yet unknown to Don. Four years younger than Don, Kathleen does not know that when she first arrived at Waratah, her future husband was being educated at St Gabriel's. How busy are the dragonflies! They dart through the dangling gum leaves and mysteriously join the dots of life patterns.

* * *

Don has spent nine of his thirteen years of education at St Gabriel's School and he leaves the school with a trade and with considerable work experience. He is ready to take his place in the outside world. Before he leaves St Gabriel's, Don and his friend ride their bikes to Newcastle and on to Rosary Convent, Waratah, to see their former school again. For them it is a nostalgic journey. They park their bikes against the familiar building and walk expectantly up the stone steps as they had done as small boys. With a very warm welcome, the Sisters and Deaf teachers greet them, as do the young women they knew as small children. The boys secretly charm

the girls, who write up the visit in their personal journal in 1931: *12th July, Don Wallis and Paddy Kenna came to see us. They came by bikes from Sydney. We enjoyed their visit. Don is a fine gentleman.*[xii]

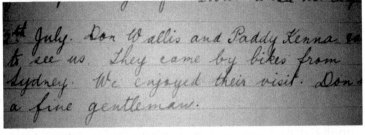

From the diary of Agnes Lynch 1931, University of Newcastle Archives

Kathleen is in the building at Waratah that day but Don does not meet her, nor know of her. In the same year, 1931, they both leave their footprints behind at the schools that shape their lives and where they form friendships for life. They leave behind the rivers and the bush and the land they have temporarily walked lightly upon, only to be awakened in the Country where their families live.

Kathleen and Don complete their education prior to the beginnings of major changes in the Catholic Deaf education system in Australia. By the mid 1930s change is in the air as various influences affecting Deaf education filter through.

---

[i] *http://www.thehills.nsw.gov.au/IgnitionSuite/uploads/docs/Aborigines%20in%20The%20Hills.pdf*

[ii] Christian Brothers' Educational Record, p.208

[iii] The Christian Brothers' Educational Record, 1923 p.208

[iv] The Advocate1939 Catholic Deaf Melbourne with Archbishop Mannix 13 January 1941

[v] Annals of St Gabriel's, 1926 p.51

[vi] The Catholic Press, Sydney, 22 October 1925

[vii] *John C. Wallis' Letters to his Parents 1927-1943*, Missionary Sisters of Service Archives, The Wallis Centre, Hobart, Tasmania, December 1927

[viii] The Advocate, *St Gabriel's School for Deaf Boys*, February 2, 1928, p.31

[ix] Johnston, Brian James has researched Patrick Joseph Corr in a private paper 2015. He also refers to Corr in *Memories of St Gabriel's – 75th Anniversary Commemorative Book* printed by NSW Government Printing Service, 2000, p.151

[x] Ibid. p.50. The photo welcoming the new Irish Brothers shows Patrick Corr as the last man in the second back row in a grey suit.

[xi] In an old treasured book, published in 1923, in St Louis, Missouri entitled, *How to Talk to the Deaf* by a Redemptorist priest, Father D.D. Higgins in the U.S. is found in the bowels of the Redemptorist student library in Melbourne. While it gives a description and picture of American signs based on the French Sign Language from the 1700s, it has pencilled markings showing which of the signs are familiar to Waratah and which are common to St Gabriel's. An earlier Redemptorist priest in Australia obviously studied Sign language. Held by author.

[xii] *Diary of Agnes Lynch 1927* Waratah Archives, University of Newcastle Library

Emma and Abe's Response

They are relieved
with the depth of concern for their children.
They anger
when their children are compared
with other children and
considered as less.

They know their children
as strong, intelligent children and
like others in every way,
except for their language
and the fact that they hear differently.

They are full of gratitude
for the specialised care and skilled education
that is given to their children.
They work hard to pay for it
— board, care and education.

They resent their children's support
described as charity,
Justice, yes,
the right to education.

They live on a small holding of poor land
at Homewood — that does not pay well.
Emma takes on extra work
She supplements their income lolly-making,
and selling them to shops in Yea.

Then while Abe stays on the farm,
Emma establishes the café
on the Hume Highway in Seymour
to draw further financial support
for the education of their family.

Bernadette T. Wallis

PHOTOS

Marie and Don Wallis at Waratah 1918

Don in St Gabriel's school uniform 1924

Charles Wallis 1932 – he is 10 years younger than Don

Waratah boys move to the new St Gabriel's School for Deaf Boys, Don front row 1923

St Gabriel's boys and Brothers, Don second row, third from left, Don second row, circa 1925

St Gabriel's soccer team: Don holding the sign, Alex Anderson in second row, second from left 1923

St Gabriel's confirmation group, 3 December 1926:
Back: William Reeves, Reg Pocock, Albert Jackson, John Hargrave, Arthur Spratt, Gerald Lund and Hubert Jacobson
Front: Cyril Derby, George Wilbow, Don Wallis, Bede Sheekey, Jack Beath and Pat Coolahan

The boys were confirmed by Archbishhop Kelly at St Mary's Cathedral, Sydney

Don Wallis in soccer uniform

St Gabriel's boys and Brothers 1926:

Back: Br Esmonde, Des O'Reilly, Jack Beath, Don Wallis, Albert Jackson, William Reeves, Reg Pocock, Gerald Lund, Jacob Augustine, Br. Kinnaird, Merty Jackson, William Coffey, Hubert Jacobson, Arthur Spratt, Pat Coolahan, George Wilbow and Br. H. Green

Second Row: Cyril Derby, George Smith, Jack Brundell, Frank Farrelly, Allen Boody, Joe Wren, Mary Thomson (Matron), Harry McArthur, Bede Sheekey, Mick Della, Ron McKay, Bede Stack, Stan Pocock and Frank Tyquin

Third Row: Les White, Roy Edie, James Hartigan, Bill Flaherty and Tom Houlcroft

Front: Br Hayes, Br Nunan, Frank O'Connor, Gerald Phillips, Thomas Holloway, Jim Tyquin, Br Allen and Br O'Farrell

Abraham and Emma Wallis with, from left 1932:
Charles, Brian, Don, Marie, John and Chester at John's ordination at St Patrick's Church, Kilmore Victoria

Don with his dog at home at *Wirrabong*, Homewood near Yea Victoria, circa 1930

Brother-in-law Harold Fulton, Don and Charles Wallis at Deaf Retreat, circa 1944

Don playing golf

Kathleen with baby brother, Kevin, Nhill Victoria, circa 1923

Waratah: Kathleen back row third from left, 1927

Waratah Drill: Kathleen far right in second row, circa 1928

Kathleen with book and her sister Monica, circa 1928

Waratah: Kathleen third from left, in a play 1928

Waratah senior girls, circa 1931: Kathleen second row second from left

Kathleen feeding the calf at *Carlyle*, Mt Gwynne

The Walsh sisters Molly, Monica and Kathleen

Waratah, circa 1930: Dressed for a play, Kathleen second from right

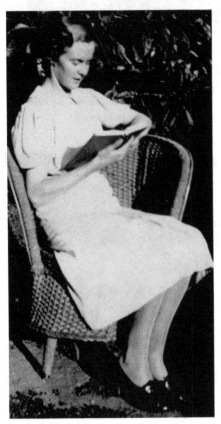

Kathleen, circa 1931

Kathleen, circa 1940

Kathleen at *Carlyle* Mt Gwynne, feeding the horses, circa 1935

The Walsh family:
Back: Brothers Jim, Dick, Bill and Kevin
Front: Mary Adeline (Centre) – to her right sisters-in-law Audrey, Marie and Anne – to her left daughters Kathleen, Monica and Molly

Kathleen (left) with Emma Wallis mother-in-law, and her parents Mary Adeline and Richard Walsh, circa 1941

Don at *Wirrabong*, Homewood near Yea

Kathleen at *Carlyle*, Mt Gwynne near Mulwala

Don (centre) and friends

Kathleen and Don, Melbourne Victoria

PART II

Chapters 8 – 13

THE ADULTHOOD STORY

CHAPTER 8

LIVING AT THE MURRAY AND THE YARRA

As they pick and peck on the ground

In the bush by the River

The two Wonga Pigeons

Find grubs and insects

In between mulched leaves and debris

They stay close together

They watch each other without knowing.

It is December 1931. With smiles sixteen year-old Kathleen leaves school and institutional life behind. She is feeling excited about the year ahead at *Carlyle* homestead on the Murray River, where two dragonflies chase one another, in and out, up and down along the river bank. The summer light streams through her window as she wakes in the morning and Kathleen lies there at peace. She is home in *Pangerang* Country. Later in the day, she walks on her own to orientate herself and reconnect with the land. She stops and gazes at the gum trees and notices the bird life. As the Wonga pigeon jumps along ahead of her on the track and takes a low flying leap to the branch of a tree, it allows her to pass and watches its new mate further down the track.

One of the farm dogs finds her and begs for a playful pat, and then follows behind as Kathleen returns via the stables and the dairy, where she finds her mother at work separating the cream from the milk. Glad to be home she bends towards her mother, touching her on the shoulder. Kathleen steps back so she can see her mother's hand signs and facial expressions when her mother turns to face her. Her mother knows she has to stop everything and have face-to-face encounter in order to communicate well with her daughter.

Tasks are set as Kathleen prepares for her future life. She is still known as Girlie at home, and her mother insists she continue to develop her home duty skills, as well as to work on the farm, including in the dairy. Her desire is to explore what everyone else is doing inside and outside the homestead. She is curious. Where is everyone and what they are doing? Of course it is important that she sees everyone; it is her connection to the world. She doesn't hear the normal conversations that go on between people as they move around the house, the sheds and the yards and she does not want to miss out!

With her mother's encouragement and explanation she realises that her trousseau must be prepared. Crocheting doilies in many different patterns she stores them in her glory box until they sit under vases of flowers or sacred statues in her future home. She proudly finishes tablecloths of various sizes with different fancy work patterns, including the willow patterns, and she crochets a royal blue wool dressing gown for herself, a skilful work of art. Keeping the extended family links she sends a piece of fancywork with the words *Greetings from Yarrawonga* to her godmother Aunty 'Leen back in Horsham.

Girlie's sisters develop these skills too. Each day they have their special chores in and around the house. Monica cooks in the kitchen, young Molly and her mother wash and iron and Kathleen cleans, sweeps and washes the floors, keeping everyone at bay while she does so. Her finger wags when someone enters to walk on a wet floor. The girls share creative ideas and recipes for preserving, cooking and presenting food. They knit and sew baby clothes and children's clothes with smocking and they make hats to wear to Sunday Mass. They enjoy the pressure of looking nice and well presented in public, even during times of economic hardship.

Her father, Richard, values her presence on the farm. She notices the activities that are taking place and looks for him. Sometimes she sees him at the stables attending the Clydesdale horses that are in the process of being broken in or being harnessed for ploughing in the paddocks. Springtime brings forth new foals, and Kathleen stands at the fence watching them playfully prance with the mares in the paddock.

As the poddy lambs and calves are brought in she holds them close as she teaches them to feed from a bottle. Later, teaching them to drink milk from a bucket, she gently lowers their heads into the bucket, and as she puts her milky fingers into their mouths their tongues feel like various levels of sand paper. The pressure of their sucking gives an indication as to their strength and wellness. Their tails wag excitedly until the bucket is empty.

Some days Girlie makes butter at the dairy. Other days she notices men arrive at their newly fenced sheep-yards for the regular sheep sale, for which her father is responsible. Down the road the new Irrigation Scheme and its supply channel, the Mulwala Canal, is already being excavated with Clydesdale horses and trowels that scoop the soil to the side. Men come from all about to find work and camp nearby. Kathleen watches the kindness of her father at the end of the day, as he takes his own chaff down for the hardworking horses that are tied to the fences for the night's rest.

Harvest time is a tense period with heat, dust, flies, chaff bags for feed, hessian bags for storing the grain, big iron needles and string as thread to sew the hessian bags together. Different types of machinery and processes are required for harvesting hay, oats, wheat or barley. Horses and drays are loaded with the harvest, some of which is kept for the next season. It is hard work with long hours for everyone. Girlie is part of it all.

The women are busy in the kitchen preparing food for morning and afternoon tea, as well as for lunch and dinner. Girlie balances lunch in a sack and rides down to the men in the paddocks. The men stop to eat and roll a cigarette, while yarns are told. She loves to spend the time with them as they take their food breaks. It is her brother Bill who converses in sign with her and laughs and teases her. She checks the horses, rubs down their necks reassuring them. They already have with them their hessian water bags for drinking water.

The work on the farm is endless and the labour is intensive. Girlie's father and brothers also lease land on other farms for further planting of crops, including hay. While Bill plays a significant part on the farm at this time, the farm cannot

Kathleen Walsh, circa 1935

provide for Girlie's young adult male siblings. They eventually all move on, except for Bill and the youngest, Jim, who continues to attend the local school.

Girlie scans the open sky. She notices the birds migrating in formation. She studies them and wonders from whence they came and where they go to rest. Watching the movement of the clouds she learns their message for the day and night and indications of a dust storm on the horizon. She gains a healthy respect for lightning and thunder and learns from her mother the old wives' tale of covering mirrors in the home on an approaching thunderstorm. Girlie sees the seasons come and go and the rivers rise and fall.

Hospitality and neighbourliness are important values in the country. People are welcome and often stay for a meal or overnight. There is always room. In the evenings with friends from properties nearby, Kathleen and her siblings play cards – Kathleen partners with Bill because it is always easier for everyone else for communication purposes, especially when they play Five Hundred. She is considered a good card player – little do others realise that a subtle sign she makes and her brother sees, and his return sign to her, go a long way to a winning game. Quickly or nonchalantly she moves her hand to point towards her ring finger to indicate her dominant hand of diamonds or makes another sign to indicate she has two Aces or the Joker. Arriving home she laughs with her family. So while she is competitive, she breathes in the normality of being with people who accept her, as a fun-loving, attractive young woman, as she wins the hearts of everyone with her smile.

As her visual humour and practical jokes are shared in the family, such humour shapes the type of entertainment and activity that engages her and brings enjoyment and satisfaction as a Deaf person.

* * *

At nineteen Don leaves school and an institutional way of life too – a life he has known since the age of six. He finds the adjustment difficult. He also leaves behind the Sydney he knows so well and the face-to-face daily encounter with his school friends. They are like brothers to him – they are his school family.

At Homewood near Yea, Don lives with his ageing father – he has no one around who can communicate with ease. Of his hearing brothers, John is in the seminary at Manly, Chester is away working and Brian is at boarding school. Charlie is away at school too – at St Gabriel's. His mother Emma, and his sister Marie together create a spirit of hospitality at *Wallis' Café* in Seymour, Victoria where Marie is known for her pastry cooking.

Emma opened her own café, Wallis Café in 1927 on the Hume Highway, Seymour Victoria

In his loneliness, Don is brought face to face again with the tragedy that occurred during his last holidays at home. He graphically explains to his friends all that happened:

It was a sunny day and some young people were swimming at Sunday Creek Bridge. I was swimming too and I saw my friend James in trouble further up the creek. He was trying to stay afloat. I swam over to him and I tried to help him. The currents were strong in the water and he kept disappearing. I could not find him so I shouted making a big sound and waved my arms to the other people. With gestures I tried to make them understand that my friend was drowning. I shouted loud again. They heard me. No one understood me. They could not sign. I had no pen and paper with me. I felt alone and desperate and very upset. Police divers came and searched everywhere in the fifteen feet of water and James' body was never found.

A very sad day and a tragic event! His friends go over the story with him and they express their sorrow.

While Don has a family with Deaf siblings and is well respected in the Deaf community, he resents his deafness. He imagines and dreams of possibilities for a new life raising his hope to be like others in the world. He is blocked by what other people see as an impairment and disability – he is refused an interview to join the Army.

With the Great Depression and its aftermath in the early 1930s, work is scarce. With almost thirty-two per cent of Australians out of work Don toils around home at *Wirrabong*. He digs and builds a rabbit-proof vegetable garden that he is proud of. He milks the cows and looks after the chooks to ensure a plentiful supply of milk and eggs. To provide further sustenance, he shoots rabbits and catches fish in the Goulburn River.

Don compensates for his loneliness at home – he involves himself heavily in local sporting activities and by doing so he challenges everyone to cater for a Deaf person. He shows them that Deaf ways and needs are different. He enters the marathons in the district of Yea. How is a race to begin fairly when a Deaf person is in the line-up with other competitors? Ready, Set, Go! A shot fired or a whistle blown? Don does not hear a shot fired or a whistle blown, so they require something visual as a trigger to start the race. It is agreed – the race officials drop a man's large handkerchief and Don is gone. You cannot see him for dust – he is off like a hare, an onlooker declares. With his win another trophy sits on the shelf in the shed with other memories of his sporting achievements.

With the support of his mother to contact people, Don searches for work in his tailoring trade in Melbourne on the Yarra. Initially, he works as a tailor in a small Jewish family business in Parkville. The Jewish family is good to Don and he reciprocates by being interested in them and willing to learn differences between people and their cultures and to accept them for who they are.

However, Don lives in boarding houses and he is hungry day after day. There is never enough food. He looks forward to the weekend when he can sometimes go to his mother's café in Seymour and enjoy her fresh pies.

Soon he moves on to work for the prestigious store Buckley's in Bourke Street Melbourne, before working at Myer Department Store in the same street.

Fulfilling his need for friendship and communication, he mixes widely with Deaf people, including those whom he meets at the Victorian Deaf Club at

Jolimont. He easily becomes fluent in the *two-handed* Sign language[1] and integrates socially with Deaf people of all ages. Older Deaf men especially, become mentors for him, in particular Bill O'Bryan who had been at school at St Kilda where a number of Catholic children had been to school and formed close friendships and had begun to attend retreats from the 1920s. Don also attends the social gatherings and retreats organised by the Catholic Deaf Association. Kathleen is not there.

It is 1934 and the Catholic Eucharistic Congress takes place in Melbourne with many events being organised. Don attends the reunion for Waratah and St Gabriel's students at *Siena* at Camberwell, where the Dominican sisters have their school for hearing children. He catches up with so many friends including his teacher from his primary years, Miss Hanney. What a pleasure! In his mind memories of his years at Waratah reverberate. She is pleased to see her students as

Reunion at *Siena*, Camberwell Victoria 1934:
Back: Jim Campbell, Jack Newton, Jim O'Gorman, ___, Alex Anderson, Father Phillips, Don Wallis, ___ Holloway, Vosper Wilson and John Murphy.
Middle: Herbert Wilson, Nellie Byrne, Doris Wilson, Mary Elligate, Pat Counsel, Nellie Elligate, Olive Anderson, ___.
Front: Mrs Wright, ___, Mrs Thompson, Marianne Hanney, Mrs Cunning, Annie Holcroft (children unknown).
Very front: Mabel O'Gorman, Eileen Derby, Maud O'Bryan and Esther Hutchinson.

---

[1] British Sign Language is the basis for what becomes Auslan, Australian Sign Language.

young grown-up men and women making their way in the world. But Kathleen is not there either. He has yet to meet her.

Being passionately interested in sport is a way he extends himself, whether he participates in the sport himself, observes it as a spectator, discusses it with anyone in sign or by writing on paper, or reads about it in the newspapers. As a Deaf person in sport, he is on an equal footing and sees himself on an equal playing field.

With his left-handed golf sticks, he plays at the Royal Melbourne Golf Club. He brings home a trophy from the Catholic Young Men's Society Amateur Athletic Club (CYMSAAC) that uses facilities at Olympic Park in Melbourne. While he joins in the inter-club competitions, he complains to his mother that the amateurs who pay fees to use the facilities at Olympic Park are not permitted to use lighting in the dressing rooms after dark, yet professionals are permitted. With his pen and notebook Don sits with the authorities and writes his problem that when he cannot see he cannot communicate – since his pen and notebook are of no use in the dark. The issue is resolved with the trustees of the park.

* * *

Don's sister Marie has high expectations and wants to have her own car – few women drive at this point in time and she never does have the opportunity. In her hope she is clearly influenced by her father, who even though the family struggled financially, is one of the first to have a car in the Homewood district.

After working in Wallis' café, Marie moves to Coburg in Melbourne and obtains employment where she is a seamstress and makes parachutes for the army. She knows her work is well done and she is proud of her efforts. But the young girl who works beside her takes advantage of her as a Deaf woman. She claims Marie's competent work as her own – Marie is deeply upset and stays silent. With their sewing skills, Emma and Marie find second-hand adult coats and skirts. From the fabric they make warm clothing for poor children and send them to Jack who is now a young enthusiastic priest in Hobart, Tasmania.

Marie reads prolifically and walks to the shops each day for the newspaper. This provides her with current political and general news. The newsagents know her well, as she buys every magazine that comes into the shop. She is hungry for information and knowledge. Nothing satisfies her thirst to know more. As she walks down the street, she meets various people – neighbours who are people from all walks of life – and she interacts with them with such interest. She fills the pages of foolscap writing pads with industrious conversations on all types of interesting subjects. With her inquiring mind she includes many questions.

Marie mixes with various Deaf people and attends the Victorian Deaf Society social groups, as well as the Catholic Deaf Association, which is often known as the Catholic Deaf Club. She meets Harold Fulton, originally from Rockley, near Bathurst NSW, and an ex-student of the School for Deaf children[i] in Sydney. He signs in the *two-handed* alphabet. Marie then becomes familiar with the *two-handed* fingerspelling and Sign language based on British Sign.

* * *

On the weekend Don returns to Seymour to see the family and he asks his mother about the re-union at Waratah that she and Marie had attended. Emma smiles and signs to him how wonderful it was to see so many girls there. She looks intently at him and signs that she met one girl who lives in the country without any nearby Deaf friends. Surely she is lonely. She puts Don in no doubt that she thinks he should visit this girl. For the next month Don thinks about his Mother's strong suggestion and then makes plans – yes, he will ride his bike to the Murray River and visit this girl.

Having crossed the river and as he walks down the dusty roadway towards *Carlyle* homestead, he already knows from his mother that she is a Waratah girl, which also meant that she knows many of the people he knows. He also knows immediately her mode of communication, her cultural, religious and social milieu. Knowing she is familiar with the Catholic ethos with the likelihood of an Irish background helps him understand who she is and the common ground they share. Her friends are Australian-Irish signers and it is understood in the Deaf community that Australian-Irish Sign Language is the Catholics' Deaf language in Australia.

Don feels the magnetic force between Kathleen and himself, and every chance he gets he finds himself at *Carlyle* on the Murray. Attracted to one another by their common language they are at ease with and understand each other, expressing emotion and reading each other's facial and body language. He enjoys holidays and long weekends hanging out with Kathleen and her family.

As ex-Waratah students and with Australian-Irish Sign Language being their primary language, they look to the Catholic community for the vitality of social interaction, life-giving mental stimulation and spiritual support – those who share the language, history, culture, values and faith. How sharing a language and culture attracts and unites!

As a Deaf man, Don stands tall. He sees himself as a proud, independent and capable individual well able to look after himself and his dependents. Accordingly he puzzles over the concept of charity on behalf of the adult Deaf community. Yes, it is true the Deaf will never hear music or hear their children's voices, birds sing or the sound of ocean water pounding on the rocks. Nor will they voice clearly in the spoken word or sing with choirs. Yet as young adults, Kathleen and Don avoid pity from people in their regard. They do not want to pull on the heartstrings of people and they squirm in the presence of those with condescending attitudes. They fill their minds with the beauty of images – of children's expressive eyes, birds in the pink evening sky, water that forms an exquisite patterned cloth over black rocks. Kathleen too is proud and does not see herself in need of entitlements because she is deaf. Both shake their heads if described as afflicted or considered deserving or impaired, but otherwise keep silent keeping their hurt hidden deep in the caverns of their psyches. While as adults they reject charity, they remain extremely grateful for the generous charitable donations that supported their educational needs.

Don and Kathleen, like other Deaf people, sometimes experience lack of understanding from hearing people particularly, in work places. Staff meetings happen without the provision of an interpreter effectively preventing them from participating in decision-making. Decisions are often made without them being present or without their input. Don and Kathleen find it is not always comfortable for people living in a society with difference.

During their four to five year-courtship, Kathleen and Don are reserved, their eyes twinkle – they love one another and visualise a future together. The two dragonflies land and flow along the river on a slender gum leaf. Don and Kathleen celebrate their wedding in the Church on the Hill. They honeymoon in the cool air of the holiday village of Marysville at the base of the mountains north east of Melbourne Victoria– they set up house together in Melbourne on the Yarra.

---

[i] It was called the Deaf and Dumb Asylum.

CHAPTER 9

SETTLING NEAR GARDENER'S CREEK
FLOWING TOWARDS THE YARRA

As they purposefully and industriously

Peck and pick

The two Wonga pigeons

Satisfy their hunger for nurture

Never out of sight

Watching for each other

Moving as one and yet apart.

The Yarra River, originally the Yarra Yarra River, meanders into Melbourne from Mt Baw Baw in West Gippsland through open land and farming properties via Warburton, Woori Yallock, Yarra Glen, and Healesville to Chirnside Park. From there it flows through Templestowe, Abbotsford, into the city of Melbourne and on to Port Melbourne and into Port Philip Bay at Hobsons Point. The Wurundjeri knew it as *Birrarung*, which is thought to mean the mists and shadows of the Yarra River.[i] In the Boonwurrung language *Yarro-yarro* means *ever-flowing*,[ii] a river that on its journey quenches the thirst of plants and trees, animals and peoples.

Kathleen and Don buy a house in the small, two-square mile, suburb of Hughesdale. Their house is right on Dandenong Road, the main thoroughfare between Melbourne and its far eastern suburbs and is about three kilometres from Gardeners Creek, a tributary of the Yarra. Gardeners Creek was originally known as Kooyongkoot Creek which from the Woiwurrung language of the Wurundjeri-Baluk group means *the haunt of the waterfowl*.[iii]

* * *

In their new home in 1941, Kathleen and Don learn to live together and for the first time since she leaves school Kathleen uses her Australian-Irish Sign Language constantly. While her mother, father and siblings all sign, she is forced to accommodate their lack of fluency by slowing down her signing so she can be understood clearly by the family. Also they mostly concentrate on fingerspelling with some signs. In fact both Kathleen and Don often have to slow down their interactions with hearing people. As their signing slows, so also does their facial expression. This means their communication is stunted and drawn out, so different from two people familiar and versatile with their own language.

With Waratah educated women like Kathleen, Don signs differently from the way he signs with Deaf men from St Gabriel's. The Waratah women sign with less fingerspelling. They are quick, gentle and graceful. For those who attend St Gabriel's, more emphasis is on fingerspelling with one hand. Don signs with strength as he commands presence and attentiveness. When he is conversing with Deaf people, who have not attended the Catholic school system with the Australian-Irish Sign Language, he uses the *two-hand* fingerspelling and local signs. Don then interprets for Kathleen in a mixed Deaf group[1] setting. She knows the *two-hand* alphabet but she cannot read it back easily. This means she can miss out when the conversation is flowing.

Early on weekday mornings, Don walks to the nearby Hughesdale railway station in silence, accepting smiles and gestures of hello from people who come to know him as he travels by train into the metropolis. Sometimes he rides to work on his well-worn bike – a ride of seventeen miles along Dandenong Road into the city. Whatever the mode of travel he uses, Don presents for his workday as a tailor well dressed in his work suit, hat and tie.

Wherever he goes, Don's top pocket always holds a small notebook and pen. He writes short questions and statements about everyday events in his conversations on paper. He expects the person to respond on the same notepad. This is a crucial means of communication in his everyday work life and is particularly important in the work with his clients.

Don's notebook is complementary to gestural means of conducting and clarifying conversation. He knows he needs more in his repertoire for interacting with the hearing world than just a smiling wave to indicate *Hello, how are you?* So he looks to the sky to indicate whether it is a good day of sunshine, a bad day of rainy weather, or a sad day with no rain, or it's too hot to be working. He gestures – pointing here or there, telling someone that the train is late, as he looks down the train line and then looks at the clock with a frown on his face. The train is late! Or he smilingly points to his new Ford Mainline with the number plate ASC 263 and lets them know how pleased he is with his new purchase. Of course more complex communication requires time, concentration, patience and commitment from both parties.

In a Deaf visual language, sentence construction, syntax and grammar, is different from English so they find themselves in need of assistance. From the

---

[1] This means both the one hand sign and the two-hand Sign languages.

drawer in the sideboard, Kathleen and Don consult a tatty but treasured little guidebook on letter-writing etiquette. It assists them with their English phraseology and they are comforted to know that their little book shows the appropriate wording to ensure their letters follow the norms of professional, business and personal communications. How do I write clearly and with courtesy? They consult on questions such as, how do I address the bank manager, the accountant and the doctor? Dear Sir/Madam, Dear Mr Leonard, Dear Teacher, Dear Sister, Dear Miss Bailey, Dearest Aunty Jane or My dearest Daughter? And how do I sign off? Is it with warm regards, yours truly or yours faithfully or is it something else? They not only want to be competent but they want to be seen as competent in their literary communication with the hearing world.

* * *

Kathleen, the country girl who worked on the farm, spends lonely days in her new home at Hughesdale. The house is timber and freshly painted white with a tiled roof. The garden is bushy with a little lawn and a vegetable garden in the backyard and while being a wife is a novelty, Kathleen is a competent homemaker. Don is the beneficiary of both a loving home and the freshly cooked cakes and biscuits that appear every day in his work lunch box. She washes in a fired copper tub, drains the washing in a concrete trough and wrings it out with her strong wrists and hands. She manages with the very few resources of a young married couple in wartime when food is rationed by coupons. She misses a house-cow in the back yard for milk and butter, but is pleased when a daily egg supply materialises after Don builds a chook house for their Rhode Island Red hens.

What a luxury, Kathleen and Don think as towards evening they turn on the electric lights. They remember the kerosene lamps in the homestead at *Carlyle* and at the home at *Wirrabong*, where the faint light generated by the lamps makes it more difficult to see expressions on people's faces in their family interactions. Now, at night with electric light, they see more easily their conversations in Sign language with hand and finger movements, as well as facial expressions and body language. While Kathleen is focused on her knitting or cooking, Don attracts her attention by turning the light on and off, as he enters the room.

On Sundays, filled with faith, Kathleen and Don walk to Mass at the Oakleigh Sacred Heart parish Church where they are familiar with the décor of statues and sacred icons. For them, even with the Church full of people around, all is silent as they pray but they are attuned to the movement of people – in the liturgical celebration and in the church. During the sermon they watch the priest and his facial expressions – is there kindness or humour? They wonder what is being said.

* * *

111

As they are building their dreams for their future life, Kathleen becomes pregnant. Kathleen and Don go to the Victoria Market with their war ration coupons to buy a calico bassinet. Questions arise, questions emerging from ignorance and fear: *How will deaf Kathleen go through the birth of the baby? How will she manage as a mother?* Don and Kathleen are confident. They pray and trust that all will be well.

In the winter of July 1942 the baby is born. Molly, Kathleen's twenty-two year old sister and best friend, is beside her at the hospital and tells Kathleen what she understands the medical professionals say after the birth. The baby is yellow and jaundiced but all is well. Kathleen and Don proudly take home their first daughter Carmel Mary. She is the first grandchild on both sides of the Wallis and Walsh families and many photos are taken.

The name, Carmel, is not a name in their family heritage, but Mary comes from both sides of the family – from great, great grandmothers, from great grandmothers and from grandmothers and Kathleen's sister, Molly, whose name is Mary Margaret. Kathleen has a Prayer Book for the Deaf[iv] that has a limited list of feast days in the Church's year. One of them is Our Lady of Mt Carmel. Is this where they find the name for their daughter? Did her Deaf friends discuss the list of feast names that were allocated in this particular prayer book? A number of Kathleen's friends are having children too.

Extended family members who feel responsible, and the medical profession ask the next questions of one another. Is the baby deaf? Carmel is not deaf[2] – they learn that Sign language will be her first language in a Deaf home and that her second language will be spoken English. Her speech will probably be developmentally delayed. She will be bi-lingual and become fluent in both languages.

Further questions arise. How will they manage the parenting of a child? Kathleen is experienced in looking after babies and small children, after all she is the first daughter in her own large family, and it was her role to nurture younger siblings. She is confident with babies and is watchful and aware. Don is less experienced. Really he has no experience.

At night, Kathleen sleeps close to the edge of the bed, so her arm hangs into the calico bassinet close beside her bed. She sleeps lightly and when she feels movement she knows that baby Carmel stirs or wakes and that maybe she is crying and is hungry. This continues through every night. Soon they move Carmel into the cot apart from the bed. This is more challenging. The baby cries, but they have no way of knowing when she is crying. Kathleen finds her baby sobbing and very distressed. The separation is too much. She anguishes over this and holds and cuddles her baby to attempt to ease the pain of not being there – and ease her own

---

[2] About 90% of Deaf people who have children have hearing children.

pain of not hearing her child – only for it to happen again and again.

Don is at work each day and Kathleen is at home with the baby. As she changes the baby's nappy and smiles and makes her special loving sounds as the baby focuses on her, she sees the baby suddenly turn her head towards the window. Kathleen looks towards the window as well and then moves to see what is outside; the dog barking and looking towards the porch at the front door. Kathleen opens the door and finds her neighbour who has a telephone message for her from her family in the country. They are coming to visit tomorrow! The baby grows and continues to be instrumental in giving her mother clues as to what is happening around her.

As Carmel is their first child, grandchild or niece, the grandparents and aunts and uncles become involved and give support and advice. Don's mother, Emma, enters from the back door, because there is no doorbell and there is no use knocking because she will not be heard. Everything is quiet, no movement anywhere as she looks for them in the house. She goes to the bedroom where the baby is in the bassinet and there she finds Don and Kathleen kneeling either side of the baby, eyes closed and in silent prayer unaware of anyone. She looks on for a moment and senses her intrusion, so tiptoes back to the kitchen to avoid making vibrations on the floorboards that may disturb them. She waits, deep in thought, until they return to the kitchen and she greets them and discusses how things are. Everything is good.

It is particularly challenging for both Don's and Kathleen's mothers, who have put so much energy into the support of their Deaf son and daughter. As new grandmothers, they struggle with how to achieve a balance between being there for their adult children and letting go to allow Don and Kathleen to find their way of raising their own children and family. In the past, the mothers have been spokesperson, advocate, interpreter, educator, as well as mother. Emotional ties are strong. To see their adult Deaf child take on responsibilities in their work and social life and then as parents requires trust and belief in them and trust that they have been successful in preparing their Deaf children for their role as parents. They need to tread a fine line between support and interference. Walking that line requires great sensitivity, self-knowledge and wisdom – traits that even the best of people fail to have in full measure.

For Don and Kathleen, the potential for the line to be crossed between help and interference is exaggerated by the reality that Don has a strong emotional attachment to his mother Emma and by the fact that his mother has always been his source of advice and support in financial and business matters. While Emma continues to freely provide advice and support driven by her natural concern for Don, Kathleen and their children, she crosses the line from Kathleen's perspective. Kathleen has a different approach to managing babies and children. She dislikes Emma's methods of teaching children to behave.

Even though Emma has had three Deaf children, she does not always understand either Deaf ways with children or the psychosocial development of children with Deaf parents. She believes in harsher punishment while Kathleen believes the opposite. Kathleen is quietly annoyed and angry and feels the interference of a mother-in-law who does not trust her as a Deaf mother and a Deaf woman. She asks for support from Don, as she believes that the conflict with Emma is destroying her confidence.

This is a cause of tension. Don remains dependent on his mother – the emotional attachment to her remains strong. She is always there when the need arises to negotiate to buy a more suitable house or when he wishes to establish the new business. Of his parents she is the one he relies on, since his father never grasps the language. It is difficult for Don to distance himself and support Kathleen as they form a team together in life apart from interference from others. Kathleen in turn continues to make return visits to her mother-in-law as she realises that Emma plays a vital role as an interpreter in their business dealings.

Grandmother, Mary Adeline, who still lives in the country, does not involve herself so intensely in matters of discipline. Her methods are more gentle and with a softer expression. She remembers how she disciplined Kathleen as a small child at Sunday Mass, sitting her on her knee and letting her Rosary beads tickle and drop into the sensitive palms of her daughter's tiny hands. Now she sees Kathleen doing the same for her daughter.

However, Mary Adeline is concerned about her granddaughter's language development. She devises a plan. She and Molly take Carmel to the farm for a long holiday to encourage her to vocalise in speech. They are successful until Carmel returns home and reverts to her first and silent language in sign.

Hands Hold the Memory

Hands hold the memory
The feel of the gentle
Slow fall of Rosary beads
Into the palm of sensitive,
Waiting hands
In the loving silence
Of a mother.

Hands hold the memory
The conscious sensation
Perceptibly receive
The blessed beads
From small hands held high
Pouring them back into hands
Of a mother.

Hands hold the memory
A mother who sits her on her lap,
Keeping stillness and quiet
Plays silently
In centred meditation
Rosary beads and ritual
Amid pews of people and children
Discipline held by a Mother.

Bernadette T. Wallis

It is 1943. Kathleen misses family and is troubled when her father suddenly falls ill with post-surgery complications after an appendectomy – an appendix removal at the hospital. She is called home to *Carlyle*. With baby Carmel, she travels through the day by train and is met at the railway station by her brother Bill, who is anxious that Girlie arrives in time to see her much loved father and say her good-byes. She is in shock – she cannot believe it. *Is he dying?* She asks questions and more questions. *Why? What happened? How long?* No one can explain exactly what is happening. The responsibility of her child is handed around the family and she spends many hours with her father, as she holds and gently squeezes his hand expressing her love in silence.

She ponders the words on her father's gold watch on which is engraved: *Presented to Mr. Richard Walsh by his friends of the Horsham district as a token of esteem on his leaving McKenzie Creek, Horsham. 16.3.1912.* That is thirty-one years ago. He is a good man. He treats people well. It is a matter of days when he dies. Don comes from Melbourne for the funeral and joins her as she sees her father laid to rest in Yarrawonga cemetery.

Gold watch belonging to Kathleen's father

* * *

Family is still important to Kathleen. Her sister Molly, her life confidante, now an aide at the Mercy hospital, is a regular visitor – she often stays and spends time with Kathleen. Her brothers, Jim and John, ride bikes from *Carlyle* homestead to Melbourne to see her and Don. Don introduces Jim to skating at St Moritz in St Kilda Road. Jim and Don are great mates. They enjoy one another's company and a beer or two or more. Jim's humour and his ability to sign, basic though it is, helps in their friendship and he refers to Don as a great bloke, an interesting character and a lot of fun.

Don notices that young Jim needs a good suit. Always thorough in what he undertakes, he measures up Jim and in his spare time in the winter evenings, he drafts a pattern and makes him a double-breasted brown suit, which Jim treasures and wears for many years. Kathleen is always anxious to visit her younger brothers, Kevin and John in the Franciscan religious order at Box Hill and Kew. Kathleen and Don choose Kevin to be the executor of their wills until their children are adults.

Don's brother, Charlie, ten years younger, looks up to him as a mentor. They are close friends and their conversation ranges from politics to the intricacies of building bridges and stories of risk-taking adventures. For a short time, Charlie lives with Don and Kathleen. Don's brother Chester visits occasionally – he is in the Lighthorse Regiment and lives in Broadford.

In October 1945 soon after World War II and after the sadness of two miscarriages, Bernadette Therese is born at Bethlehem hospital, South Caulfield. The hospital is a reasonable taxi trip away from their home. Knowing she is in labour Kathleen arrives at the hospital only to find that the staff do not believe her. Rather than looking at her, the nurse directs conversation through Molly. *Tell her that she is only eight months and has another month to go – go home!* Kathleen is emotional and indignant that no one at the hospital understands her and no one believes her. Next day when Don arrives home from work he finds her in the advanced stage of the birth process and in great distress. She insists that Don take her back to the hospital immediately. They arrive in time – the doctor is too late. Within half an hour Sister Carmelita, a Little Company of Mary nun, delivers the four-week premature baby.

Don and Kathleen choose the name Bernadette after the saint and in memory of Miss Marianne Hanney – a name that is not a family name. The name links Don and Kathleen to their school at Waratah and their teacher and mentor, who has died several years earlier. In memory of Miss Hanney, a number of Deaf ex-students had gathered to place a statue of St Bernadette at the grotto with the white statue of Our Lady of Lourdes, whose story allures them.

Three-year-old Carmel bears the responsibility of alarming Kathleen and Don of anything that needs their attention. When the baby cries, she alerts them to sounds: *Baby – cries!* and she becomes an advocate, interpreter and teacher.

It is November 1945. The premature baby is one month old when Don is called home to *Wirrabong* at Homewood because his father is dying. This is an emotional event for him. Kathleen stays home to care for the baby so he misses her presence and support.

Don's mother, Emma, looks tired and distressed as she waits for Jack to return from Hobart. Marie who married Harold two years earlier has her baby, Mary, with her, and Chester, Brian and Charlie are also there. As Don arrives he sits in the bedroom where his elderly father lies and Don laments yet again that he cannot communicate with him and say to him things he wants to convey. He remembers Charlie and himself playing cards with him. He knows his father's love for books, reading and poetry and his father's love for his car. He appreciates his father's thirst for knowledge and understanding of how things work in the world. This passion has been passed on. He wants to thank his father for insisting that he get a good education in difficult financial times. He wants to tell him of his new baby, another daughter, born just a month ago.

Everyone is called to dinner around the table. They leave Abe alone. Don quickly finishes his main course and quietly slips back to his father. Business between them is not complete. As he enters the room this time, he kneels down close where he can see his face in the evening twilight. He senses it is as though his father is waiting for him. It is his father's personal time with him – an intimate moment. His father looks steadily at him and smiles with full recognition. In this way he shows his sorrow and remorse that he cannot communicate. He has done all he needs to do now. He closes his eyes and soon breathes his last. Don hurries to the dining room and signs for everyone to come – and his father dies. In this precious time with his father, Don feels reconciled and is filled with gratitude for that last smile that helps to wipe away the hurt and resentment towards his father. Jack celebrates the Requiem Mass for his father and Abraham Knight Wallis is buried in the Yea Pioneer cemetery. At the Wirrabong Creek, a dragonfly hovers and hurriedly moves along the creek.

Before long Emma finishes up on the land at *Wirrabong* and eventually buys land and lives near Broadford. Some years later still, she buys a home in Melbourne at West Brunswick. Charlie lives with her there.

* * *

---

[i] *http://aboriginalhistoryofyarra.com.au/14-language/*

[ii] *http://en.wikipedia.org/wiki/Yarra_River*

[iii] *http://en.wikipedia.org/wiki/Gardiners_Creek*

[iv] *The Prayer Book for the Deaf* was compiled at Waratah for the Catholic Deaf Schools with the encouragement of Bishop Gleeson of Maitland.

CHAPTER 10

NEARBY MERRI MERRI CREEK

From far above the trees

A shadow forms a big shape

Onto the pathway of the floor of the bush

As hawk-like and mysterious

And the Wonga Pigeons

Stay in sight and safe together

In the garden of the bush.

At the northern edge of Melbourne, where Wurundjeri of the Kulin nation lived, Don and Kathleen choose their new middle class home. It's on Sydney Road, Fawkner, a location up from Merri Merri Creek. While the Creek begins at Wallan north of Melbourne, it flows through rocky boulders in a southerly direction into the Yarra River and then into wide Port Philip Bay. The area around Merri Merri Creek, its aboriginal name meaning *very rocky*, was well populated before white settlement. Aborigines hunted kangaroo and emu in the grasslands nearby. Possums were also a source of food and their skins were sewn together for treasured soft waterproof clothing. Here the ever ancient dragonflies continue to fascinate the children as they dart here and there with no seeming pattern to their activity.

While Kathleen and Don walk home from the tram stop in the evening moonlight after being in the city, they see the ring-tailed possums balance nimbly on telephone cables along the street. They do not hear them jump on the roof while they are in bed at night, but they do see evidence of them clambering into the ceiling of their timber built home and the children tell them of the scary noises they hear.

Don and Kathleen are now closer to the city for work, for shopping and for their meetings and social life at the Catholic Deaf Club. They are also close to Deaf friends in the next suburb, Alex and Olive Anderson and Bill and Eileen O'Bryan and their families, whom they visit regularly. The O'Bryan's name their son Donald, whose godfather is Alex Anderson. The Deaf families are important to one another and they form a big Deaf family. The community activities are their life-blood. This is post War in the late 1940s and Don and Kathleen notice that many new immigrants, mostly Italians and Greeks, have settled in the local area in Fawkner.

Don and Kathleen's home Sydney Road, Melbourne Victoria, circa 1950

They check that St Mark's Catholic Church and school is within walking distance from their home. They notice that during the week the Church becomes a classroom on weekdays. Soon the parish priest and the Sisters of Mercy notice them at Sunday Mass – they are easy to spot in the congregation as they communicate in sign with their daughters who look up at their faces and use their hands in communication. A family that is different. Kathleen is pregnant again, sick and unable to attend Mass, so the priest brings communion to her.

The Sisters who run St Mark's school have suggested that Carmel start school at an earlier age than other children, so that she can develop her somewhat delayed spoken English. She is four. The Sisters are young and full of energy and their school has large numbers of migrant children. They are therefore used to teaching children for whom English is a second language. Having the advantage of a well-developed language in Australian-Irish Sign Language, Carmel easily grasps her second language. Before long she voices stories to her younger sister in bed at night in the dark.

As they observe her as a hearing child, Don remembers the importance of the radiogram and music to his hearing siblings. *Yes*, he thinks, Carmel is four years old, so it is time! He buys a plug-in wireless so she can listen to programs that belong to the hearing world. He is fascinated by it and how it works. Kathleen is intrigued by it – she places her hand on the wireless and feels the thrill of the vibration. Don tries to think what a hearing child needs and discusses the issue with his Deaf friends because he wants the best for his hearing family. Yes, one day he will encourage his daughter to play the piano.

Don has his own set of the red encyclopaedia – he regularly looks up various items. His thirst for knowledge never leaves him. He is conscious of his fathering role and wishes to share his desire for knowledge. After tea is storytelling time and he sits his five-year old daughter Carmel on his knee as he pages through the atlas section of the encyclopaedia. Sometimes he tells stories of his life growing up. They sign together in their visual language. He enjoys the inquisitiveness of a child open to learn and make meaning of life. He helps with homework and Carmel tries to work out how her Dad can *hear* her spelling. This is a problem when he asks her to spell the word he has to spell to her first! It is never a satisfactory outcome but they laugh together and somehow Carmel learns her spelling. In the spelling class, her hands go under the desk and she first of all spells the word on her fingers before confidently writing it down. Her brain is wired – her fingers know how to spell before she speaks or writes.

Up the Hume Highway at Clonbinane on Sunday Creek near Broadford, Don's mother and brother Chester have property. On the farm at *Glenelgin* in Clonbinane, his brother Chester breeds and breaks in horses that he sells far and wide. He later has a riding school. He owns hunting dogs and ferrets that hunt rabbits and foxes on the property. He also has sheep and cattle. This is where Don loves to ride – and Chester always has a horse ready for him. Here, he escapes the city life and feels the freedom of riding the horses up into the hills. He has already introduced Carmel to the horses having placed her in front and put her tiny hands on the end of the rein, as they headed into the bush. A walk and a gentle canter! She becomes a horse-lover and the sensation of both horse and land captures her too.

Life at home is dynamic and spirited. The rectangle fishpond that spawns goldfish and water-plants outside the old washhouse provides reflective entertainment. Kathleen often stands and watches – a serene way to pass time. Two-year old Bernadette wants to touch the fish – she takes an unplanned dip as she topples over into the pond. Don and Kathleen do not hear the splash of water but Kathleen, who is forever attentive, sees it happen, rushes across and quickly rescues the blubbing child. She is fearful of the dangers posed by the water and imagines herself inside or hanging the washing on the line and being out of sight of the children, when such a thing happens – a child drowning. Together they realise the risk is too great for them. The fishpond goes and in its place a garden of cactus plants grows.

Down the street to the quarry the children in the neighbourhood run to search the puddles for spawned tadpoles, which they trade with one another. Carmel trades ten black tadpoles for a big silver one. She takes her tadpoles home to the laundry tub so they can watch them develop. Soon legs appear and the tail disappears and frogs are found jumping about moving into the fernery outside. Kathleen disapproves and forever discourages such practices in her washhouse.

Walking towards the tram with one hand firmly in Kathleen's hand and the other one free, Bernadette drags a stick and plays music along the green-painted old corrugated iron fence that runs almost a block before the tram terminal. The vibration flows through her fingers and into her hands and arms. Kathleen feels the vibration too and hears not a sound – not so for the passers-by who are only too well aware of the din.

In 1947 Don's brother Brian is ordained for the priesthood for the Melbourne archdiocese. He visits from time to time and, while he signs in a swift and stiff manner, he becomes a support by interpreting in business situations after his mother is less able to attend to this for Don.

* * *

It is the 1940s. Don normally travels to work at Myer Department Store [i] in the city by train, the closest railway station being Merlynston. The Myer slogan is *For Value and Friendly Service*. *The Myer News Store Magazine* is published a number of times through the year for the staff. While it conveys personal news of the staff, the births, deaths and marriages, it also serves to build *esprit de corps* among the staff, a sense of cooperation and good will, as they work together. In the magazine various executive appointments and departures from the business are announced. Staff members are encouraged to serve the customer with dignity and friendliness. Examples are given of how they can better themselves in their work and do's and don'ts are outlined, while they encourage staff to know their merchandise. Don sees these are clear guidelines and understands their ethical stance.

Stories are told in the magazines of the senior staff and their travels overseas to attend meetings and develop their particular area of expertise. As well, different cities of the world are written up for the interest and education of staff readers. Lunch-time discussion groups on current affairs take place and among the topics are: Growing More Food, Black Africa, Secrecy in Science, Pakistan, and The Cold War. This information is so interesting to Don. He never stops learning.

Support for staff includes free legal advice and the Myer dental care program. Staff sports are encouraged – cricket, basketball, table tennis, badminton and fencing, including a women's fencing club. Opportunities for social life together are created – the Christian fellowship, the Myer Theatre Club, The Myer Choir and the staff children's Christmas party.

While staff members and their families are invited to use the Myer holiday venue, preference is given to those without such opportunity. Don's family belongs in that category. Carmel and Bernadette excitedly anticipate their first holiday at the Norman Lodge, the Myer holiday home at Mt Eliza – and it is Christmas.

They begin the journey by tram to Flinders Street station and train to Frankston where they climb on the bus to Mt Eliza with the luggage. Don realises he has left his best and very good hat on the train. Upset at losing his new and expensive hat, Don looks around for help. The girls are tuned right in and wonder if they will be called on to interpret or to speak to someone themselves. *What do they need to do?* There is nothing that can be done – his hat is lost and someone else would have it by now!

On the first morning they walk along the windy beach. Even though they live in Melbourne the beach experience is new and unfamiliar to them. They are river people – holidays and outings usually take them north to the Goulburn or Murray Rivers where extended family live, rather than to the beach. Carmel is curious and runs up to a huge blob of jelly with jellylike streamers to investigate. This is so interesting. Then some men from further down the beach yell at her to keep away from the jellyfish – they are dangerous. She stops – shocked and puzzled. No one told her before!

Nearby the Myer holiday home is the Franciscan monastery where Kathleen's brother John, a Franciscan student is on holidays too. On Christmas Eve, Don and Kathleen and the girls with a number of holiday people walk in the dark down the monastery driveway for Christmas midnight Mass. The excitement is tangible and they look forward to seeing uncle John. While Christmas carols are sung in the chapel, Kathleen and Don watch the organist and the choir – hearing nothing. Back at the holiday house, Kathleen has hidden in their luggage two dolls that are clothed in beautifully crocheted white woollen dresses. She is sure the children will love their Christmas gifts this year.

After the holiday Don returns to work at Myer. He continues to be an eager student of his trade. Don is greatly interested when they offer a course for staff on textiles. Various experts in the field are brought in to discuss the origins of the nature of fabrics such as wool, linen, silks, cottons, rayon and nylon. Don recognises good materials and knows how to use them – he hopes for a bright future as a senior tailor within the organisation.

Tailoring is a big department within Myer and there are other Deaf men also employed there. This gives Don the opportunity to further develop his career as he is able to discuss tailoring issues more easily with co-workers and is able to become a mentor to other Deaf men. One of them is Jim Moloney. Young Jim is forever grateful to Don for recommending him for employment at Myer and in doing so giving him a great start to his working life.

1948 is a watershed year for Don. Myer advertises for young men to learn the art of traditional English Tailoring from master craftsmen. In glowing terms they describe it as a craft with its superb cut and style, which has been handed down from generation to generation. It goes on to suggest that the successful applicants can become the highly paid skilled tailors of the future. Don is not selected. He finally realises that as a Deaf person, he is not going to be given big promotions to senior roles in the trade. No advances in his job are offered, even though he is more skilled than most of the staff.

He must prepare for a life after Myer. In the evenings, he takes on private clients for whom he makes suits, coats and jackets, especially for people who differ from the average size. Initially clients are seen in the kitchen where there is good light. Don soon builds an extra room onto the house, where he can see clients at night and do his work. He is very particular and professional about how he serves his clients.

As well as the huge mirror for his clients to see themselves during the fitting process, Don has huge tailoring scissors. The girls are warned with the index finger wagging towards them – never touch the scissors. The hand sign for scissors is a sideways opening and closing of the index and middle finger. They are sharp and they are meant to be sharp so as to crisply cut various fabrics. They are not to be used for any other purpose – certainly not paper.

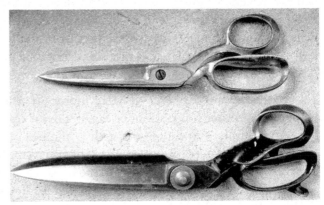

Don's tailoring scissors. Photo: Joseph Percy

Don makes suits, coats and dresses for the girls – Kathleen willingly helps out. He does this with pride while the girls revolt and complain about having to stand on the kitchen table for fittings and while hems are being pinned.

* * *

It is springtime in Melbourne on a Saturday morning and Bernadette will soon have a birthday in the year 1949. Her father signs to her as he has done since she was born. She understands these signs. He now wants her to fingerspell, that is, to spell words with her hands and fingers, because it is time she grows up in her language. She is hurt because she thinks she is grown up and because she will soon be four! Her father comes from the school of thought that believes in the importance of fingerspelling and he considers it a more sophisticated method of signing – that is what he was taught or that it was subtly inferred.

Downhearted and determined, she goes to her mother and insists that she teach her – now! It is urgent in her eyes. There and then her mother sits her down with her on the timber floor in the hallway, as she patiently and gently teaches her the *one-handed* Australian-Irish fingerspelling. She begins with the words: *cat C-A-T*,

mat M-A-T, sat S-A-T, rat R-A-T, then cap C-A-P, map M-A-P, tap T-A-P, lap L-A-P.
She practises with her for a few minutes it seems, or was it longer? The child feels
the pulsating excitement in her veins of a new found achievement and she runs
outside to her Dad, who by now is mowing the lawn with a push mower, without
electric cords or batteries. She tugs at his legs to alert him of her presence and he
stops and looks at her with full attention. Then she tells him forcefully that she can
sign like a grown-up. Just watch me. He waits patiently and surely, smiling inside
himself, he watches his little daughter sign each word, *cat C-A-T, mat M-A-T,* and all
the other words. He signs encouragingly in reply and her confidence rises.

He is right. She already signs in her communication and the fingerspelling
of words was ready to tumble out of her. She has observed it since she was born. He
treasures communication through fingerspelling, an appreciation he gained from his
schooling with the Brothers, who emphasise its value in their method of teaching.
The conversation between Don and Kathleen that evening, when she is out of sight,
is one of pleasure at the ordinary event that has just occurred – their daughter
fingerspelling for the first time.

* * *

Life in a Deaf family is made up of ordinary interactions and poignant
moments. In the middle of an ordinary day Bernadette looks up and in sign asks her
mother, *Tell me about when me born.* Kathleen smiles and tells the story in sign, *You, so
tiny, so small, so frail – I look after you and keep you safe at home – I don't go out in the cold or
in the heat of summer until you are strong enough.* Bernadette asks her mother again in sign,
How big me when baby? Kathleen conveys tenderness and the notion of how precious
life is. She reaches into the kitchen cupboard and brings down a cup. She points to
the circumference of the cup and circles her finger around the top. She signs almost
softly, *Your head – that size, the size of the cup circumference.* Her daughter relishes the
intimacy of the moment and signs again, *But how big was I?* This time Kathleen picks
up an orange, *Your head – size of this orange.* The little girl giggles. Imagining her head
as an orange is worth a giggle. Kathleen holds sacred a time when the birth of a
premature baby was precarious.

Kathleen has a further two miscarriages before their new baby is born in
1950 at Sacred Heart Hospital in Moreland. This time all goes very well. The name
for the baby is discussed with the responsible eight-year old Carmel. They trust her
judgement before they take the decision to call the baby Margaret Anne. A great,
great grandmother came from Ireland on the boat called *The Margaret* and Molly's
second name is Margaret. Anne is the name of Don's favourite cousin, Anne
Douglas in Northcote. Although Don is proud of having another daughter, he signs
to the neighbour and shakes his head sideways, *No boy! Three girls!*

In faraway Tasmania, Jack, as a diocesan priest, is involved in establishing a new community of Sisters[ii] who will work in rural and isolated areas of Australia and with people who live beyond the normal supports of the church. In 1950 he travels to Rome with Archbishop Tweedy of Hobart to organise the official approval at the Vatican for the order of Sisters. He rarely sees the family, but on his way back to Tasmania he and the Archbishop call to see the new baby, Margaret, and Don, Kathleen and the girls, giving each of them rosary beads blessed by Pope Pius XII. The family treasure this visit and their time with Jack.

As she grows Margaret is dressed in her red riding-hood cape captivating everyone as she signs her first signs – *more, dinner, toilet, milk, cat, drink, finished.*

* * *

Kathleen's sister and confidante, Molly, is given the task to introduce Bernadette to the school grounds and kindergarten. En route, the little girl kicks and screams in protest. School is a foreign country – a different environment. When she comes home and has a quiet time with her mother, she signs in confidence about school. *It is noisy*, she signs and then she puts her hands over her ears. So many children are talking at once – *it is all confusing* – the teacher speaks to everyone not just to one person. Bernadette is used to face-to-face conversation – it is normal to her at home – she has grown up with it. *You look at me and sign to me – I can understand you. No one looks at me when they talk* she says. She cannot understand what is going on. She does not realise that instructions given to the whole class are intended to apply to her as an individual person. It is such a relief when she meets someone's eyes as they talk – she then knows what she is expected to do.

As her children take leave of Kathleen each morning for school, she asks three regular questions: Firstly, have you been to the toilet? Secondly, have you said your morning prayers? Thirdly, have you a handkerchief in your pocket?

The sign for *toilet* is the 't' of the alphabet, shaken sideways in front. *Finished* is the 'a' of the alphabet with the thumb in an upward position, shaken sideways vigorously, two or three times. *You* is the index finger pointing towards the person. *Prayers* is where the palms of the hand touch one another as in clapping and held upright. *Handkerchief* is formed with the thumb and index finger that touch the nose and brush past it in a forward direction. *Pocket* is formed with the hand entering an imaginary pocket on the side of the hip.

With these signs and her facial expression of eyebrows raised in question, Kathleen conveys the message in perfect syntax and grammar. *Toilet – you – finished? Prayers – you – finished? Handkerchief – you – in pocket?* With a nod in a downward *yes* direction, she gives a kiss and a wave good-bye. She follows to the gate and watches them walk along the street in their school uniforms. How do you put visual language in spoken words? You can't, otherwise it looks like broken English.

While Don and Kathleen's daughters learn English and other subjects at school, no linguistic education is available for them in their first language, Sign language. No one considers how beneficial it would be for them to learn the linguistic elements – the grammar, syntax, lexicon and expression even when they use the language every day at home. It is not understood or thought as necessary or desirable in an educative setting. The result is that the girls do not have an intellectual knowledge or depth understanding of the language and the story of their Deaf heritage. The knowledge they gain is by osmosis in the home and in the Deaf community and is very dependent on how much they are involved with family and community.

Don and Kathleen value the benefit of having their children as *on tap interpreters* – they are strong bridges that link Don and Kathleen's intelligent minds to the other person who wishes to communicate with them.

Sometimes hurtful things happen. After shopping, Bernadette walks through the street towards home with her mother – she is six. A young boy in the town rides past on his bike and he calls out, *Your Mum and Dad's dumb and can't talk! Stupid!* She puzzles over the taunt and learns that her parents really are different – Deaf – and she does not want her mother to be hurt. In fact she is hurt and keeps it to herself.

Bernadette gains peace of mind when she reasons that the boy's parents fail to sit around the table at dinner and inform him that there are many different languages for different peoples. French, Spanish, Korean, Gaelic – and Sign Language for Deaf people. The difference is that it is not a spoken but a visual language. She learns that adults in families say derogatory words in front of children about people who are different and that children easily catch parental attitudes.

In signing, the concept of being stupid is conveyed with a closed fist that knocks on the side of their forehead. *Don't be stupid*, they sign as the children are playing up and need to be called to order. Or it can be a derogatory sign. *Stupid! He's stupid! They think we are stupid!* The strength of the closed fist knocking on the head and facial expressions to various degrees go with the sign to indicate the intensity of the intent.

The sign for not being able to speak is made with two fingers, the index and middle

Dumb

Words are shouted
Simple name-calling
A stigma placed
In my presence.

Shockingly embarrassed
Hurt held and carried
A heart pierced
Deeply within.

Puzzled in mind
Feeling something wrong
Ignorance pervades
Here and now.

I have a secret
I cannot tell
I stay silent.
Not stupid!
Not dumb!

Bernadette T. Wallis

fingers, placed flatly on the lips. Don knows it is interpreted as the English word *dumb*. He discusses English words with his friends and they ponder over meanings and what is disrespectful or offensive to Deaf people, including the word *deaf-mute*.

Deaf people rightfully feel resentful and angry when referred to as *deaf-mute*, *mute*, *dumb* or are called *Dummy* – meaning to them that they do not speak and that they are also stupid. How dare the word and concept be used for people who are deaf or for any human person! Their daughter writes a letter to God to complain.

> *Dear God,*
>
> *Today I heard my Mum and Dad called 'dumb' and described as 'deaf-mutes'. What does that mean? I know when I hear it, inside of me freezes. I don't say the word 'mute' or 'deaf-mute' ever, even though lots of people do. I feel they limit my mother and father and they think that a person unable to clearly speak orally is also deprived of language and meaning. I feel offended. I know Mum and Dad communicate extremely well with me in Sign and Mum makes meaningful sounds. She is playful and she sucks in her lips and makes sounds, cooing sounds that express her spontaneous affection. They are sounds that are comforting and loving. She does not do this in public but just in our family. The word 'mute' really doesn't fit. And she is not 'dumb' – she is 'cluey'!*
> *Thanks for listening,*
>
> *Truly yours,*
>
> *Bernie*

Kathleen and Don also find it puzzling and hurtful when a hearing friend says that he would rather be blind than deaf. He goes on to explain that Deaf people are much more isolated than someone who is blind. Initially, Kathleen and Don do not understand but suddenly they realise that their hearing friend really does not understand them as Deaf people, even though the person knows them well. For Don and Kathleen their worldview is gained predominantly through sight and they cannot imagine being without it. Kathleen feels such sorrow as a young woman who is blind walks down the street. She calls her daughters to have compassion for those who have such trials, believing that being deaf herself is not such a trial.

* * *

It is Friday – the end of the week. Don finishes work at Myer and ritually calls into St Francis Church, genuflects and slips into the side Lady Chapel, lights a candle and kneels as he looks at the framed picture of Our Lady of Perpetual Help. He prays for his young family. He walks past and places his hand on the picture as a tangible sign of his trust in her care for them.

In expressing their Catholic faith, all is in silence for them as Don and Kathleen attend faith-filled events and Sunday Mass at St Mark's at Fawkner or

St Francis' Church in the city. They reach out to people in hospitality and enjoy friends in the community and more especially in the Catholic Deaf community with whom they form deep relationships from school days and in their early marriage. Don treats his work place with honesty and respect and his customers appreciate the way he serves them. Kathleen visits relatives and Deaf friends in their need. She cares for and nurtures her family as her primary responsibility – she shares her experience of God and reminds them of God by uplifting her eyes, her arm raised and her index finger pointing upwards to the sky.

Don becomes president of the Catholic Deaf Association and the front door is left ajar so the committee members can come into the house without knocking and disturbing the girls who are in bed. They gather to sit around the oval kitchen table for their discussions and are unconscious of the noise of their footsteps, chairs sliding across the linoleum floor, the deaf guttural sounds, as well as sudden laughter after the telling of a story. There is silence for minutes – except for hands shuffling as if chaffing – another sudden burst of laughter and the girls are comforted to hear their Dad's laugh among the laughter of everyone else. They wake again just when falling asleep until exhausted they finally give in to deep sleep. The meeting proceeds, issues are discussed and events are organised.

Archbishop Mannix endears himself to the Deaf community when he arrives on the feast of *Ephpheta* each year. He gives a personal blessing to each person present, including the babies and children, who marvel at receiving a sixpence coin from him. The anticipation is palpable as the crowd waits in a long queue for each individual's turn to stand before this great figure of the Catholic world in Australia. Everyone looks up to him. He extends his ageing hand for each one to kiss his ring. Carmel is over-awed by the experience – she gets to sit on his knee and never forgets the privilege. After Benediction – with spirits, minds and hearts enriched by the day – people make their way home in the winter darkness.

The Archbishop also attends the annual Deaf family Christmas party that has a Deaf Father Christmas who signs to the children. Organised by the Catholic Deaf Association, with the volunteer support of the Catholic Women's Social Guild,[iii] it is also held in St Francis Church hall.

* * *

Kathleen's siblings all move on from Melbourne. She misses her family and feels the loneliness of city life as a Deaf person. Molly marries Laurie Whitty from Boomanoomna, Dick marries Anne Walsh from Yarrawonga, Monica marries Jack Toohey from Barooga, Bill marries Mary Lonergan from Cobram, Jim marries Marie O'Dwyer from Barooga and Kevin marries Audrey Whitty from Boomanoomna, and her Franciscan brother John soon leaves for Papua New Guinea as a missionary. Some of the in-laws struggle to master Sign language and feel inadequate and frustrated when their communication is limited.[iv]

Chester marries Sheila Slavin from near Yea. Their five children are in the minority among their Wallis cousins because all their seventeen cousins have Deaf parents. The children are matter-of-fact about it and treat the difference as part of their life. This is shaped by the constancy of the visits of the Deaf aunts and uncles. One of the children, Moira, asks Don and Kathleen, *How do I sign my name?* They teach her the letters, M-o-i-r-a, and patiently and gently adjust her fingers to a more accurate form. Uncle Don and Aunty Kath teach her and her siblings to express: *Hi! Thank you, please, cat, dog, good, bad, good-bye.* The nieces and nephews are so pleased with themselves and sign to one another showing their new and developing skill.[v]

Sheila wants to communicate well enough to have meaningful conversations with her sisters and brothers-in-law and their Deaf friends, so she learns basic Sign language too. How frustrating for all concerned is this process of teaching hearing people to communicate when they only give limited time to the process! It is excruciating! Yet, there is not a flicker of an eyelid that shows impatience on the part of Kathleen and Don.[vi] They are so eager that more people know their language especially family members and they are always ready to induce any young person to learn. This perseverance creates the possibility of fair, good or fluent communication either now or later – and relationships are formed.

* * *

It is 1951 and Don and Kathleen celebrate ten years of marriage and review their lives. Don turns forty soon and he is tired of the monotony of his life at work with little challenge. His secure job in the city of Melbourne from pre-War, during the War and post-War has not eased his restlessness. While thorough and meticulous in the tailoring trade, Don is not satisfied at Myer. With his vision to employ Deaf people himself, he writes to the Brunswick Council for permission to establish his own tailoring business. While he receives the authority to go ahead, this dream does not eventuate – and his yen for more in his life, and for the land, stays with him.

And what of Kathleen when all the children attend school? What will she do? Even though they live in a middle-class home with a big backyard and a car, have a secure nine to five job and a healthy family with three children, their dreams are bigger! They think about what they really want in their life together as a family. All the while, Don holds the dream to have his own business on a farm where he is his own boss.

And what does it mean to leave the city of Melbourne? They make a most momentous and courageous decision. Together they decide to make the break and move on to where Don's heart lies – on the land, where he can be more closely aligned with the earth and feel a different challenge and freedom. For Kathleen it is also a return to the land she knows so well. They take the opportunity to venture forth and be more in control of their working life – and for Don, Kathleen is by his side. For her, the move is closer to her family, where she can discuss family issues with them. And he feels at home in a small rural community.

With the significant improvements they have made, they sell their house on Sydney Road, Fawkner in Melbourne and arrange financial assistance through a small loan from his mother, Emma, to purchase a dairy farm at Berrigan in the Riverina, about forty miles from where they originally met near the Murray River.[1]

---

[i] The information about Myer Department Store is taken from material in The Series of the *Myer Store News* from 1947 – 1954 held in the Myer Collection of Archives, Baillieu Library, University of Melbourne.

[ii] The new Order founded in 1944 was originally known as the Home Missionary Sisters of Our Lady and later this was changed to the Missionary Sisters of Service. In Victoria, they were often known as the Caravan Sisters, because for a period of time in their early history in Tasmania they used a caravan to move from parish to parish.

[iii] The Advocate, *Christmas Party for Deaf Children*, 20 Dec. 1951 p.19

[iv] Interview with Jim and Marie Walsh in Wodonga 2013

[v] Interview with Moira, daughter of Chester Wallis, Melbourne 2014

[vi] Ibid

---

[1] Emma dies three years after the move, by which time the loan is repaid via her solicitors in Seymour.

Sign Language

In my face in the silence
In the creases and crinkles
I have adjectives and adverbs
Tiniest of muscles crunched and stretched
Every fibre of skin and sinew, alive with tones of colour
In my living face

Personal pronouns point outwards and inwards
Nouns in my arching arms and my flying hands
Verbs in my life-filled body
Words in my whirling fingers
Light in my expressive eyes
Lips that form and shape

They rage or endorse
Glow with joy or fade with sorrow
Dance in a waltz or jerk in satire

No matter
Silently
Looking
Seeing
Touching

A myriad of messages
An answer filled with emotion that lights up a mind
A picture that draws itself on a vacant canvas that has waited its time
A story of love and war, hope and joy
In my space
In my face in the silence

Bernadette T. Wallis

CHAPTER 11

BERRIGAN ON MULWALA CANAL
FLOWING FROM THE MURRAY

As in slow momentum

The Wonga Pigeon

Lifts up on branches

Higher and higher

One day he goes out of sight – and is gone

The Other

Worries and frets with anxiety

She had warned, do not go again

Let us watch each other and stay close.

Berrigan is Wampa Wampa – Prepa Prepa Country. The Wiradjuri, Yorta Yorta and Baranga tribes lived and cared for this Country for thousands of years. Once a quarry and once a picnic area, the old Green Hills with their rocky outcrop on the eastern side of Berrigan were surely sacred to the Aboriginal peoples – they knew the place as *Bari-gun.* Has the name developed into Berrigan? Berrigan exists among place names such as Nangunia, Lalalty, Mulwala, Barooga, Boomanoomna, Cobram, Jerilderie, Narrandera, Tocumwal, Yarraweah, Yarrawonga, Wangaratta, Wodonga and Walla Walla – words and meanings from Aboriginal languages.

It is 1952 and Berrigan town has a population of approximately two thousand people. With well-established family identities and a strong Catholic Irish culture, Berrigan offers a rural community spirit of hospitality and tolerance. In this post-War era, the economic climate is difficult and life is simple.

Don and Kathleen with their three daughters aged nine, six and eighteen months settle at *Forest Vale*, a property of one hundred and ten acres with a dairy farm and milk delivery business along Finley Road. A kilometre on, the Mulwala Canal flows under the bridge on its route from the Murray River at Mulwala/Yarrawonga past Kathleen's old home at *Carlyle* through extensive farmland and eventually to the Edward River at Deniliquin.

The irrigation water from the Mulwala Canal, which supports local agriculture, flows via many channels including one that flows alongside the *Forest Vale* property. The dragonflies appear on the channel in the summer.

* * *

Don and Kathleen's arrival ensures that initial curiosity in the small town is high but the myths, ignorance and misconceptions about Deaf people and Deaf families common in wider communities rapidly decrease and then dissipate over the following fifteen years. People seeing the new family in town notice an ordinary couple with children but something is different – hearing children and Deaf parents. They also see the family communicate in a completely different way – in Sign language with hands and fingers moving in intense face-to-face encounters. This family unit sets up a business in the town.

Don and Kathleen exchange a regular city life-style of a nine to five, five day a week job and indoor night work at home, for the unpredictability of farm life in the elements, and long days that begin at dawn. They settle for less comfort, more financial risk but a freer life-style that echoes the life of their parents and grandparents on the land in Australia.

Don's creativity is unleashed with the support of Kathleen's down-to-earth practicality and common sense. Each morning, gone are his suit, tie and good hat to be replaced by old trousers, a hand-knitted wool jumper, gumboots and his wide-brimmed farmer's hat – a hat that develops a unique odour from his hardworking sweat. He walks down the paddock, opens the gates for the waiting dairy cows before returning to the dairy to turn on the milking machines. He does this both morning and evening – a commitment he makes to the cows. After morning milking, in his horse and cart, he delivers the milk to the people and the cafes in the town – a commitment he makes to the local people.

Within days of their arrival in Berrigan, they visit the convent to enrol Carmel and Bernadette into St Columba's Catholic school run by the Presentation Sisters. Initially, they pay the Sisters sixpence a week for the education of each daughter. The Sisters take a special interest in the girls while Don easily monitors his daughters' progress and their behaviour in the school setting since he delivers milk to the convent every day.

On Sunday mornings, Don leaves a half pint of cream at the convent with the normal milk order. Next morning the cook Sister Camillus writes a hand-written note for him with money wrapped in paper for the day's required pints of milk, leaving it with the empty bottles. *Dear Mr Wallis, Thank you for the cream you left for us. We appreciate your generosity. Can we have two pints of milk today? Thank you.*

* * *

The *Forest Vale* home is a small three-roomed, un-lined, timber cottage with a partly fibro sleep-out and a corrugated iron roof. The girls hear the rain falling and automatically pass on the information to Kathleen and Don. *Yes, it's raining!* With hands and arms and facial expression, the girls interpret its softness or intensity. Immediately Kathleen and Don go to the window or door to see it themselves. On the land they watch the weather because of possible consequences for the day's activities.

Two small huts stand beside the cottage, one is the laundry and the other for various tasks. For two or three years, a young migrant farm hand is housed there. He has very little English but he joins the family for the evening meal. Don communicates with him through gestures or the girls attempt to interpret. In the house yard are two special rainwater tanks for drinking and activities such as washing the dishes or washing hair. Outside is also the dam-water tank, which is used for bathing and the laundry, as well as gardening and water for the dogs and cats.

Chooks, ducks and turkeys are part of life around the household. Don buys day-old chicks, which arrive by train and are collected at the railway station. In the second hut in the yard, a container and a lamp for warmth is set up to enable the chicks' survival until they are old enough to advance to the fox and dog proof chook-house.

Eggs are collected daily for baking – biscuits, sponge cakes, bread and butter puddings and pavlovas. Kathleen packs a dozen eggs, wraps each of them in newspaper and places them into Weetie boxes. Through Don's contacts on the milk round, she sells the eggs, bringing a little extra cash into the household. The local Catholic Church has cake stalls and Kathleen cooks her cream sponge – it is sold before it arrives on the table.

Pleasures are delightfully simple. Life is uncomplicated. Milk and cream come directly from the dairy, bread from the baker and meat from the butcher. Mail is collected from Box 28 at the Post Office. To fuel the kitchen stove, they collect wood from the farm or gather coal after it falls from the goods train carriages to fuel the kitchen stove. Kathleen is excited when the new fridge arrives, an important asset for family life on the farm. In the yard surrounding the house they grow a variety of fruit trees including a blood plum, apricot, nectarine, a fig-tree and a quince tree. The farmland is bereft of native grasses and bushes.

Kathleen enjoys the companionship of her girls as they explore the land and discover new things. They know every tree and bird[1] and on finding nests they

---

[1] The local birds: pee-wees, magpies, plovers, top-not pigeons, crows, welcome swallows, twelve apostles, grass parrots, galahs, the willie wag-tail, white cockatoos, tom-tits and the occasional robin red breast, eagles, hawks and boo-book owls.

study their designs, materials and methods of construction. They relax and climb high in the Currajong tree to keep cool, eat a banana and read a book. They cut a spindly branch from a Murray Pine for their Christmas tree.

As well as working on the farm, Don develops his skills as a carpenter, a builder and a plumber. He puts in benches and a sink in the kitchen, a bathroom and porch, as well as significant windows for more light in the cottage. This allows them as Deaf people to see what is happening outside of the house and gives more light to see their conversations more clearly inside. The familiar oval kitchen table that comes with them from their home in Melbourne also assists with conversation as it enables everyone around the table to see one another.

Instead of a door-bell at the front door, a door-light is installed. Press the button and a bright light shines on and off in the house. This for the first time allows Don and Kathleen to know that they have a visitor at the door at the same time as their hearing children. It is new and different for them to know immediately rather than depending on their children for that information. It means also that when the children are at school they know someone is at the door.

Don and Kathleen need the children to use the telephone primarily for the family dairy business and for contacting relatives. They trust the capacity of their daughters and set up the telephone in the lounge room on the wall with a fixed mouthpiece at least a meter high. The hand-held hearing piece is attached to a cord and held to the ear. Because the girls require something on which to stand to reach the mouthpiece, Don builds them a solid stool. Their number is double-one-two, 112. As they stand to speak into the phone, they hold the earpiece with one hand, while they use the other hand to sign to their parents who want to know who is on the phone and the content of the conversation.

At the Berrigan telephone exchange Thelma Ryan, the telephonist, is aware that on the phone number, double-one-two, children make and receive all calls for Don and Kathleen. When the children are away and Don is desperate for a business call, he drives into town to the exchange at the back of the Post Office and asks Thelma who is generous with her time to make the call for him. He has the information and the message already written on paper and he waits patiently for her to consult or finish the call.

* * *

As she smells the diesel fumes of the tractor coming over the rise, Kathleen asks the girls to set the table for the evening meal. *Your father – coming home! Hurry up!* The girls refute the fact and sign that they can't hear him, yet within a few seconds they reluctantly admit she is right. They hear the tractor. *How you know?* She laughs, *I smell him!* Besides her well-developed sense of smell, Kathleen develops her sense of sight too – her eyes constantly at work. She finds the lost tennis ball in the long green grass after everyone searches. On dark evenings when she takes the children outside to view the stars, as she loved to do at Waratah, she is the first to spot

Sputnik 1, the first artificial Earth satellite, in the sky while they stand gazing upwards.

For both Kathleen and Don, the dogs that live outside are a special part of their lives. They are watchdogs and companions trained in the ordinary rituals of daily life on the farm. They give cues for Kathleen and Don as to comings and goings on the farm. Tim, a black border collie with a white strip down his face and white sox, lies lazily beside them – he suddenly twitches one ear – they immediately look around to see what alerts the dog. *What does the movement mean?* They see him bark and ask themselves *What does that mean? Is it a snake or a sound of someone coming and if so, is it a car coming down the driveway or someone right outside?* They learn to interpret the meaning of Tim's responses. They learn, too, that Tim will not settle until they take notice of the possum!

Don goes down to the shed a distance from the house. Tim follows and stays by his side. Kathleen turns to the girls and signs, *Go fetch Dad for dinner.* They stand outside and call loudly to Tim, who jumps up and looks towards the house. Don is alerted and looks in the same direction – they wave and sign in big gestures to him: *Dinner – ready – home – hurry – come!* Don obeys. He likes food.

The water channel near the house, the chickens, eggs in nests, cool places under the water tanks in the hot summer – they all attract snakes. Don knows his snakes from around the Goulburn River: copperheads, tiger and red-bellied snakes. He is unaware of the venomous and sometimes savage nature of the ordinary brown snake, until he finds himself between the mother brown snake and her young. It rears up in front of him ready to strike its weapon of poison. Kathleen, who knows them well from life on the Murray River, warns him to keep his distance and while he wards off the snake and eventually kills it, he is well shaken and develops a healthy respect for them – he learns that they are part of life in Berrigan. The girls draw imitation tracks of the snakes across the driveway and run inside to their fun loving mother, as they feign fear with their whole bodies: *Come, quick – see on road – tracks – snake – come, see!* Kathleen detects on their faces a slight curl in the corner of the mouth where she sees a smothered laugh – and joins in the playfulness taking her part to be surprised and alarmed.

However snakes are a constant worry. From the kitchen window the girls see a healthy and shiny brown snake slithering along the ground between the house and the laundry where Kathleen is working. In panic Bernadette tries to catch her eye because her twelve month-old-cousin that they are caring for has crawled outside to look for her. The snake is between them and their mother and she has her back to them. There is no use calling out to her so they throw a tennis ball towards their mother that bounces in front of her and attracts her attention. As she turns around as they expect, they sign to her telling her frantically in sign about the snake and she runs to the baby and places him in safety. She then finds her ever-ready shovel, follows the offending snake and extracts it from under the tank stand. Her children are now safe from this particular snake.[2]

Water is precious on the farm. As the irrigation season begins, the girls excitedly follow Don to the corrugated iron pump hut that will draw water through to the smaller channels on the farm. As the pump starts with great noise Don hears nothing but feels the machinery rattling and vibrating heavily. The girls stand bare-footed in the small dry channel and wait with anticipation for the water to spurt through the pipe and towards them. The flow of water trickling down the channel is a miracle to their eyes. Don smiles a big smile – he thumps his hand in the air with the sign *good*, his thumb upwards. He watches to ensure the water flows into the designated paddocks.

Beside the dam, which is surrounded by eucalyptus trees and feeds off the irrigation channel, stand a windmill and a water tank on a high tank-stand. This windmill supplies water for the household. In the summer when the water levels in the dam are low, the water is brown and muddy. Clothes that are washed take on a red-brown tinge so good clothes are put aside to be rinsed with water from the rainwater tanks. Bathwater is brown and shared, so when the plug is pulled and water flows out, there are red mud traces along the bath.

A serious challenge presents itself – there is leakage in the tank by the dam and no water is flowing to the house save from the rain-water tank that is kept for drinking and special use. Kathleen is cross and frustrated by the leak resulting in no water and nags Don to do something about it immediately. Down to the tank they both go to fix the problem. Soon the girls take on the job with him – they are nine or ten years old. While they climb up the ladder onto the tank-stand, their father places a piece of leather and a bolt through the leaking hole in the tank and their job is to hold it tight in place. Kathleen is amused when she finds a composition that Bernadette writes:

Well, the usual happened, there was a leak in the tank at the windmill. I went down with Dad and it was dark, but Mum wanted the job done. Dad climbed into the tank, which meant I could not see him to communicate. I held the bolt and piece of leather, while he sloshed inside the tank in his rubber boots, then with his torch, he found where the nut was to go on the bolt. I held it tight while he twisted it. He made his guttural sounds from inside, but I didn't know if he approved or didn't, whether it was working or not! His sounds did not tell me anything but that he was there. I just waited and waited. It seemed ages in the dark until he climbed up and I could see his face above the tank in the little bit of light from the torch. Then putting his torch in his pocket we connected hands in the dark and he signed that we had to do it again, so he climbed back in and out again. Next time he showed his face in torchlight, he smiled. Was I glad! We connected hands and I felt his thumb in the 'good' position and he spelt out, 'Windmill...ok...good wind so water will draw up to tank...tank full with water tomorrow. Mum pleased tomorrow.' And he laughed.

---

[2] In the 1950s, no rules and regulations to protect snakes applied. They are now on the endangered species register.

Kathleen and Don encourage their young children in freedom of spirit. They believe them and trust them in many ways – and they entrust their confidences in the girls. In turn, they expect them to be trustworthy. In the summer, Don allows his daughters without supervision to swim in the Mulwala Canal with friends and the local children – until the Council bans it at the First Bridge because of the associated risks.

As the family sits in a café in the bigger country town of Wagga Wagga, they enjoy the semi-privacy of a booth where they sign together in conversation. A group of young men see their difference and chat with one another in hushed tones. With bravado in front of his mates one of them walks over to the table, bends his face in front of Don and asks: *What time is it, Mate?* Don speeds a lightning glance towards Bernadette across the table and her electric response in sign tells him that he wants to know what time it is. Don's dignity shines through as he calmly looks above the counter at the oversized clock on the wall. No words – he points to it, there for all to see. Look at the clock and you will find the time! The children snigger when they see their Dad has outsmarted the group of ill-informed men. A good lesson for them, they think. Fish and chips with salad made up of iceberg lettuce, tomato and tinned beetroot follows. They return home to Berrigan on partly gravel roads.

* * *

Time passes and Don's professional tailoring days are well behind him. The youngest daughter Margaret with no memory of him as a tailor takes up her interest in making doll's clothes. She freely uses the precious scissors that previously had been banned from children. Her tiny hands cannot lift them, so she brings the fabrics to the scissors on the redwood dining table, rather than take the scissors to the fabric. Then she stamps her feet on the timber floor making vibrations so her mother, feeling the noise, turns her head and approves of her good work.

Life is busy on the farm and with commitment to the cows and the townspeople, Don and Kathleen's social life is now considerably limited. They miss out on some family events although Kathleen returns to Melbourne to visit family and friends through the year. In 1954, the year the new Queen Elizabeth II comes to Australia for the first time, Don's closest brother, Charlie, marries the radiant woman, Valerie Hayes. He is disappointed when he cannot be present at St Mary's Cathedral in Sydney for the occasion but he encourages Kathleen to go by train on the route she knows so well. Charlie's brother, Father Brian, a priest from the Melbourne archdiocese, officiates at the wedding.

Don's sister, Marie and her husband, Harold have a family of six hearing children, who learn the basic Australian-Irish Sign alphabet in order to sign with their aunts and uncles, but in their family naturally communicate with the *two-handed* fingerspelling which became the dominant Sign language in their family.

It is the mid 1950s. Sunday is a day off except for Don milking cows and delivering milk. In between milking time is family time. Kathleen looks forward to visiting her sister Molly and brother-in-law and Laurie Whitty at Lalalty where her mother Mary Adeline now lives. The girls are glad to see their cousins. Molly and Kathleen with their mother walk around the garden sharing cooking ideas and news of their children nourishing one another in their communication and friendship. The children play together and bring the Shetland ponies into the yard for the day's activities. The seven Whitty cousins all learn basic Sign language and more particularly the Australian-Irish alphabet to communicate with Aunty Kath and Uncle Don. They think this is the only Sign language in the world.

Kathleen is keen to also keep visual contact with her other siblings and their families. She wants to actually see them and their growing children so during school holidays Kathleen and Don take a drive and call in often unannounced, especially when an event has occurred in the family and she wants to share or know about it. They know each niece and nephew and follow their lives with a deep interest. The need is strong in Kathleen and it supports her mental and social health to be with those she loves and cares about.

Conscious of her teeth Kathleen discusses her concerns with Molly, knowing she lacks calcium in her diet. So in her late thirties and with her charming smile, she fronts up to the dentist in a bigger centre over the River. With no interpreter – and no explanation or full understanding of the consequences, the dentist extracts all her teeth and plans for full dentures for her. She returns home shocked and devastated – and three weeks later she receives new teeth that don't ever fit.

It is winter and not being well for some weeks, Kathleen at forty-one realises she is pregnant and signs to Don the surprising news. Their youngest daughter is already six years old. *Is this the boy!* With excitement she passes on their news to close relatives four months into the pregnancy, but within the next month disappointment strikes again. Tired and upset she comes home from the dairy and lies on her bed. Bernadette goes to her and Kathleen asks her to ring the doctor now, the same doctor her sister Molly went to. Pointing to her stomach she signs: *Tell doctor – baby – died.* She does not realise that her daughter does not have all the English words but is old enough to worry about translating into good English or more sophisticated language, like using the word *miscarriage*.

Bernadette lifts the earpiece of the telephone, as she stands on the stool to speak into the mouthpiece fixed to the wall, and calls the doctor in Finley to report, as her mother instructs. Her mother watches her through the door from the bedroom, anxious that her child is being brought into an adult world. The doctor says to bring her to the hospital. Bernadette says her father is still working and won't be home until late. He says it does not matter how late but bring her tonight.

It is Friday night about eight thirty and Don comes home from the milk factory. He and Kathleen sign together out of sight from the children. In the car with the girls in the back, all is quiet and serious as Don drives Kathleen to Finley to the doctor, who immediately sends her to hospital. The girls wait in the car in the dark until their Dad returns and they drive home without their Mum. She stays in hospital without anyone to interpret and her daughter worries about her. Now in the adult world, she wants to know what will happen and what will they do and what happens to the baby. The baby is real to her – after all, the due date was set to be 19 March.

The morning comes around quickly and Don with disbelief and sadness rises and attends to the milk delivery in town. The girls sleep in a while then eat some toast and ride into town to find their Dad and stay with him while he continues with his rounds. Their minds focus on what happened the night before and what is happening with their Mum. He is glad of the company – they have a family secret. Kathleen comes home the next day, yet to recover after her fifth and last miscarriage. No one talks about it. Kathleen walks along the channel with a bucket to water the native trees she has planted. The dragonflies are playfully skimming the water in the channel.

* * *

It is 1956 and Don continues his interest in sport, of course, since this is the year of the Melbourne Olympic Games. With workmen organised to look after the dairy, they have two precious days to see the action. They take the opportunity to visit Deaf friends and one in particular, Patricia Caleo, who invites them to her parent's home in Essendon to see the new invention – the television. Their Deaf friends gather around it and see pictures of news of the day and cartoons. Don is captivated.

Besides the marvel of actually seeing famous athletes at the Olympic Games Don returns home enthused about the possibilities of seeing the news of the world each evening through a television. He makes the acquisition of a television a priority although it is five years before it becomes available in the country. In 1961 when they buy the timber framed set they become the third household in the town of Berrigan with a black and white television and an antenna high above their home. A new world opens up to them. As the horse race results are shown on Saturdays at the end of the evening news, Don quickly pens the winners and place-getters, first, second, third. They turn off from channels with dancing and musicals and find visual stories with action pictures. Within a short time, closed captioning is added as a possibility and Don presses the text button permanently. As soon as the girls walk into the room, they turn on the volume. Don and Kathleen turn it to zero when the girls leave – they don't need sound.

* * *

As Charlie and Valerie establish their family of eight hearing children in Melbourne they bring the children up to the farm. They are younger than Don and Kathleen's children – Christopher, Bernard, Gabrielle, their first daughter who is named after St Gabriel's school for Deaf boys, Gerard, Pauline, Karen, David and Loretta. All their children sign in their first language – Australian-Irish Sign Language, communicating easily with Uncle Don and Aunty Kath. A strong sense of belonging pervades. Enjoying one another's company, Kathleen and Don with Charlie and Valerie converse in sign long into the night and early morning around the oval kitchen table, so eager and hungry are they for familial communication.

Deaf friends and their families come from Melbourne to see Kathleen and Don on the farm too. Alex and Olive Anderson, Gert and Chas Hennessy, Stan and Myra Batson bring their families who experience farm life, the adults thoroughly enjoying the company. Some of the younger people in the family join Don on the milk round first thing in the morning. Other friends, who travel in holiday time, include good friends Darcy and Patricia Counsel, Ron and Eileen McKay, Pat and Dorothy Coolahan, Herbie and Dorrie Wilson who are all ex-students – or married to ex-students from Waratah and St Gabriel's, their extended school family. Into the early hours of the morning they again sit around the table regaling accounts of times past with loud laughter spurts and using their fists banging on the table to emphasise the feeling or the issue – or something. No one realises the noise and vibrations that intermittently reverberate through to the timber floor and throughout the household.

* * *

Praying is part of their everyday life. Kathleen signs *God-is-with-us-and-sees-us*, as her index finger points to the sky and then comes down and touches her eyes. She tenderly tells the girls that God watches over them and takes care of them. God for her is a personal and relational God. Seeing is important – she believes she needs to be face-to-face in order to communicate as she

My Children

God – up there – looks at you
God – watches you – cares for you
God – loves you – loves everyone
You – love God too?

looks to the sky. The girls see their father in the lounge room on his knees in prayer and they do not interrupt him. Instinctively, they tiptoe through the room and ensure not to make vibrations on the old carpeted timber floor and they do not touch him or disturb him just now. When he rises from his knees and goes to work on the tractor, his rosary beads automatically go with him in his pocket. Mary, the mother of Jesus, means a lot to him as he relates to her as an intermediary for his hopes and dreams of life.

To My Dad on the Land

The yearning and forgiving land calls to you

Come into anonymity beyond concrete and city bounds

To open skies and starry nights

That twinkle in the darkness

Of space and aloneness

In Love.

The lengthening and changing seasons call to you

Come into freedom and beauty beyond streets and towns

To open paddocks and mature gum trees

That lead into unexpected no-thoughts and dreams

Of eternal oneness and stillness of being

In Love.

Bernadette T. Wallis

143

CHAPTER 12

CROSSING THE MURRAY
TWENTY-TWO MILES TO COBRAM VIA BAROOGA

What more might there be?

Together and apart

Wonga Pigeon is gone.

The Other with courage,

Anger and love drives her on

Ventures high to find him.

There in big skies beyond

A shadow quickly descends

Hawk pounces, claws and lifts her high.

The native bush rose, *eremophila longifolia*, is also known as *Berrigan*; it is a shrub or tree that thrives in the hot overhead sun and dry conditions and is found in many parts of Australia. Was it in great proportions on the old Green Hills – Bari-gun?

Both Don and Kathleen work hard. They want the dairy farm to become a successful business. The townspeople of Berrigan puzzle as to how their milk vendor, who is known as Mr Milky, comes from seemingly nowhere into the district, sets up his business on a dairy farm and provides for his family by becoming the dominant milkman in town. They know nothing of Don's past and they know little of his life with Kathleen and their three girls.

Early in the wintry morning in his rubber boots and with his old hat on his balding head, Don heads for the dairy. Kathleen, who sleeps lightly, has already made sure he is up on time. He has already prepared and devoured his breakfast of hot milk on six Weetabix with two spoons of sugar, while the rest of the family lie cosily in bed. The aroma of his breakfast is comforting for the children as they hear him moving about in the kitchen.

Before he delivers the milk to the townspeople and the cafés in Berrigan, Don milks his forty cows in a four-stand milking machine, so that four cows are milked at the one time. Don marvels at the progress from milking by hand to milking by this modern machine. He watches the little glass container above the bales, which shows the quality of milk from each cow, before the milk travels along the pipes to the milk vats and into the steel cans of various sizes: three gallon, five gallon or eight gallon. Kathleen sees the girls off for school and then takes over the dairy duties. She is very much at home as she separates some of the milk for cream, cleans up and feeds the poddy calves – all unenviable tasks especially in the thick of winter and the heat of summer.

Under a huge gum tree down in the paddock, Don keeps pigs that are fed with the food scraps from the cafés in town and with the skim milk from the dairy. Kathleen demands that the pigs be as far away from the house as possible because of the heightened degree of the sense of smell that she has developed. She does not want the odours of the pig-sty wafting towards the house. On a windy day Don comes home hatless and explains to her that his old working hat has blown off his head into the pig-sty. Upset at losing his favourite hat, he further explains to Kathleen's amusement that the pigs had chewed it up and eaten it. Pigs eat anything.

Don bridles Dot, a gentle half Clydesdale, puts her into the milk cart and with his old brown leather money-bag over his shoulder delivers the milk to people's homes in the town. As people rise and come out to collect the milk Don interacts with them with a wave and smile – a Good Morning! He goes down laneways and back streets throughout the town stopping at different places to pour the dipper of milk of one, two or more pints into the billy or jar just as each customer wants. Lastly, he drives Dot down the main street to the cafés in town and delivers the gallons of milk for them to make their milkshakes through the day.

Don's other horse Bazil, a large bay gelding with attitude that requires skilled handling, also learns the routine and the route for delivering milk to the various customers. Bazil is known in the town – he was once the local Jack McGrillen's racehorse. Since he was somewhat flighty and always invariably anxious to move on so he can return to his paddock and be fed chaff, incidents happen. Don shares the stories with Kathleen who eagerly waits for him to return home. So what happened, she asks when she sees that Don is upset. He tells the story in sign:

This morning was brisk and I managed to catch Bazil, because I wanted to give him a work-out. All was going well until I got to Cobram Road near Chanter Street – almost the end of the delivery round. As I walked around the back of the customer's house with the milk I did not see the children come out on the street – some men told me that the children made a noise and Bazil startled and reared up in fright. The milk-cart tipped up and cans of milk spilt onto the street. More frightened, Bazil bolted down the street and tried to gallop for home. The locals knew Bazil and they came out from the café and pub and everywhere to form a cordon across the road and catch him. All the milk was gone! Cans were everywhere. Some people missed out on a delivery today. I was glad to get Bazil home – I will take Dot tomorrow.

Kathleen offers compassion – and lunch. At the end of the milk delivery and when the milk-cart is lighter, Don always lets both Bazil and Dot have their rein and they enjoy their gallop home along Finley Road.

Some weeks later, Don returns home with another horse and milk-cart story told by the café owner:

Mr Wallis arrived in his horse and cart about ten thirty to deliver the milk. His horse, Dot, waited patiently while he came into the café and poured the milk into the café cans. As soon as Mr Wallis came onto the street, he sounded his particular guttural tone and Dot moved on while he jumped onto the back of the moving cart – all timed very well. On Saturday mornings children sat outside and watched the routine. Just before he came out of the café, the children imitated Mr Wallis' deaf guttural tone for the horse and it moved on. In his gumboots, Mr Wallis ran behind to catch up without realising what the children had done. He was annoyed with his horse. Next day I told him to warn him, so it would not happen again. At first he was surprised but it all made sense to him as to why Dot went on without him. He laughed at the children's prank and he watched eagerly next time for any of them who tried to take advantage of him.

* * *

Don communicates with customers, solicitors, insurance companies, bank managers and accountants. He writes on his writing pad and he expects the same response from others. Ted Ryan, the bookkeeper at Jack Hickey's butchery, stops his work and takes time to have a conversation on paper and with some very basic sign with the *two-handed* alphabet. Don joins him at the pub in the evening and learns more of the news in town and takes it home to Kathleen. He trusts Ted, and he and his family become trusted friends. On the weekend Ted's daughters Helen and Geraldine regularly come to the farm and join the girls in whatever is happening. With their brothers they also swim at the first bridge swimming spot in the Mulwala canal. Their mother, Nell, becomes a hearing mentor and offers advice and a listening ear to the girls.

Don meets with Henry who has a dairy and stud sheep across the road and relates well with him as a friend. When he gives him the famous card with the Signed alphabet on it with the *one-hand* on one side and the *two-hand* alphabet on the other, Henry takes it seriously and learns basic signs so that between himself and Don, they can have a basic conversation without resorting to pen and paper.

Don values him as a mentor in relation to dairy farming in this part of the world as well as other farming and family issues. Henry and his wife, Jess, watch out for the girls and ensure they are safe on the road. Their three boys, Ian, Malcolm and Bruce are the same age as Don and Kathleen's girls. Hearing the girls squabbling on their way home from school, Henry reports their behaviour to Don who communicates the incident to Kathleen. She is seriously not happy and signs crossly to them. For *good girl*, the sign for *good* is the thumb in an upward direction; and then the hand thumps downwards, sometimes gently sometimes with energy. For *girl*, the index finger brushes forward on the cheek. For the word *bad* the little finger and hand thumps in a downward movement. No distinction is made about the less important and the more serious swear words. Swearing is swearing and whatever a spoken word it is, it is bad, very bad in their eyes even though they never hear it. Good is good and bad is bad – nothing in-between.

Don, Kathleen and girls combine to run a dependable and professional milk production and supply business. The girls take all the phone calls for the business. The customers call saying they will be away on holidays for the next ten days and not to leave milk, or ask to change their order from two pints to four pints because they have visitors. But from time to time mistakes are made. Bernadette hangs up the phone and tries to spell out the name of the person who rang. She cannot spell names like *Gillespie* or *McPherson* or *Monaghan*. Neither Kathleen nor Don recognise from Bernadette's spelling the name of the person who is cancelling milk for the weekend. Finding it difficult to understand men who mumble with broad Australian tones or people with accents, she is stressed. It is not part of her experience. She fails to accurately pass on vital information from the customer.

As an outcome to this dilemma, Don and Kathleen insist that the girls let them know before answering the phone. Wherever they are, the girls run to find them, tap them on the shoulder or wave from across the room to grab their attention and then they sign that the telephone is ringing. Running ahead, they answer the phone and ask the person how to spell their name, even if it is *S-m-i-t-h*. Learning extra spelling at school in grade two helps Bernadette to be more effective in her fingerspelling.

* * *

Occasionally Don is the victim of deceit. Someone has told him how good the Ayrshire cows are and promises they will add quality to the dairy herd – Don believes it! He buys the huge Ayrshire cows on this recommendation and waits in anticipation for them. When they arrive, chaos reigns. They are wild, have big horns, jump fences and disrupt life in the dairy and on the farm. He realises he has been duped in the purchase. The cows have come directly from the bush – untrained and cannot be managed. Greatly disappointed, Don sells them shortly after. *Who has taken advantage of him?* – his pride is hurt and his dignity offended.

Through the stock agent in town, he buys six heifers to replace the Ayrshire cows. They are a mixture and fit very well into the dairy herd. The children discuss the names for each of them, Baldy, a red shorthorn, because she has no horns, Peachabel because of her colour, Buttercup, Brindle, Blackie and Goldie. They are proud as they watch their Dad write the names of the cows in his big official record book.

On a cold night, the girls wake in fright as they hear a terrible commotion and scramble out of bed to wake Kathleen and Don. *Scared... big ferocious noise... the bulls fighting... big noise!* They convince them there is trouble – they are always believed. With his torch Don ventures out in the night to sort the problem. Henry Rendell's Guernsey bull and Don's Jersey bull moo and paw the ground threateningly towards one another in protection of their own herds. They push through the insecure farm fence and begin to fight. The Rendell's wake to noise of the bulls too – Henry is quickly on his feet and drives his tractor down the paddock. With Ring, his skilled and treasured long-haired border collie, he calms the situation. Kathleen prays Don is safe and waits for the girls to report to her when they hear the bulls settle down – then she knows Don will be home soon.

Don builds a relationship with the bull but the bull terrifies the girls. Carmel is chased across the paddock and Kathleen watches on and waves encouragingly as her daughter runs around the dam to come home. Separating the bull from the cows Don quietly leads it down the laneway to the back paddock. He closes the gate and turns to walk home along the same laneway. As he reaches the end gate he turns to find that the bull has jumped the fence and is gently following him back. Don has not heard it and is very glad of his good relationship with that particular bull!

* * *

Don witnesses great changes in his dairy business and in the milking industry from 1952 to 1960. He does away with his horse and cart and drives his utility to deliver milk. With various improvements in government health regulations, he takes the milk for pasteurizing and bottling to the Goulburn Valley Butter factory at the southern edge of Cobram twenty-two miles away. As he drives past the little church on the hill at Barooga, it reminds him of his wedding day and his marriage to Kathleen. Every night he crosses the old timber Barooga Bridge and the Murray River Bridge into Cobram in Victoria.

Excitement rises when the Murray is in flood. The river is turbulent but picturesque. Urgent questions arise and Kathleen asks: *Are the roads closed? Is Don able to cross the bridge safely tonight? Will he be able to collect the milk for the town?* The questions simmer through the night until he returns and she sleeps peacefully again. The river settles and the wetlands in the river flats allow the Red River gums to drink deeply in readiness for another drought. The dragonflies make the most of still waters and hover with ease increasing and multiplying.

At night the Butter factory is lean on staff and the machines rumble along with various outcomes, including the production of vast vats of cheese. The cold cement floors are still wet from the evening's hose wash. Don arrives, unloads the crates of empty bottles and reloads the filled pasteurized milk bottles. Returning home he stores the milk overnight in the cool-room at the dairy in readiness for delivery to the townspeople in the morning.

With the workload increase in the milk delivery business and the constant commitment to milk the cows, Don and Kathleen sell the cows, cease the dairy activity but continue going to the Butter factory to collect the milk for delivery in the town. The pigs go too. Kathleen and Don buy beef cattle and a few sheep that graze on their land and sell them when the prices are right. This decreases the physical workload.

Late in the summer, Don borrows Henry's truck to transport hay-baling machinery. As he drives slowly through the middle of the town near the Post Office, a young man in his youthfulness runs across the street and flicks the truck with his hand. As he does so, the hay baling equipment spins him around and flips him to the ground. While Don does not hear the yelling and screaming, he feels the thump on the truck. He immediately looks in his side rear vision mirror and sees the young man fall to the ground in the middle of the street. He is horrified, deeply upset and fearful. Witnesses, collecting their newly sorted mail, stand stunned in horror. The young man has made a big mistake in his life and court proceedings follow. Though no charges are laid against Don his confidence is shaken. He discusses it only with his confidante, Kathleen.

* * *

Deciding to buy a new tractor, Don arranges for the salesman to come from the nearby town to the farm and asks Bernadette, who happens to be home, to be with him to interpret for the salesman and himself. She is no professional interpreter but the interpreter she is – a professional child of Deaf parents. Besides knowing everything that is going on with the farm she crosses all the boundaries of interpreting rules. Well there are none really! She asks her questions of the salesman – not her Dad's. The salesman explains to her the choices her father has and the advantages of each brand of tractor as well as their cost. She puts her own interpretation on the discussion. As the salesman does his pitch, she listens carefully and tells her father what she thinks the salesman says and judges for herself which deal is the best. She surreptitiously tells him which tractor they should buy. And yes, her father buys the tractor she thinks she recommended. Don's decision is assisted by his own intelligence. He knows what he wants. However in her young responsible mind she prays incessantly that she made the right decision and that nothing goes wrong with the tractor. True, she is not responsible – her father is, but when the salesman returns to his office, he says to his female administrative assistant: *I've just sold a tractor to a ten year-old girl!*

Time moves on and Don buys more machinery. He enters the hardware and machinery store in Berrigan where sixteen-year-old Max McLaughlin works. He writes on his notebook that he wants to buy a plough and Max writes in return, *Second-hand or new? Do you have any second-hand*, Don writes as his eyebrows rise in question. Max shakes his head sideways. Don writes, *New* with a smile on his face. Max and Don go to another customer's farm to see how a particular brand of plough operates. Don seems happy with the plough's performance so Max transports the new plough to Don's back paddock, puts it on the tractor and adjusts the discs. After a test run up the paddock, they stop and young Max looks at Don wondering if he is happy with it. Don thumps his hand in the air, his thumb upwards. Max asks himself what this means and re-adjusts the discs on the plough in case Don is not happy. Again after another test, Don thumps his hand in the air with his thumb upwards.

They return from the paddock to the house and Kathleen comes out and as quick as lightning signs to Don, who replies that the plough is very good and that he is very happy with the service. With a big smile she looks towards Max and thumps her hand with her thumb upwards. Max finally understands that it is a sign saying all is fine, all is good. Max learns more basic signs and grows in appreciation and admiration for Don. Whenever Don comes into the store, Max moves towards him to serve him.

During the repetitive work of ploughing the paddock Don, with space in his mind, reaches into his pocket for the old leather pouch that holds his rosary beads and prays as he thinks deeply – which turns into thinking nothing. In this state he feels refreshed and notices the shapes of clouds and movement of the breeze in the gum trees. He sees the blades of grass, the bees, wasps and insects – and all around him in the silence as he continues circling the paddock.

* * *

The people of the town come to know Don and support him with communication in significant ways. From the telephone exchange Thelma rings the number, double one, two hoping that one of the girls answers the phone. Little Margaret is too small to take the call and points to the phone and signs to her mother that the phone is ringing. Kathleen touches the bells on the phone and feels the tingling under her fingers and relates it to Don. Because of the persistent ringing, they discuss what to do.

Don drives back into town and down the main street towards the exchange. It is Saturday afternoon and Bernadette is with her girlfriend Geraldine and Geraldine's mother, Nell. She notices her father's utility and she knows immediately something is amiss. It is out of character for her Dad to be in town at this time of day. She runs down to the exchange to investigate. She knows there is an urgent message. Thelma puts the call through to the red telephone box outside the Post Office and Bernadette answers the call that says Grandma Emma Wallis has died. She turns to her father and breaks the news in sign: *Grandma in Mercy Hospital Melbourne – died*. There is a big pause. *Who phoned? Your cousin – Anne Douglas.*

Tried to ring earlier. Wanted tell you Grandma low – a stroke. She died just now. Another pause. *Funeral Monday in Yea – Anne said.* Tears well up in Don's hazel-coloured eyes and his daughter puts her arm around his waist hiding her face for a short time. Then she looks up at him for communication and they drive home to Kathleen to share the news and make plans. They note it is the 5 June 1955.

Ten-year-old Bernadette is part of the discussion and says she is willing to stay behind and do the milk delivery with her uncles. *How else can Don get away quickly to be with his family and for the funeral in Yea?* On cardboard from a VitaBrits box he draws a mud-map of the milk-delivery route and explains in detail what has to happen and what she needs to do. He trusts his daughter knows the business and the milk round well enough. She guides her uncles, Kathleen's brother John, the Franciscan priest who is home on holidays from Papua New Guinea, and Molly's husband Laurie Whitty from Lalalty.

Laurie drives his truck and John puts on the old brown leather money-bag and feels what it is like to be Mr Milky for two days. They enjoy the challenge and talk to every customer. Bernadette sits in the front of the truck with the mud-map and the record book on her lap and gives directions where they are to go. She patiently waits for them to inform her of correct payment and she writes it in the big book. All is recorded. The milk-delivery takes an extra two or three hours. The cafés expect milk by eleven o'clock and for two days they wait until well after lunch.

* * *

It is natural for Don and Kathleen to think about sending the girls to boarding school for their secondary education, because they knew the experience – and they want the best for them. Carmel wins a diocesan scholarship, which makes the decision easier as to where they might go. Difficult though it is for Don and Kathleen as well as the girls, they attend the boarding school at Mt Erin High School in Wagga Wagga – a school run by the Presentation sisters who taught them in their primary years in Berrigan.

With the loan from his mother long paid off, Don enters into a mortgage for farm machinery and another vehicle. In order to keep up with repayments, he develops his business for a better return and turns to his brother Brian for advice on investing in the property next door, the property *Rosedale*. It is the end of 1958. Kathleen worries about financial commitments and Don's future health with further farm responsibilities. Don wants Rosedale where there is a more comfortable home for Kathleen. Everyone is involved in the discussions – and they purchase the property from Paddy Schweicker.

Kathleen and Don settle into *Rosedale*, the original Berrigan maternity hospital, with its four reasonably sized bedrooms and a wide corridor, a lounge room and an open kitchen and dining room. The morning sun shines on the front verandah where the old oval kitchen table stands and where Kathleen and Don sit for morning tea together. Kathleen now washes in an inside laundry with the bathroom near the entrance of the back door. She notices it is easier to house their relatives and friends who visit – and the girls have their own rooms. The last three holes of the Berrigan Golf course are adjacent to the paddock near the house where the girls play with their father's left-handed golf clubs. In the corner of the paddock stands a stile over the fence, which makes for a short cut when walking into the town.

At the gate to the house yard is the meat house with a cellar that now houses the tools and such things. The kurrajong tree, a different shape from the one at *Forest Vale*, offers shade for the car on the sandy soil. Nearby is a huge ant-bed. Further down the yard and paddock is the silo, an unused dairy and a fowl house with a big yard for the chooks to run. The haystack is near the stand of trees and the wetland area.

Don enters the new outside timber toilet with its luxurious cement floor and corrugated iron roof, and in the deafening torrential summer rain and wind he feels the vibrations but does not hear the sound. With the noise, an agitated red-back spider bites him on the backside and he lands in the local hospital suffering from the poisonous attack that is more serious than jokes indicate. The milk round is in chaos for days.

While Don continues the milk delivery business and the farm work, he and Kathleen find it difficult on their own with the heavy work of lifting crates of milk day after day. They employ Max McLaughlin and other young local boys to collect the milk from the Butter factory in Cobram and do the milk round in Don's grey Holden utility. Don instructs them how to give good service in the town. Don trusts Max who he has known from buying goods at the machinery store. Max likes Don and is happy and keen to pay off his new car with the twenty-five pounds a week he receives – a good wage. The boys do well and Don is pleased with their sense of responsibility. Soon he buys a Volkswagen van for the boys to use – and Don allows them to put in a radio for themselves. The people in the town let Don know how they view the way the boys are conducting themselves in the job. In this way he keeps up with what is happening and what the gossip might be!

With interest, Don opens a letter from the Goulburn Valley Butter factory manager who is unhappy about the loss of milk bottles and insists that they be returned to the factory. So Don sits down with Max and explains that the customers must return their empty bottles. They write a note to customers to this effect with the rule – no returned empty bottles, no milk!

Anxious to see what happens with one customer who is very lax in returning bottles, Max waits. Yes, the customer requests three pints of milk, but there are no empty milk bottles. The boys have their instruction from Don – no bottles so no milk! They drive on not leaving any milk. Next morning they arrive at the same customer's home and twenty-one empty bottles appear on the verandah. The boys leave twenty-one pints of milk on the verandah and quickly drive on – this will teach them. Later in the day, Don goes to see Max. He is serious and writes on his notebook that he has a complaint from a customer. Why were twenty-one pints left for them? Max replies and explains in writing that because of the *no bottles, no milk* rule the customer next day left twenty-one empty bottles. He then admits they left twenty-one bottles of milk. Max worries that he may lose his job. The side of Don's mouth turns into a grin and they both laugh loud. Don keeps his sense of fun in the most serious of situations.

Max looks up at him and thinks of Don as fair and just, astute and a good businessman with a good sense of humour. He tells his mates that Don is highly intelligent and he is amazed how Don assesses situations with such accuracy and responds accordingly. He adds how adaptive Don is in in all mechanical and everyday things. *I am inspired by his conduct and call him a legend in our town, he says.*[i]

With the constant worry of the demands of the business and in the face of Don's increasing inability to continue hard physical work, he and Kathleen make a further business decision to sell the original farm, *Forest Vale*, together with the dairy and milk delivery business. On *Rosedale*, they run sheep and put in grain crops to bring an income for the year. Kathleen keeps watch in lambing season to prevent the horror of black crows attacking the newborns lambs while continuing to maintain her country garden through drought conditions. With his workload reduced Don joins the Berrigan Bowling Club and enjoys the local companionship.

* * *

Don and Kathleen trust their daughters and emotionally support their future plans. Carmel comes home and discusses her hope to be a teacher with the Presentation sisters – she has been teaching her young siblings for years. Don and Kathleen recognise her gift for education. She leaves home in 1960.

A little apprehensive, Bernadette finds an opportune time when no one else is around to talk with her parents – she wishes to join the Missionary Sisters of Service in Hobart, Tasmania. She worries, *it is so far away* and that she is to be the second one to join a religious order. But she feels right about taking the step to join the order of Sisters started by Don's brother Jack, although she knows some relatives and other people will think she is crazy. *What will her Mum and Dad think and feel?* She reminds them of the two Sisters who called in with Jack on their way north to begin a foundation in Parkes NSW – they were so friendly, normal, modern looking and interested in people and the work on the farm. Kathleen and Don know this group of Sisters and have followed their development since their beginning in 1944. Sadness still enters their hearts and Don sheds a few tears – she will be so far away. Still Kathleen and Don encourage their daughters to follow their desires in what is right for them. Bernadette leaves her job in the solicitor's office in Berrigan to go to Tasmania in 1965. Soon, the youngest, Margaret, moves to Albury for further study and work. They then follow, with great interest, their daughters' paths in life, supporting, visiting and writing letters.

Kathleen and Don celebrate their silver jubilee and again reflect on and review their lives. They are lonely and isolated on the farm without the girls and miss the daily interaction of the milk delivery business. Don becomes more debilitated with his rheumatoid arthritis, and with medical advice he resigns himself to major hip surgery – a serious decision in 1966. The business life for Kathleen and Don in Berrigan comes to a conclusion after fifteen years. They realize their time in Berrigan has been an important part of the journey of their life of service and contribution to the wider community. They also realise that Berrigan is not the place for retirement for them but they surely want to be close to the river where the Murray cod and Red-fin river fish thrive.

Reluctantly selling *Rosedale*, they leave behind in the town of Berrigan a rich legacy of inspiration and hope. A short time later, the *Rosedale* house and the old timber oval kitchen table, inadvertently left behind in the move, are destroyed by fire. Among the wattle trees, golfers on the Berrigan Golf Course play the fifteenth hole in the shadow of where the old farmhouse stood with the cellar, the kurrajong tree and the ant-bed.

---

[i] Interview with Max McLaughlin, January 2014.

The Land

How can I let go of my dream

Life on the Land?

My body is broken

On the Land

My blood is given up for all

On the Land

In this town,

In this Country.

I have no sons

My daughters are gone

My heart shared in Love

Aches

And I take up a new dream

A new earth

A new hope

With proud thoughts

Of a past well-lived

And forever reaching

Toward new Life in Love.

Bernadette T. Wallis

CHAPTER 13

RESTING PLACES ON THE OVENS AND KING, THE MURRAY AND MURRUMBIDGEE RIVERS

Wonga Pigeon struggles for Life

She pulls away hard from Hawk

Her breast torn open bleeds

Onto the white Waratah below

As she jumps from Waratah to Waratah

All the Waratahs turn red

With the blood of the Wonga Pigeon

Flowing from her heart.

The Ovens and King rivers meet at Wangaratta where wetlands bring birds aplenty. From here the mountains can be seen in the east, in the north and in the south. The *Pangerang* people lived in this beautiful valley. The name *Wangaratta* is derived from an Aboriginal word meaning *the resting place of the cormorants*, the bird that stands in stillness and holds its wings open to breezes and sunshine.

In 1967 Don and Kathleen move into their new home in O'Leary Street in Wangaratta with Tim, the black Border collie. Tim is faithful and sits adoringly beside Don wherever he is. He is always ready to be directed in sign or gesture to any menial task that requires attention. On their first night Don and Kathleen sit at the redwood dining table and converse together. Life is new and different. Don allows Tim to sleep just inside the laundry rather than outside to reassure him that all is well.

With his gnarled working hands on the arms of the redwood timber armchair, Don sits attuned and sensitive to sensation and movement. He feels the vibrations of the garbage truck as it passes by in the street. In this new situation in town, he looks out the window and watches it, remembering the sensation for next time.

Kathleen cannot believe that so many of her dreams are fulfilled. At last she can luxuriate in a solidly built and comfortable house. She wakes with the thrill that she can water from the abundant town water supply her full garden of prized hydrangeas, fuchsias and roses, as well as violets and cannas that she has transferred from the farm. She rejoices in her ability to walk down a few blocks to see her best friend, her sister Molly.

Don and Kathleen's home, Wangaratta Victoria
1967 – 1986

Kathleen enjoys the everyday company of extended family members communicating in sign. She is uplifted by her conversations with them on all kinds of interesting issues. She walks down the street to be with her ageing mother and shares further responsibility with other members of the family for her mother's care. Kathleen remembers that her mother learned Australian-Irish Sign Language while she was on that eventful holiday with her father only to find it was no holiday – she was left at Waratah for her schooling. She remembers on returning home how she and her mother were able to communicate in a new and meaningful way so their encounters were alive with interaction.

In Wangaratta and free from the onerous duties of the farm, Kathleen now finds she is more available to attend family functions, including extended family funerals. Her sisters, Molly and Monica, sign to her and she learns the stories of the relatives although she still grieves the reality that as a child she did not understand that they were her aunts, uncles and cousins. Now she understands their significance in the family context and at last it all fits together.

Don and his exuberant dog are disoriented. Being used to the extensive land of the farm, Tim dislikes his lead and finds the house yard in a street and in a big town limiting and most confining. Don also feels lost and constricted. Tim wants to be with him and waits for him to come outside into the backyard. Instead Don gets into the car and backs out of the garage. In his enthusiasm Tim jumps the fence and runs onto the street. It is too late. Kathleen calls to Tim in her deaf voice and a vehicle on the road swings to avoid him and he is killed. Don grieves the loss of Tim and the loss of space and land.

Don goes fishing in the Ovens River and sits on his canvas chair in the beauty of the bush along the banks of the river. Here he draws together a semblance of meaning to his life after feeling the stress of the move – the auction of machinery and Rosedale, the farm itself that he loved. He says goodbye to the people and the lifestyle. Watching the currents in the river, he allows his eyes to transfix him and transport him into being at one with all of nature around him and where he feels everywhere and nowhere at once. Refreshed, he returns home with one fish, a Red-fin that Kathleen cooks and he eats.

He establishes a lavish vegetable garden in the back yard, where he sets up his shed for his tools from the farm and adds further tools for various hobbies he develops. From the local tip or elsewhere, he gathers behind the shed a growing pile of timber, corrugated iron, tin and bits and pieces that he believes he may work with or that may come in handy one day for some reason unknown or unimagined at the present time.

In Wangaratta Don looks for work. Only in his fifties but with his arthritis, heavy work is not for him. In no way does he wish to return to work as a tailor, although he does continue to renovate Kathleen's skirts or such things. He applies for a job at Cohn's Cordial Factory as the cleaner, the grounds man and general dog's body, who tidies up after everyone else. He relates well with his immediate boss, Mr John O'Brien, who sits down and communicates with him by pen on paper. Hardworking and thorough in his job, Don polishes the old linoleum squares in the offices and with the ride-on mower cuts the extensive lawns. John is inspired by both Don and Kathleen and enjoys conversing with them. In turn Don appreciates John's respect and affection.

But John's boss does not cope with Don's deafness. Under instructions from him, John arrives at work distressed and does the most difficult thing he ever has to do in his working life. With regret and sadness he asks Don to sit down. With pen and paper in his hand he writes to Don that his job is finished and to leave the premises. Don, shamed and mystified, drives home and explains to Kathleen all that happened. That night John tells his mate at the pub: *I told a Deaf man, a thorough gentleman with whom I have a great relationship that he polishes the floors too well. That was the excuse of the big boss to put him off work.*[1]

Kathleen walks everywhere. Healthy and full of energy she cleans one day a week at Whitty's Produce where she is comfortable working for her brother-in-law and nephews. She also washes and irons clothing for the boarders at the Marist Brothers' Champagnat College for boys bringing in a little money for immediate needs. Out shopping with the girls when they are home, Kathleen proudly signs to the regular shopkeepers as she points to her daughters and points towards herself – *Mine! Yes, my daughters!* She introduces them to anyone she knows and extends the communication with her *on-tap interpreters* by her side so the person learns more about her and she can learn more about the person.

Don and Kathleen establish rituals around communication and keeping abreast of the news of the world. They buy the newspaper every day to keep their minds alive and active. Kathleen explains with convincing facial expression as she points to her forehead, the locus of her mind: *If we don't read, our minds will become smaller, dull and slow – whereas if we do read, our minds keep active and we are more interested in everything*. Don begins reading the paper first, never finishes it in the day and picks it up again at night – to read every detail of every section. Kathleen reads it cursorily and Don relates to her all he reads and what he thinks about it. While Kathleen hovers in the kitchen cooking the meal, Don watches the news on television and he adeptly matches the newspaper items with the TV items without knowing the words spoken. As they sit for dinner, Don informs her of all the world news and they discuss it further through the evening.

Nieces and nephews surround them in the town of Wangaratta and nearby. Eight-year-old great niece Cherie of the next generation ritually learns her *one-hand* alphabet from Aunty Kath as do her siblings. Can anyone imagine thirty-five years later as she sits in a London café with her ex-pat mates that an English Deaf man collecting for the Deaf Foundation approaches her with his collection tin. From the closet of her memory of childhood experiences, Cherie pulls out her signed alphabet and signs *H-e-l-l-o!* He, in amazement, looks at her and addresses her in sign, *How on earth do you know Irish Sign?* Very few people know that language now. She responds that her great Aunty Kath in Australia taught her when she was eight years old – her friends watch on with mouths wide open. After a fascinating few minutes of communication between the two of them from different sides of the world, he genuinely thanks her – *for what?* Learning something of a Sign language – and Deaf culture.

Don and Kathleen take a trip to NSW and Queensland and visit their Deaf friends at various places including at Ipswich, Bill and Eileen O'Bryan, formerly of Coburg. As well they endear themselves to the Missionary Sisters of Service at Parkes and Toowoomba and some families of the Sisters, when they call on them as far as Bundaberg – now that they are connected to them through their daughter. The Vichie family offers great hospitality there – one of the boys shows him his artwork and the other takes him to the back shed to show his surfboard. They enjoy the travel and meeting these people who are prepared to take the time to communicate with them.

It is the 1970s and Kathleen and Don experience the changes in the liturgy at the church since Vatican II. They learn from Deaf friends about the church's new Rite of Reconciliation[ii], and that they do not need to write their personal confession on paper. For years in preparation for the Church ritual, they have written their part of the conversation and handed it through the little window in the confessional box to the priest, who responded by writing on paper.

Now Kathleen confides in her sister that she is so relieved that her daughter, Bernadette, went with them to St Patrick's and explained the process and interpreted the common ritual that included readings, songs and examination of conscience. She and Don chose to go to the young priest at the back of the church for their individual time for absolution. She tells Molly that Bernadette went to the priest first and told him that they were next in the queue and that they were deaf. He said to her, *what do I do?* She responded, *absolve them!* Kathleen signs and explains to Molly she is more relieved that the next part was different from any other time. Then Kathleen smiles and describes to Molly what happened: *I go in to small room to priest and kneel down. His hands – on my head – gentle – he prays.* She comes out, looks at Don who is waiting, nods, and he knows that all is good, very good! No more stress to write out her confession in her second language. The sense of touch, important to them, conveys the healing of forgiveness and human compassion in the way this second rite of Reconciliation is conducted.

* * *

Don and Kathleen's daughter Carmel moves to various places in her educative role – to Wagga Wagga, Hay, Drummoyne and back to Wagga Wagga. They are proud of her and like to converse with her directly about her life. Bernadette works in various parts of Tasmania and finally she moves to Parkes to work in the rural parts of western NSW. This pleases Don and Kathleen, because she is closer to them. When she later moves to Melbourne, they are more pleased because she is much more accessible – it is important to them to see their loved ones face-to-face for meaningful communication. They are also very interested to know what their daughters are doing, the value of what they undertake and what inspires them.

Don and Kathleen's teenage daughter Margaret, at home for a while working in Wangaratta, announces her plan to go nursing at the Mercy Hospital in Albury. Not long before she finishes her study, she falls in love with David and they announce their engagement. In the summer of 1975, Kathleen and Don polish the old Valiant as the bridal car and place white ribbons on the front. With feelings of pride Don walks the stunning bride down the aisle at St Patrick's Catholic Church in Wangaratta. His mind slips back in time to the day he received his beautiful bride at St Joseph's in Barooga. Now he witnesses his daughter step into her future. Years pass quickly and the three grandchildren become the iridescent light of Kathleen and Don's lives.

* * *

Don sets his mind to numerous hobbies. He does his woodwork and attempts an adult education course where he finds the communication too difficult and too frustrating to continue. He goes into shops and studies various items that give him ideas for his woodwork. He makes a spinning wheel, rocking horses – one for his niece, Donna – an unfinished rocking chair and toys. He orders patterns through the mail including a pattern for a doll's house that he wants to make for his granddaughter.

He starts a tapestry that depicts a country scene of horses in a paddock with gum trees. He frames it and places on the wall of the lounge room. He continues his tapestry work as he finds that the movement of his hands and fingers as he threads a tapestry needle in and out helps to keeps them supple. Eventually he finishes his prized tapestry – a masterful piece of work that emerges as the Last Supper. This he also frames and the family gathers to have a Mass in the home when the tapestry is blessed. Tom Robert's shearing shed tapestry is never finished.

Kathleen cares for Don in his long illness. His arthritis is advancing its invasion of his body and more surgery takes place. He shuffles along and pain gnaws away at him. His signing is hard to understand. His fingers are bent over towards his thumb and his *one-hand* fingerspelling suffers succinctness and clarity.

In 1985 Don is seventy-three and more than anything, he likes being with the three grandchildren and dreaming good things for them. He hobbles out to his men's shed with his eldest grandchild who is nine and they stand together at the bench exploring whatever is in such a shed. Coming back inside for lunch he takes the baby in his arms and looks in awe as he holds him. The three-year-old takes her turn on his knee as she clasps on to him and reaches for his pen and notebook in his top pocket and draws a picture for him. He sits with David, his son-in-law, as a mate and they have a beer together.

After they have gone and with thoughts of his granddaughter still in his mind, he brings out the plan for the doll's house and studies it for some time. He feels an urgency to begin and he places the floor of the house on the big outside work table. This is all he can do – bring it out and remind others of his hope to build it for his granddaughter.

Kathleen walks outside and sees Don unable to move. The ambulance takes him to hospital and the girls are called. He signs that the Doctor asked if he was at peace. *Are you?* And he fingerspells a profound *Y-E-S*. He fingerspells to his loved Kathleen, I am sorry for his shortcomings in his life. Kathleen asks her daughters, *For what?* In her mind she loves him beyond life's shortcomings. She is unprepared for his death and grief takes over like a dark, low-lying cloud, but she never regrets his dying. Intimately she knows his pain and knows relief in saying goodbye – *Into Your hands, I commend his spirit.*

* * *

Within nine months, Kathleen sells the house in Wangaratta and moves to a unit in Hume Street, Albury, closer to her married daughter Margaret and her grandchildren. As she settles, she longs to communicate and share her joy with Don. As she lies in her bed she sees him as in a dream. But she is not dreaming. He is there, and he smiles. She is initially startled, but his momentary presence in this vision gives her courage and the confidence in the rightness of the decisions she continues to make. On the wall above the redwood dining table, Kathleen hangs

Don's framed tapestry of the Last Supper.

As the blackbird scratches the mulch onto the path in the front garden, she complains of its behaviour, but in the backyard her compassion shines through and she feeds it. The lonely Kathleen blossoms in a new way of life without Don by her side at every moment. She is magnetic with her smile and forms acquaintances and friendships with people wherever she goes, whether it is the butcher or the banker or the sister of her sister-in-law in a coffee shop in the shopping centre.

Kathleen sets the table with an embroidered cloth, delicate china cups and saucers, sugar spoons and a plate of Salada biscuits with cheese and tomato and a plate with her homemade fruitcake. She is to be visited by Father Greg Bourke. While the chaplains for the Deaf community in Victoria visit her in Albury they all sign in Auslan. Father Greg Bourke at least learns the Australian-Irish alphabet, which suits Kathleen. Pleased that he respects her language, she readily engages in conversation and welcomes the rare opportunity to trust someone outside her family and explain her truth about how she is presently feeling, and how she feels about her schooling and early life. As she tells her story, her shoulders swivel and she grimaces as she tells of Sister Martina and her troubles with her and then she smiles and laughs.[iii] She holds the experience of sharing with Father Greg close, as it warms her heart when she is understood, or in hearing language that she is listened to.

Now she is free and available, she visits her daughters and goes on holidays with them. She now signs all the cheques, makes decisions without consultation about clothes that she buys for herself and gifts she buys for the grandchildren. No need to declare how much her hair perm costs. Margaret and David provide on-going support assisting with body corporate issues, the care of the house and negotiating the best deals for a new television with captions.

Her Serbian neighbour hangs a few vegetables in a plastic bag over the fence. When they go to their letter boxes on the street they meet and greet with a wave and smile. Even though he has no Sign language, they manage to communicate. She tells her daughters that he has the pension. *How do you know, Mum? Tell us how you know these things!* her daughters ask. She explains that she and the neighbour communicate with charades and gestures. He had shown her the windowed business envelope containing his pension, circled coins on his hand, placed his hand in his pocket and pointed to the gods in the sky in gratitude. She understands. *He gets the pension!*

At Sunday Mass in St Patrick's Church, she kneels, sits and prays while she observes the whole community as well as the priest. With dry humour she signs privately to her daughter, *I don't have to listen* when she realises the homily is less than desirable, either boring or theologically unbalanced. Firing their hearts with her engaging presence she extends the sign of peace in a handshake to parishioners who form a community at the back – and she waits for this silent moment of face-to-face acknowledgement and deeper communication each week.

After Mass, her niece and nephew Bern and Michael take her to MacDonald's on their way home and she happily announces to her daughter that she has been to Mr McDonald's place for breakfast. When the girls offer to take her out to a coffee shop she refuses and signs, *I don't like coffee.* But, Mum, they explain in sign, that's just the name of the shop and they serve cups of tea too.

Kathleen misses meaningful conversation when her sister Molly can no longer communicate with her, as she is in advanced stages of Alzheimer's disease and has moved into residential care. She can no longer speak and has ceased to recognise her family and friends. On a visit to Molly on a very warm day, Kathleen shows her photos and signs to her. In the silence, Molly suddenly looks up at her and with her index finger points to her throat and runs her finger down the front of her neck signing that she is thirsty. No one else notices the meaning of the movement of her hand and fingers. Kathleen immediately turns and lets the nurse know that Molly is thirsty and requests a drink of water. Kathleen is glad she is there that day.

Molly

In an unfamiliar wheelchair
And with no speech now
She sits in the dazzling sun
The broad shading tree nearby.

Her index finger is lifted up
Deliberately slowly
It touches and glides
From her chin
Down her neck and pauses
I thirst.

Her attuned sister
With full empathic response
Turns to anyone — everyone
And signs
Bring her water
She thirsts.

Water that soothes, quenches, refreshes
Someone understands
The richness of kindness
Releases and flows
Making water into wine
The wine of friendship and love.

Bernadette T. Wallis

Kathleen stands by watching intently, as her daughter speaks to one of her other daughters on the phone. She asks for the news and tells her own news to be passed on. The three-way conversation is hardly a conversation with her, but she observes the body language of her daughter talking and listening on the phone and asks, *What did she say? What are you laughing about? Why are you so serious? What's wrong?* Before the end of the phone call, her daughter gives her the hand piece and she speaks in her deaf tone, *Hello, hello!* that sounds nothing like, *Hello, hello!* She hands the phone back. Her daughter on the other end of the call waits for this moment to hear the intimacy of her mother's Deaf voice.

Developing new skills in her seventies and eighties, she allows her life to open up further. Taking her fingers to a typewriter she readies herself for the new invention of the teletypewriter, a telephone with a typewriter. The phone flashes a bright light on the bench and she excitedly hurries to answer it as her daughters have done in the past. Slowly she types in her second language – English, as she writes *Hello, this is Kathleen here. Go ahead. Hello Mum, It's Bernadette here. How are you today? GA.* For the first time she converses directly on the phone with her daughter without anyone interpreting for her. On the receiving end Bernadette feels her heart warm with the freedom too in having direct access to her mother from a distance. Her mother signs off *Lots of love. Good-bye, Mum.* Now she feels confident she connects more easily with the family on her terms and when she wants to.

It is of great benefit on a warm day towards evening when Kathleen walks into the back bedroom to close the window when she finds a young intruder attempting to climb in. She screams her Deaf scream, runs to the window and jams it closed. What courage! Just as shocked as Kathleen, he jumps down out of sight and disappears while she hurries to the phone, calls her daughter and types: *HELP – man, window at back. Tried to get in.* Her son-in-law David, and his brother John drive straight away to her. No one can hurt Kath or the children's Grandma!

Now Kathleen enters her next phase with a fax machine. Now she communicates with anyone and sends her news via a fax. She writes her fax message in her own time, rather than struggle in the immediacy of a teletypewriter conversation. In her reading she finds articles and newspaper clippings and feels connected and involved in their lives as she faxes them to her daughters – things about making garden compost, a recipe using beetroot or a picture of children in the Iraq war that she is concerned about. The grandchildren excitedly fax their drawings with l-o-v-e.

Kathleen seemingly does not age and resists the thought. Finally to satisfy others she puts the senior's personal alert system pendant on a chain around her neck. Pressing that red button will alarm someone somewhere in a central office and in turn they will alert Margaret, David or the police. She hates wearing it and she feels burdened and intruded upon.

But one day she uses it to her advantage. For Margaret's birthday she buys a gift and card and waits for her to call in. Working, Margaret plans to see her later but David phones urgently: *Can you go to your mother, she has pressed the alert system, otherwise the police will go.* Margaret reluctantly and hurriedly excuses herself in the middle of a meeting – her mother is number one priority. What has happened to her? As Margaret arrives at the door, Kathleen opens it with open arms and signs: *Happy birthday! I – waiting for you all day! Here – my present for you!*

Life becomes lonelier for her. Joseph, her grandson, calls in and cheerfully shows his new sports car and beckons to her to get in – yes, they drive around town and she feels so proud being with him. She feels even younger again. Taking his leave in the evening, Joseph communicates his goodbye with his sports car lights that blink and wink as he drives off, and waving she laughs with a warm feeling of love.

While experiencing sadness when all her Deaf friends die before her, Kathleen meets younger and new friends at the Catholic Deaf community – at the John Pierce Centre where Bernadette works in counselling and pastoral care. Staying with Bernadette she meets the local Deaf people particularly the few who sign in the Australian-Irish Sign Language and communicate easily with her.

* * *

Is she safe and is she eating properly at home? No, not really. She leaves her home in Albury and she moves closer to Carmel in Wagga Wagga, the place that means the *place of many crows.* There the Murrumbidgee River flows through the traditional lands of the Ngunnawal, Wiradjuri, Nari Nari and Muthi Muthi tribes.

Kathleen signs with her thumb in a downward direction describing the residential aged care unit as not being to her liking. No one signs, except for make-do gestures. Over ninety herself, everyone is old around her yet she still walks around to cheer everyone up with her smile. She wanders into other rooms, gives nods and smiles and signs a goodnight, wishing them a good sleep – without a spoken word. When she meets staff she reassures them with her *good* sign, her thumb in the air with a gentle thump that indicates that the

Kathleen's Forever Prayer

God
You are a forever God.

Wherever I am
Wherever you are
However my circumstances
Whatever I am doing
Or whatever I am not doing
You are there
You are part of me – of all
You are my life – you are life
All that I am
And all that surrounds me
You are joy of beauty
You are beauty of landscape and moonscape
You are fullness of sea and sky
Ever reaching, ever arching.

My eyes look for you forever
I plead with you forever
For all who suffer forever
For all disrupted and crushed –
For the children
For the poor
For justice for all
And compassion for all
In the world forever.
Yes,
You are a forever God.
AMEN.

Bernadette T. Wallis

residents she visited are doing fine. She cannot but help those who appear to be frailer than her. Members of the staff are frustrated by her going into people's rooms when she is not supposed to – and yet she is so kind and meaning well. She can charm some of the staff and annoy others. She in turn is also frustrated that she has no meaningful communication with them except on a surface level.

Carmel brings her home to ErinEarth during the day as often as possible where Kathleen entertains herself and involves herself in the comings and goings of life at ErinEarth,[iv] with a wetland and frogs, a dam, windmill, native trees and shrubs, vegetables, two dogs, Megs and Lizzie who adore her, chooks that lay eggs for her to collect, and many birds that play in the birdbath and nest in the trees. Carmel communicates with her as an intelligent woman, who understands concepts of climate change, compost, eco-systems, drought and fire, plants and trees, wetland systems and spirituality.

Soon she no longer moves around easily and her ageing catches up with her. She is ninety-four. Carmel continues to bring her to ErinEarth during the day and sits her in the big cushioned armchair in front of the big window where she watches the moving trees in the breeze, the gently whirling windmill and the birds diving in and out of the birdbath. She finds it difficult to eat and her daughters entice her with soft foods that she might like. They accompany her closely as she gradually loses energy and her will to live.

Two of the grandchildren, Joseph and Michelle, come from Melbourne to visit their Grandma at ErinEarth. At the end of the day they help her into Joseph's proudly owned Hilux 4-wheel drive and take her back to the residential aged care unit. But on the way they take an alternate route and pause on the banks of the Murrumbidgee River and let her spirit rest in seeing the beauty of the gum trees and the sunset. Murrumbidgee means the place of *big water* in the Wiradjuri language.

As Kathleen deteriorates, her daughters offer continuing care with a signed prayer ritual and communion each day. In slow, rhythmic sign and eyelids closing out any interference in her encounter with God, she prays the mantra, *Jesus, Mary, Joseph – mercy on me.*

In the autumn of 2010, the day after Kathleen dies is Mother's day, and her grandson, Mark and his wife, Jennifer, announce on Skype from Denver, USA., they are expecting a child. They tell us Grandma knows – they gave her the news a few days beforehand. With sweet news of new life in the family, they grieve a beautiful life's end.

The girls ensure the daughter of Don's friend, Alex Anderson, interprets in Auslan[v] the Mass of Thanksgiving for the life of Kathleen Agnes Walsh. It takes place in the familiar St Patrick's Church Wangaratta with the chaplain for the Deaf Community, Redemptorist priest, Father John Hill, as main celebrant. People flock to farewell her – to honour both Kathleen and Don and to walk beside their family.

Her nephews from both sides of the family lower her into the grave beside her life companion, who sought her out at *Carlyle* on the Murray River. The three daughters fingerspell in their first language, *Good-bye, Mum!*

The family no longer uses Australian-Irish Sign Language at their family Christmas or at birthday celebrations. Wait, watch and see: in the middle of chatter and noise, a daughter throws a sign across the room and another daughter visually catches it and responds with her hand fingering in the air. No one notices. With a knowing smile, a feeling of intimacy touches them. On the first anniversary of their mother's death, the three daughters meet at the Ovens and King Rivers, where the aqua coloured dragonflies skim the water as the sun sparkles their wings. In silence they picnic together using their first and treasured language, which is now disappearing – Australian-Irish Sign Language.

Kathleen and Don's burial headstone in Wangaratta Victoria

---

[i] Interview with John O'Brien, Wangaratta, 2014.

[ii] The document *Constitution on the Sacred Liturgy* from Vatican II (1962 – 1965) led to many changes in liturgical practices.

[iii] Bourke, Gregory, Thesis *The History of the Catholic Deaf Community of Melbourne, 1997*

[iv] ErinEarth is an education centre for sustainability and eco-living managed by the Presentation Sisters, Wagga Wagga NSW.

[v] Most of the Deaf people present at the funeral signed in Auslan.

Lament

Where has my Deaf Language gone?

My heart aches and sighs aloud

Sounds that reach beyond the unending horizon,

My language, intimate friend you are,

Where have you gone?

What have they done to you?

They know not what they do.

My Language, heart-to-heart you know me

Through and through

My fingers are numb, they wait and wait

My hands are stilled, they long and long

To form my innermost thoughts

And most precious of emotions

Inexpressible without you

My Language, my Love.

Bernadette T. Wallis

PHOTOS

Donald Corcoran Wallis and Kathleen Agnes Walsh married at St Joseph's Church, Barooga NSW
16 August 1941

Kathleen and Don on honeymoon at Marysville, Victoria

Kathleen and first child, Carmel

Kathleen with first baby, Carmel

Kathleen crocheting babies' clothes

Don at a function with the Catholic Deaf Club
in Melbourne

Don with first child, Carmel on horseback

Don with second child, Bernadette

Three Walsh sisters: Kathleen, Monica and Molly and their children, Bernadette, Carmel, twins Des and Mary Toohey, and Laurene Whitty

Don and Kathleen with Carmel and Bernadette, showing new baby Margaret to her Franciscan brother, John at Box Hill, Melbourne Victoria

Bernadette and Carmel Wallis in Melbourne Victoria 1947

Carmel and Bernadette in dresses made by
Don, ready for the school ball held at
Collingwood Town Hall, Melbourne 1951

Carmel and Bernadette
going to school at
St Columbas' in Berrigan
NSW 1953

Carmel with Margaret and Bernadette at Sydney Road home, Fawkner Melbourne 1951

Don on milk cart with horse, Dot at *Forest Vale* in Berrigan NSW 1952

Kathleen in the sorghum crop on the Berrigan farm 1961

Don harvesting on the Berrigan farm, circa 1963

Bernadette at the steering wheel of the tractor with Margaret, Berrigan NSW, circa 1956

Margaret with Don and some local men stacking hay, Berrigan NSW, circa 1959

Kathleen and Margaret beside silo, Berrigan NSW, circa 1960

Bernadette, Margaret and Carmel in *Mt. Erin* High School uniform with Kathleen in the vehicle 1955

Don and Kathleen with their Valiant car and Tim the dog, Wangaratta Victoria, circa 1968

Don and Kathleen farewelling their daughter Bernadette at Essendon airport, Melbourne en route to Hobart to join the Missionary Sisters of Service 1965

Bernadette, Don, Kathleen, Carmel and Don's brother Jack (Fr. John Wallis) 1980

At Penna, Tasmania 1968: Margaret, Fr John Wallis (Jack), Kathleen, Bernadette and Don Wallis (signing)

Margaret Wallis and David Percy's wedding

Kathleen and Don at the wedding

Don walking his daughter Margaret to
St Patrick's Church, Wangaratta

At Penna 1990:
Back: Carmel, Kathleen, Bernadette Wallis
Front: Wallis brothers – Chester, Jack (Fr John), Charlie and his wife Valerie

Don with grandchildren Mark and Michelle

Michelle wanting her grandfather's notebook and
pen from his top pocket

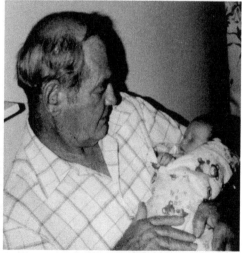

Don with granddaughter Michelle
the day she was born

Don (signing) going to
bowls in Berrigan NSW

Kathleen with her grandson Joseph

Kathleen with Bernadette 1994

Kathleen aged 84 in her back garden at Albury NSW 2000

Kathleen at *ErinEarth*, Wagga Wagga NSW with Lizzie and Megs, the resident dogs who watch over her 2009

Kathleen in the gardens at *ErinEarth*, Wagga Wagga NSW 2008

PART III

Chapters 14 – 20

UNCOVERING A SILENT HERITAGE

CHAPTER 14

DISCOVERY OF IDENTITY

Uncovering a silent heritage

Finding its expression

Its form

Its rhythm and silent music

In joy and liberation

In my Other world.

I have been on a journey of discovery. The realisation dawned on me that I have lived a life that has been indelibly influenced by Deaf culture and Deaf language. Various events through my life have drawn me into greater understanding of this Deaf heritage, which has led me to be involved in the Deaf community for a significant part of my working life. I am grateful for that heritage – and now I actively reclaim it.

The journey begins with the question of identity: Who am I? Yes, I am Bernadette Therese, the middle daughter of Don and Kathleen. My older sister is Carmel Mary and my younger sister is Margaret Anne. These are our written names, which were chosen by our Deaf parents. Our Deaf names have the letters from the Australian-Irish signed alphabet 'C' for Carmel, 'B' for Bernadette and 'M' for Margaret – all signed with the hand held at chest level and shaken sideways. Our parents chose these visual names as our identity within the family and within the Deaf community.

On one occasion I attended a professional personal development workshop. As I arrived I was greeted and the question was asked: *What do you want to be called?* The choices of response could have been Bernadette, my formal, professional and written name; Bernie, as I was called by siblings, cousins, aunts and uncles, teachers and childhood friends; or Bern, which my siblings and close friends often called me as an adult. I paused. An interminable blank space encircled me and I thought, *I don't know*. I spoke the word *Bernadette*, the adult name from the hearing world. That would do for now.

At the end of the conference, we formalised the experience through a ritual. As we stood in a circle each person was encouraged to speak out her name with the strengthening intention of reclaiming her identity. The question echoed. *What do you want to be called? What is your authentic name?* Without a word I looked around the circle of faces and in silence signed my name, the 'B' of the Australian-Irish signed alphabet at chest level and shook my hand gently and surely from side to side.

This was my visual name given to me by Kathleen and Don, the visual name known to me from my birth, the visual name that held the emotional content of my identity. While this action was empowering for myself, I had claimed my Deaf identity. It was also an enlightening moment for the group gathered.

And yes, I am comfortable that people voice my name, Bernadette. When my father wrote letters to me, I loved him writing, Dearest Bernadette. He never wrote Bernie or Bern. I would find it strange if he did.

In 1985 my father died and I was left with great grief. With memories of him emerged seething questions – questions that erupted and curled into my life. As I walked in the world of our Deaf and family heritage, I wanted to ask him questions. Why had I not asked him this or that?

Some years earlier while I was working in a Catholic parish along the Murray River my parents came to see me. We sat by the river, not fishing, but enjoying its beauty and catching up on family news. My mother always had lovely homely bits to tell me, whether it was about a different pattern for a jumper she was creating, a recipe using rhubarb or about the new plants that were robbed of life because of the snails in her garden.

My father was interested in my pastoral work and my presence in the rural parish. He wanted to know what I was doing and how my work operated. After I explained in detail he made a further request: *What more can you tell me about the spirituality and pastoral programs?* He lamented and unwittingly challenged me: *Why don't you do that for me and for us?* He meant for Deaf people, his Deaf community and for himself. *Would you believe it?* A dragonfly came into view and hung above the water for a moment before flitting down the river.

I recall the ache in my heart. Did he feel he had missed out? Was the Church not doing enough or not able to communicate with him? He wanted more in his life that addressed a hunger for depth and meaning. Maybe he had that same ache in his heart and maybe he recognised Deaf people were also looking for deeper meaning in their spiritual and faith lives. This was the challenge for me.

Just a few years later, a wise friend cast a verbal fishing line with a rhetorical question. *With your background, why don't you work with the Deaf community?* This was not just a throwaway line – it was a carefully executed cast of hook and line! My first thought was, I never thought of it. The second thought after this question was of my father, who years earlier asked the question in a different way and in a different setting. The hook took hold and I was caught.

As I moved into work with the Deaf community I learnt more about Deaf history and culture, the community's Deaf heritage – and I learned more about myself.

Unintentionally, I really had begun my search almost ten years earlier. My father was still alive when I undertook studies in the city of Spokane, in the State of Washington. Just for an interest I chose an optional extra subject – American Sign Language. While I felt at ease within Deaf culture, the language was a challenge. The *one-handed* alphabet in the American Sign Language had seven different hand-shapes from my Australian-Irish Sign Language. While there was similarity in the alphabet, its hand-shapes and local signs for words and concepts made it a foreign language for me. However, I learned the basics of the language, a new Sign language, American Sign Language.

The local American Deaf community welcomed me and I enjoyed being in their presence and part of their community. Being new in their midst, I introduced myself and attempted to communicate. They were hesitant and they asked the question: *Who are you?* They wanted more than my name. They noticed I had a Deaf way about me. They knew from my attempted signing that I had another Sign language and the inevitable question came. *Are you Deaf or hearing?* Why so, did I also look Deaf? What does Deaf look like? My expressive gestures and how I interacted showed them I was familiar with a Deaf world. I signed to them, *Me – Mother, Father – Deaf.* Their faces lit up with instant recognition and huge smiles formed.

My mother and my father were Deaf. I was accepted as part of the Deaf family. I felt the acceptance – and a sense of belonging hung in the air. They had a sense of relief, too, as I did. There was no need to explain to each other what it meant to be Deaf or in a Deaf family and what it meant to be part of the community in this way. We shared the experience of Deaf culture, its history and its way of life, as well as a visual language. My innate Deaf background gave me more of an opportunity to engage in communication and quickly establish a relationship with them.

On my return to Australia, I gladly told my father of my experiences. He was both interested and impressed that I had involved myself in the American Deaf community and especially that I had attempted to learn the language. I was surprised too, because I had no conscious agenda of learning another Deaf language but an innate pull was at work within me towards discovering more of my heritage – and it continued. At the time I had no other involvement with Deaf groups and very little contact with Deaf people, except for my family and relatives and their close Deaf friends.

Soon an opportunity arose and for many years I worked in the Deaf community in the State of Victoria, through the Catholic organisation, the John Pierce Centre for the Deaf community. My work engaged me with families – Deaf parents with children who were hearing.

* * *

In 1994 with my work I soon found myself at the Asian Catholic Deaf pastoral conference in Pattaya in Thailand. My companion during that conference at the Redemptorist Mission Centre was Myra Batson from Geelong, a Deaf woman and elder in the community. I had known her since I was a child. I noticed how the younger Deaf participants from various places in Asia were drawn to Myra who received them with openness and love. Myra understood them even though they signed in their own languages. She was their role model. She believed them and had faith in them as future leaders and advocates for their communities.

As we removed our shoes at the chapel door where incense sticks burnt, I was moved by the visual expression of the local spirituality and culture, which deepened the understanding of the liturgy celebrated in the local Sign language.

Furthermore, we visited the nearby Mission school with Deaf children who greatly impressed me, especially the ten-year old boy who was pleased to show his talent by impersonating Michael Jackson with his moonwalk, robotic and other dance movements – riveting us onlookers. In his total silence, he *heard* the music visually and matched it wildly from his own rhythmic and intuitive spinning and dancing body. I wondered, *Did my father respond to visitors with such enthusiasm when they came to St Gabriel's?* We waved our arms and shook our hands – in the way Deaf people clap another.

* * *

It was not long before I learnt about the International organisation known as Children of Deaf Adults (Coda). I attended Coda conferences in Australia for people like me, who had Deaf parents. I talked with the adult participants and there I found resonances and differences that amazed me. I listened to stories where I laughed and cried. They were often familiar to me, stories like pretending to be deaf when shopping with Deaf parents, and interpreting in times of family crises. I shared a familiar humour that bridged both visual and personal realities.

Many of participants like me also felt they lived and belonged in two worlds – a Deaf world and a hearing world. While in reality we lived in many worlds in the wider sense, here we straddled two worlds – with a visual language and a hearing language and both a Deaf culture and a hearing culture. Some participants were native Australian-Irish signers like myself, who later in life learned Auslan (Australian Sign Language) as a second Sign language, as I had done.

In the 1990s while I was working in the Deaf community I attended the XIII World Congress of the Federation of the Deaf held in Brisbane, Queensland. A profound impression was made upon me, when I watched approximately seventy interpreters who stood up front along the stage. They each had their own language group of people in view. As arms, hands and faces moved and glided in the space, the interpreters conveyed the content of the Congress for the many language groups. Each presentation was translated from the language of the country of origin into International Sign.[1] It was then interpreted for each Deaf language group and signed directly into the Deaf language required or the spoken language required. The occasion was a demonstration that potential chaos can be transformed into magic symmetry.

In 2002 the Deaf Way II Conference was held in Washington, DC. It was my first experience of such a Deaf Conference overseas. Nearly ten thousand people registered for the Deaf festival including hundreds of Deaf artists and performers. They celebrated their way of life, the history, culture and languages. Educated Deaf people from all walks of life gathered, as did hearing people who were involved in the Deaf community. They presented and responded to profoundly informative papers on the concerns and interests of Deaf communities from many parts of the globe, including South Africa, Zimbabwe, Canada, Japan, China, Philippines, Germany, Switzerland, England, Scotland, France and Ireland.

In fact, fascinating academic papers by researchers and writers, including Deaf and hearing people, brought to light facets of the life of Deaf people that are often hidden from the hearing world. They have shone further light on the Deaf world. The conclusions of the studies presented at this conference were clearly based on deep reflection by the presenters. They assisted us to reflect and examine both our attitudes and our actions.

During the Conference I shared accommodation with some interpreters in a multi-story hotel nearby. One night in the very early hours of the morning the fire siren sounded and announcements blared in our rooms. Vacate the premises immediately, take no belongings with us and go down the stairway. An emergency! We hurriedly departed taking our passports with us. We descended one floor – just the four of us – to the floor below and another floor till we found ourselves on the ground entering the footpath in front of the glaring lights of the hotel and in our pyjamas to the taxi drivers' amazement.

A few people gathered – it was a false alarm. It would have been quite amusing, if it were not for our concern for about one hundred Deaf people who were also in the building and the fact that there was no system in place to alert them

---

[1] International Sign is a contact variety of signing that arises when Deaf people from different languages meet.

except for someone who had a key to enter their rooms and switch the light on and off to wake them.

By the next evening the hotel management had put in place in every room where there was a Deaf person, a smoke detector that flashed a light for Deaf people in case of fire. A system was put in place that wherever there was a Deaf person, it was noted, so they could be alerted personally, if necessary. This was a start.

* * *

The conference experience prepared me for my visit to Papua New Guinea on my way home. I found myself sitting tight on a small bumpy plane flying over mountain ranges and mountain ravines. Someone had talked to someone on the plane to ensure I was looked after when I arrived – a white woman on my own with no experience in the country. And I was looked after.

The reason for my visit was to see where my uncle had served for forty years as a Franciscan priest. No one in the family had been there. He had died nearly two years earlier. Memorials of him hung on walls and the local people told stories with gratitude for his role in the community.

But what more brought me here? On my agenda was a visit to an educational centre for Deaf children. *That's why.* Seven delightful boys were at school that day from the age of seven to nineteen. As I sat on the old desk, the boys gathered around me. (The thought raced through my mind, I wonder where the girls are. They are back in their villages.)

I was comfortable signing with this group of boys and I did not really need an interpreter, because their signs were quite graphic and I understood the gist of the conversation. They understood me too. They were amazed that I was white and I could sign and communicate with them. *Why was that so?* How come I could sign? They wanted to know. I used my usual response: *Me – Mother, Father – Deaf!*

One of the boys repeated in sign what he thought I signed. Yes, I nodded. They looked around at each other excitedly and in simple disbelief. Are there white people who are Deaf like us? There was a sense of pleasure in their response – they realised they were not alone in the world; there were white people like them.

Then they wanted more of my story first. I showed them photos of my Deaf parents and Deaf friends. I had a photo of two distinguished-looking senior grey-haired Deaf men from the John Pierce Centre, Stan Batson and Bruno Broglio. It took their imagination to the heights. The oldest boy studied the photo for some time and then signed to me: I want to be like them. I thought, what did he really want to convey? I want to be proud. I want to be respected like them. I want to be an ok person.

Then, their stories began, starting with the tall nineteen year-old, who explained the history of his schooling: *I came to school when I was young. Big problems back in my village during holidays meant that I could not return. So I stayed home – for years. One day I said to my parents, I want to go to school again. I pestered them, told them again and again until finally they let me come back. I am now very happy with my Year Five work. I am studying extra hard so I can move into Year Six level – that will be very soon.*

The boys watched closely, as I did too, while each boy told me the story that was on his mind that day. As the youngest of them was next, like big brothers the boys encouraged and coached him, explaining how to begin his story. After all, they were like family now. Mentoring and role modelling was already in process in this little Deaf community. The young boy told his moving story about his full-breasted Mama and big Papa, his brothers and sisters, who all lived over the mountains far far away – he stretched his arm in the direction of the inland mountains. He continued, that all his family cried because his little sister had died, and they all dug the grave where she was buried deep in the earth. His hand pointed down to the ground and the expression on his face showed the sorrow of everyone in the village. He then continued as he told how his family walked and walked a long distance – for days to bring him to school. The drama of his story was compelling in his still natural *home* sign with hands and arms flailing in a wonderful descriptive narrative. The other boys took their turn too. I sensed their longing to be educated and treated with dignity.

So why was I here? While I felt the privilege of being in the country, most of all, I felt privileged to be with them. The boys taught me about trust and friendship – belonging and identity. I was very moved and I visualised my father as a little boy at St Gabriel's telling his story too – and I hoped he felt his story was accepted and respected, as he acquired the art of story-telling too.

* * *

On the local scene in Australia again, experiences of Deaf educational, pastoral and mental health conferences, and the like, were a training ground for people like me, as I studied more about the Deaf world.

While I had grown up in a Deaf family with Australian-Irish signing, I had been unaware of the extent of the Deaf world, my Deaf heritage and its deeply Catholic influences. Having re-entered the community as an adult through my work, it led me to ask further questions and unexpectedly I discovered the reality of belonging in the Deaf cultural experience, strengthening my Deaf identity.

You will see in the next chapters that my quest drew me to search for where Australian-Irish Sign Language came from and how it came to Australia. This included learning about the personalities and characters involved. As well, the journey showed me where the language was used in the Catholic milieu and why the language ceased being taught in the Catholic education system.

I also learned of my family and friends' involvement in the history—making of the Australian-Irish Sign Language community, and how we come to the conclusion that the language is now considered one of those languages that will disappear from everyday use.

CHAPTER 15

THE PILGRIM IN SPAIN, FRANCE, AMERICA, GERMANY, SCOTLAND AND ENGLAND

In 2002, I sat on the sparsely populated train that was making its way through the alluring countryside of Spain. Another realisation dawned on me; I was a pilgrim following leads almost by intuition. I recognised that while ostensibly I was studying trends in Deaf liturgy and spirituality, Deaf pastoral approaches and mental health and counselling, I was also following a trajectory towards greater integration of my life's experiences – perhaps the pilgrimage of life that we are all drawn to live.

* * *

My pilgrimage was not on the Spanish Ignatian Camino from Loyola to Montserrat, the Camino Santiago de Compostela or the Mary MacKillop pilgrimage from south western Victoria to Penola in South Australia, but a pilgrimage just the same! As I travelled from Spain, France and Ireland with diversions to other countries and then home to further experiences, I was on a journey to find meaning and to celebrate my Deaf story and my Australian-Irish Sign Language.

The conscious quest began in Spain. I learned of the two Catholic priests who were pioneers of Deaf Education. The first was Pedro Ponce de Leon born in 1560, a Benedictine monk at the Monastery of San Salvador at Ona in Burgos in northern Spain.

Pedro Ponce de Leon

According to property law of the time, individuals were required to speak in order to prove their legal status in order to own land. Since a strain of deafness existed in the families of nobility, this created a challenge: when their Deaf sons could not read, write or speak, they were forced to forfeit their inheritance.

In the care of the monks at the monastery were two Deaf boys who came from privileged families and presumably placed by their families. Dom Ponce de Leon, also from an aristocratic family, understood the issues. In his concern he was drawn to educate the boys and to teach them to attempt to articulate some words. In this way their speech, although not necessarily perfect, became the means of gaining their inheritance.

The second Spanish priest and educator was Dom Juan Pablo de Bonet[i] living in the seventeenth century from Zaragoza on the Erbo River, south east of Burgos. He too served among the wealthy aristocratic families where he met Deaf children. He also knew the importance of education in literacy and speech, especially in order for boys to inherit property. Presumably, the Deaf members in these families used *home* signs, the visual language developed organically in their environment, but the signs were not ever recorded.

Juan Pablo de Bonet

Juan de Bonet[ii] published his first book on Deaf education with a system of speech. It included pictures of a one-hand signed alphabet. When I looked at the signs, I recognised the hand shapes as similar to my own. They did indeed influence the French and ultimately the Irish and American Sign languages and my own in Australia. How amazing! This journey was not in vain.

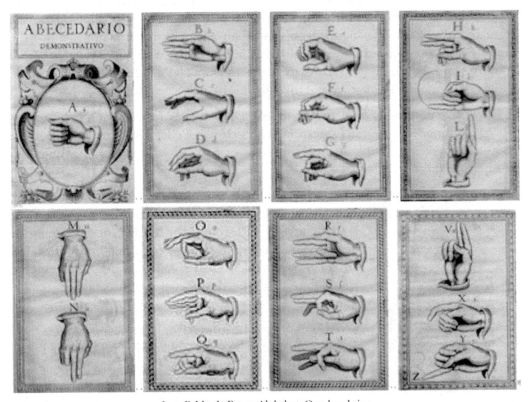

Juan Pablo de Bonet Alphabet: One-hand sign

My next discovery was equally surprising. I discovered the sixteenth century Deaf artist, Juan Fernandez Navarett,[iii] who, belonging to the upper class, became deaf from illness at the age of three. His nickname was El Mudo meaning *The Mute One* – he did not speak. Initially taught by a monk who recognised his great talent, he was sent to Italy to work under the tutorage of the famous painter, Titian. On his return to Spain, King Phillip II commissioned paintings for the St Lawrence monastery at El Escorial near Madrid. His paintings show figures making strong eye contact with each other. In a particular painting called *Nativity* or *Adoring Shepherds* (1571) all the figures are signing to each other. I realised that both Dom Ponce and Juan de Bonet began their work of education and documentation of Sign language building on the existing communication practices of Deaf people.

* * *

Next I found myself in the fragrance of France and in the loveliness of Paris with its rich artistic treasure troves. My inner urging on this journey ushered me here to explore. I immediately climbed onto the red open-top bus and soaked in the sights, alighting to view Notre Dame Cathedral and the various monuments, museums and galleries. In the evening I looked at the old matted map on the wall. Pointing to the river on the map, my Deaf companion for the day drew the river in mid-air and fingerspelt S-e-i-n-e, the River Seine. She continued to draw mid-air other rivers in France that included the O-r-n-e River. Fingerspelling the names, she pointed to towns that had stories significant in relation to Deaf people. I came to realise that a story exists behind the face of each person who responds and stands up with and for Deaf people.

Amongst those stories was that of St Francis de Sales. In the sixteenth and seventeenth century he studied law and became a leading church theologian. *Surprise, surprise!* He was named the patron saint of Deaf people. I asked why he was chosen as one who saluted Deaf people and stood in solidarity with them. The answer – he had a loyal Deaf friend, Martin.

In 1605 Francis de Sales was Bishop in Roche on the River Yon in France. Almost daily, Martin, a strong twenty-five year old man fit for all kinds of work came to the back door of the household and asked for something to eat. The dutiful housekeeper encouraged him to do a few jobs in exchange for the food. Martin could not read or write, nor did he understand the Catholic faith – he had never had the opportunity for education.

One day when Martin came again he met Bishop Francis who was moved with compassion for him and wanted the best for him. The Bishop wanted him to be aware of God, who was woven into every moment of his life. Longing to share his faith, Bishop Francis discovered that Martin was highly intelligent and astute pupil and taught Martin himself. He formed pictures with shapes and signs using his hands, fingers and body language. Through his gentle patience and persistence with signs and gestures that Bishop Francis and Martin worked out together, he taught Martin about God's love for him and for all. Martin became a Catholic, made his first communion and was confirmed.

When Francis became Bishop of Geneva and moved across the River Thiou to Annecy, he employed Martin as a gardener in the grounds and they formed a firm and loyal friendship. For years, Martin assisted at Mass until his friend Bishop Francis died. Martin grieved. He had lost a friend with whom he could communicate. He visited his grave regularly.[iv]

A prayer to St Francis de Sales begins: *Dear St Francis, friend of the Deaf, teach me to seek and to find my happiness in God, and to live, labour and rejoice in God...* [v]

* * *

Abbe Charles-Michel de L'Epee. Photo of painting at the Institute of the Deaf in Paris

In 1978 I attended a Catholic Deaf Conference with my parents, held in Canberra, Australia. It was there I first learned about the remarkable priest, Abbe Charles-Michel de L'Epee,[vi] a Frenchman born in the village of Versailles in 1712.

A friend of my parents, Stan Batson, a Deaf leader from Victoria, held the following story close to his heart and presented it at the pastoral conference with burning zeal and in full flowing sign. Everyone watched intently. Like the original story of anyone who is an inspirer, it can have mythical elements and develop accretions. With this presentation, I felt the enthusiasm, I was enlightened and my mind was filled with rich images.

The story of Abbe Charles-Michel de L'Epee began with the young French priest walking home along the River Seine through the streets of a poor neighbourhood in Paris. It was night time and very dark. As torrential rain poured down, he paused for shelter in the alcove of a house where he noticed a lantern burning through the small window. Inside the woman heard movement at the door, recognised the priest and invited him in. As they exchanged greetings, he observed two young women around the small lantern in the corner of the room with their heads bent. They were attending to their needlework. They did not look up so he considered them ill-mannered.

Their mother explained in hushed tones, as if they might hear, that they were her daughters and that they were profoundly deaf. The sisters did not hear him enter, nor did they hear the hidden discussion about them. While the mother was sadly resigned to their fate, he realised they were disturbingly isolated and uneducated. It was as though they were cast onto the edge of society, as if they did not matter to anyone. Troubled by this, he realised for the first time that there were Deaf adults and children without education in his country of France.

Deaf people were scorned and considered beyond educating. According to French and Spanish law, they were not able to own land, nor able to inherit family estates. Awakened to the gap in communication between hearing people and Deaf people, Abbe de L'Epee used his own funds and drew on other resources to implement his vision for the education of Deaf people. His endeavours addressed many injustices and by the 1760s he began to teach and care for Deaf people. He became the founder, advocate and philanthropist for education for Deaf children no matter what their status in life. He provided the world's first known public and free school for Deaf children – including underprivileged children.

As Abbe de L'Epee met and gathered Deaf people together, he closely observed their natural signs and learnt to communicate with them. Being very methodical, he was the first to collate and formalise the gestural signs. He documented a system with a simple one-hand alphabet for the purpose of education and a full language for communication with a linguistic structure for a Deaf language. While he published two well-used books, *Instruction of Deaf and Dumb using Methodical Sign* and *A Sign Language Dictionary*, he insisted that writing was an important part of their education as well. In learning of this, I think of Don with his faithful notebook and pen. He inherited this belief that being able to write was important for communication in his life and his independence in the world.

I went on to learn that Abbe de L'Epee, besides setting up his school, extended his vision to train Deaf people as professional teachers and sent them out to teach in various areas of rural France. Here for me is the kernel of the vision for his work. Deaf people for him were no longer patronised in his thinking. He saw them as taking their place in society as responsible citizens.

Seeing him as a *liberator of the soul of Deaf people*[vii] and *the father* of the language of signs, I was captured by the image that enlivened my spirit as I walked the curved street and noticed on the signpost *Rue de L'Abbe de L'Epee*. I could not believe that I had accidentally chosen to stay in accommodation so close to this street. Clearly, I thought to myself, I am not alone on my pilgrimage! It can be no other, I thought, but him – a street named in his honour for the hundreds and thousands of Deaf people and children who were educated under his system. I thought of his generous mind and heart and his expressive face. I was from Australia, a long way away. How

Street named in honour of Abbe de L'Epee

amazed he would be to know that we honoured him and that I was inspired as I wandered this street!

Further down the street I approached the school named in his honour – I was in trepidation as I entered the gates. The welcome I received was overwhelming. My heart skipped a beat as I viewed the huge painting at the entrance that showed Abbe de L'Epee as a teacher engaged with four young Deaf men all attired in the aristocratic dress of the time. As he faced the students in the painting his arms and hands are mid-air in sign; the young men focus on him in intense communication. For me, Paris was at the heart of where my first language was developed, recognised and respected. A copy of the painting now hangs on my wall in gratitude for his contribution to the world of educated Deaf people. It serves as a reminder of the Deaf children in our world who are not educated, as well as the children of parents who are ignorant of the possibilities for their Deaf children.

In a little café opposite the school I communicated from a Deaf cultural perspective with the French teachers – in my first language, Australian-Irish Sign Language. My language has its origins right here in Paris as I discovered! The teachers were hearing people, who signed in their French Sign Language, and they too were native signers like me. Our parents were Deaf. We understood one another well. The experience was unique and we marvelled at our cross-cultural experience, as we shared life stories that sounded so familiar to me.

Abbe de L'Epee died in 1789 at the beginning of the French Revolution. He was buried in the tomb in the white marble Church of St Roch in Paris. I found a local bus that took me there and as I stood mesmerised before the tomb, I gave thanks for Deaf educators and for those who continued to appreciate Deaf language, culture and education. Two years after he died, the French government took responsibility for the support of the school he founded. The National Assembly of France directed that his name be registered as a Benefactor of Humanity. It also declared that Deaf people have rights according to the Declaration of the Rights of Man and of the Citizen. This was indeed a break-through in a civil society. Yet there was still more to bring to light on this pilgrim journey.

* * *

Abbe Roch Ambroise
Cucurren Sicard

I discovered Abbe Roch Ambroise Cucurren Sicard,[viii] 1742 – 1822, another Catholic priest and another pioneer in the education of Deaf people, who was born at Fousseret near Toulouse. He succeeded Abbe de L'Epee as principal of the Deaf Institute and authored a significant book, *The Theory of Signs for the Instruction of Deaf-Mutes*, which was a handbook for many who followed him.

While for most of his life Abbe Sicard used Sign language in the education of Deaf people, he entered into the discussions about methods of teaching Deaf people, and towards the end of his life he changed his practice to the method of *Oralism* in Deaf education. A determining influence was the declaration that to be qualified to acquire land, a Deaf person must speak and understand speech in the aristocratic society. However, while *Oralism* was a method that was useful for some children, it was not always suitable for profoundly Deaf people.

* * *

Yet I was to learn more. In 1785 Louis Laurent Marie Clerc was born into an influential Catholic family in south eastern France. While his father was at work for the king as a royal civil attorney, justice of the peace and mayor of their village, his son, approximately twelve months old was in a tragic accident at home. He was burned after falling into the kitchen fireplace. The child developed a fever and it was believed that he became deaf and lost his sense of smell. On the farm as a child, he was given the job of taking care of the cows, turkeys and horses. At the age of twelve, he wanted to go to school and was taken to the Paris National School for Deaf Children where Abbe Sicard was director.

Louis Laurent Marie Clerc.
Gallaudet University Archives

The Deaf children gave Louis Clerc a visual name – a sign name. The middle and index fingers brush across the cheek near the mouth, where a scar was evident on the right side of his face. This was how he was identified in the Deaf community. It was different in Don and Kathleen's case – they were given letters from the alphabet to identify them.

His first teacher was Jean Massieu, who had five Deaf brothers and sisters and was educated by Abbe Sicard at Bordeaux before he moved to Paris. Massieu was a great influence on Louis Clerc.

Learning how to pronounce syllables and words was extremely difficult for Louis. While attempting to teach him, the assistant teacher, knowing that it was important to his hearing family that he spoke words, became angry and frustrated and gave him a slap under the chin, causing Louis to badly bite his tongue. At this, the profoundly Deaf Louis rebelled and refused to learn to speak. While he excelled in his studies he stood firm and took with him into life his belief that signing was the best method of communication to teach students like him and to gain the best results and a satisfying education. He became a most empathic teacher and proved to be a competent educator. With Abbe Sicard, Louis Laurent Clerc gave lectures and demonstrations of methods of teaching in London. There he met Thomas Hopkins Gallaudet from America.

* * *

So began another part of my journey and I learned about the consequences of the meeting between Clerc and Gallaudet. After a conference I had attended in Chicago, USA, I took the old bus out to Gallaudet University through poorer parts of the city. As I walked around the buildings and the gardens I found in front of me a prominent statue of Louis Laurent Clerc, which I was drawn to observe more closely. My question was why was this Frenchman here in this place in America – a place of importance in Deaf tertiary education? My second question was who really was Gallaudet and what part did he play here?

Alice Cogswell with her teacher Louis Laurent Marie Clerc.
Photo: Robert Adam

Thomas Gallaudet was an American Congregationalist minister. His good neighbour had a daughter, Alice Cogswell, who was deaf. That was how Gallaudet together with Alice's father became interested in Deaf children. While Gallaudet was sent to Europe for the purpose of learning teaching methods in Deaf education, he visited London and Paris where he observed the processes used in the school where Louis Clerc taught.

So it came about that in 1816, at the age of twenty-eight, Clerc was invited by Gallaudet to teach in America. He set sail to assist in the establishment of an education system and a Deaf school. On the day he arrived he met young Alice, an intelligent young girl hungry for knowledge.[ix] Her thirst for connection and knowledge could never be quenched. She wanted to see and know everything and her innate curiosity was forever active. As he thought about Alice and others like her, he was motivated as a Deaf educator. Sadly, Alice's father died in a sudden accident, and when she was twenty-five after suffering from depression she died, they said, of a broken heart.

When Louis Laurent Clerc began his work through French signs with the French *one-handed* alphabet, the American Deaf students learned the French signs and blended them with their own native Sign language. As Deaf teachers spread through the country and signs were modified, an identifiable language emerged – American Sign Language. Though Clerc, the Apostle to the Deaf People in the New World, was given a three-year employment contract, he stayed for his whole life and never returned to Paris. Gallaudet himself was director of the school until 1830, his sons following in his footsteps as educators of the Deaf.[x]

Much later, I discovered that a group of eight Sisters of Saint Joseph from Lyon, France, set sail from La Havre to America in 1836 at the invitation of the Bishop of St Louis, Missouri. One specific mission for them was to educate Deaf children. *Were they trained in France to teach through Abbe de L' Epee's school in Paris?* Dressed as nuns in full habits and after seven weeks at sea on the ship *Natchez*, they arrived in New Orleans. Because of anti-Catholic feelings they were encouraged to disguise their religious habit and wear the dress of the people. They travelled aboard the steamer, the *George Collier*, up the Mississippi to St Louis. While some sisters went further to Cahokia, Illinois to open a school, the remaining sisters settled in the village of Carondelet five miles south of St Louis where St Joseph's Institute for the Deaf was founded. This was the first school for the Deaf west of the Mississippi.[xi] It became an oral school from 1934. Shortly after St Joseph's, the Sisters founded another school for the Deaf in Philadelphia.

* * *

Next I discovered a much more recent story about Gallaudet University – a story that has an Australian connection. In 1988 Gallaudet University staff and students faced a major crisis. In an era of equal opportunity, a protest of students and staff including professional teachers, both Deaf and hearing, took place. One of three Australian Deaf people studying at Gallaudet, Therese Pierce, proudly participated in the protest as a student. They made their demands known – that Deaf people be granted leadership positions in the university, equal to their hearing counterparts. The university was closed down for seven days only opening when the protestors' demands were met. They were adamant that a Deaf president be appointed and secondly, that the board of directors consist of at least 51% of Deaf people. A Deaf man, Dr I. King Jordan, was appointed to the position of president. Deaf people had made the point and stood up for themselves, while others stood in solidarity with them. *How proud I felt as I learnt this story but why was I feeling proud?*

Still in the glow of the international conference, discovering the Deaf-French connection to America and learning about the more recent developments of Gallaudet University, I was stirred to think about my father, Don. *Did he know about a university that was dedicated to Deaf people?* I didn't know, but I still felt my father's pride that such a landmark existed in Deaf history. *Did he ever aspire to the possibilities of study or did the circumstances of time, place and responsibility simply make such an aspiration unimaginable?* After all, his earlier life spanned a major economic depression and two world wars. In any event Washington DC would have been a long way away – a dreamland away for him but not so for his grandchildren – one of them has settled in the U.S. and raises his family in Denver.

My journey of discovery continued when I read of the Deaf institute in Normandy in northern France and its importance in the story. At that point I began to appreciate the extent of the succession of significant people who over the years dedicated their lives to the betterment of others.

In 1816 a young Catholic priest Abbe Pierre-Francois Jamet founded the Le Bon Saveur Institute for the Deaf in Caen together with the Sisters of Bon Saveur.

Abbe Jamet met with educators in Paris and studied at the Institute founded by Abbe de L'Epee, where he was influenced by its well-known methods and processes. On his return he developed his own understanding of Deaf education, improving the system in Caen. Recognising that deafness was still considered a disease and a mental illness, he desperately wanted to change societal attitudes so that Deaf people could become more integrated into society.

Abbe Jamet's life commitment to the education of the Deaf grew from his own family experience – his friendship with his younger Deaf cousin.

He would have observed and interacted with his female cousin. Once he had her attention, did he point to things of visual interest? Did he learn to communicate with her through osmosis in the family and naturally use *home* signs? Did she naturally teach him some *home* signs? Between them did they make big and small gestural signs with arms and hands? Did he enjoy showing her more things through his own education, so she learned more about the world she lived in?

Among the next generation in his family, did Abbe Jamet influence his nephew Abbe Furon, a Catholic priest skilled in Sign language and Deaf education? He similarly trained teachers of the Deaf and worked with the Sisters of Bon Saveur.[1] Presumably Abbe Furon knew the Deaf cousin who seemingly influenced his uncle's decision to establish the Deaf school. Was signing natural for him as a second cousin? Did Deaf communication develop in the family? Was she as an adult involved in teaching others too? Unfortunately, I could not find any factual answers to these questions.

However, I learned of the crucial connection to Ireland. At this time Abbe Furon and the Sisters of Bon Saveur heard that at Cabra on Dublin's northwest, a Deaf institute was newly established. They knew that the Dominican sisters required training in their work as Deaf educators and invited them to come and learn. Of course, their learning would need to be adapted to their local situation, as I found out a little later.

The Cousin

I see you, Pierre-Francois Jamet
A young energetic Pierre
Sitting face to face with her
Yet no name for her.
You have her attention
You point to things of interest to her.
Was it a cat or a dog?
Children playing,
Or a drawing she makes?
You make gestural signs
With your arms and hands,
'Home' signs she designs
And you follow her lead
She understands
And a connection is made.
She learns more and more
Her world expands
You are student and teacher
Courageous and honourable
She is teacher and student
Equally courageous and
Equally honourable.

Bernadette T. Wallis

* * *

---

[1] The Sisters were devoted to the care of mentally and physically disabled children. Deaf children were included in their special care.

209

As I started to believe that I was coming to the end of this section of my journey, I took a diversion. I was invited by Pastor Benno and his wife Marion to visit them in Germany. Benno, like me, had Deaf parents and he worked pastorally in the Deaf community. He was a deeply spiritual guide to his Deaf parishioners spread far and wide in Germany. While I stayed with Benno and Marion, I shared in the Deaf community as they came to celebrate together. I relied on the pastor's English for communication – not my German. We visited his Deaf mother, who was in a deaf-friendly residential aged care centre and I was moved by the care and proactive supports that were in place for ease in communication.

Before I left the country, I called on a Catholic chaplain, who though he was generous with his time, treated me as tourist and concentrated on showing me places of local historical interest. Yes I was a tourist, a traveller, but more accurately, a pilgrim, with a different interest just now. I discovered he held a resolute belief that the oral system of Deaf education was the only way. Sign language was considered less worthy. I realised that the outcomes of the 1880 Congress of Milan that Sister Gabriel Hogan had fought against had shaped his attitude towards Deaf people. *Why was I feeling disappointed in what appeared to me to be less than compassionate and ill-informed?* It seemed that he did not want to enter into a discussion because he did not see the Deaf as needing a language or having a specific culture or being a community – and maybe coming out of victimhood. I further realised I came from inside Deaf culture. I was not a bystander. A pilgrim has highs and lows – this was a low.

* * *

Fortunately the next stops on my journey offered more uplifting insights. In London, Manchester and Edinburgh I was piloted into meetings with the local Deaf individuals and communities all of whom offered me wonderful insights. In Edinburgh I stopped for some days of silence for a prayer retreat. Each day I met with a priest who was deaf and both oral and signing – we signed in our communication. *I thought how unique this was!* How wonderful for me to have had the opportunity of expressing myself in this way in this situation. Again I felt embraced by the global Deaf community.

In London I experienced a sense of mission in their outward thrust to Deaf communities in other countries supporting teachers and Deaf students, especially in Africa. In Manchester, I again valued the experience of celebrating and communicating at length with the Deaf community and with another priest who was profoundly deaf. He prepared the spiritually nourishing homilies for the Sunday Mass and communicated directly in sign with the community. The community was strong here with a long history of pastoral attention by both a local community of religious sisters and the Catholic diocese.

I reluctantly moved on. In the next stage I found myself on a steep learning curve in Ireland and I saw more clearly the French connection come closer to Australia.

---

[i] Image sourced from *www.hhhistory.com* – Linda Farmer Harris, *ASL's French Connection*, the Bonet one hand alphabet

[ii] Ibid

[iii] Newsletter of Catholic Association of Deaf and Hearing Impaired People (Victoria) Vol. 12, Issue 11 August 1990 p.4

[iv] *St Francis De Sales: Patron of the Deaf and Hearing-impaired*, Story of Martin adapted from a paper held by the National Catholic Office of the Deaf located in Washington, DC

[v] Prayer to St Francis, The Magazine of the Catholic Deaf, *Past and Present*, Christmas 1939

[vi] Image of Abbe d L'Epee teaching students
http://www.corpus-philo.fr/abbe-de-l-epee-sourds-muets.html

[vii] Helen Keller: A political activist, writer and lecturer who was both blind and deaf and who believed Abbe de L'Epee was a father for them – a self-sacrificing friend, an angel of charity and a true liberator and Apostle. As the time of his bicentenary they also celebrated the birth of the *soul of the Deaf people* of France

[viii] Sicard image sourced from *www.hhhistory.com* – Linda Farmer Harris, *ASL's French Connection*

[ix] *www.gallaudet.edu/history/the_legacy_begins.html*

[x] Eriksson, per, translated from Swedish by James Schmale, *The History of Deaf People*, SIH Laromedel, the Learning Materials of the National Swedish Agency for Special Eduation, Sweden 1993, p.64

[xi] *en.wikipedia.org/wiki/Sisters_of_St_Joseph*

CHAPTER 16

IN IRELAND ON THE LIFFEY

Ireland was to be the enlightening keystone of my unfolding journey. *So what really happened?* On 15 August 2002 I took the short flight to Dublin from Manchester. My eyes rested on the greenness of the countryside as we approached Dublin and I felt the thrill of landing on the Irish tarmac – a thrill amplified by returning to the home of my Irish forebears who had left Ireland so long ago for the land *down under*. I was told that the Irish summer was late this year – it began that very day.

I rode the friendly bus to my accommodation. I dropped my luggage and rode another bus into the bubbling downtown of Dublin. While I saw women who looked like my aunts and cousins, I also saw people who had come as refugees and asylum seekers. They looked so different, even to the colour of their skin. The open space of my mind was ready and even though my emotions were fragile, I felt light and fresh and as if I looked out through big windows. There was a lot to see and take in.

* * *

In this part of my pilgrimage I learned about the beginning of the Catholic Church's role in Deaf education in Ireland, particularly involving the Vincentian priests and the Dominican sisters. This was at a time in the 1840s when the great famine devastated families in an already extremely fractured Irish society under British colonial rule.

The Vincentian priest, Father Thomas McNamara, became aware of Catholic Deaf children in his neighbourhood.[i] He came to realise that they were not included in the rites of the Church and missed out on the opportunity for education in faith or life. They were considered *dumb* and unable to be educated. He questioned everyone *Do they not have souls to be saved?*[ii] As I learned about uneducated Deaf children, I was questioning too. *Don't these children matter to you?* They are human beings and have the right to be educated in all aspects of their lives. *Is it a situation of out of sight, out of mind?*[iii] In 1845 Father McNamara wrote to the Bishops in a document he called *Claims of the Uninstructed Deaf-mutes to be admitted to the Sacraments.*[iv] He left the Bishops of Ireland with the positive question, *Why not have an (Catholic) Institution for the Deaf and Dumb?*[v]

In response to this challenge a diocesan committee was formed and plans were made to raise funds for a school for them. On 5 January 1846, the Dominican sisters were asked to establish the school, manage and staff it. The Prioress, Mother Columba Maher, had vision and faith when she responded: *Yes, the proposal is too good to decline and the tokens of God's providence are too manifest to hesitate.*[vi]

Father McNamara asked Abbe Furon and the Sisters of Bon Saveur in France for support in training the Irish sisters, so they could be qualified educators of the Deaf children. Their response was generous: *Send us your two Religious (Sisters), and as our gates will open, the hearts of all here will open likewise to receive our welcome guests. You are to pay nothing for expenses. We shall be only too happy to share with you the merit of founding in Ireland an institution on the model of a work, which affords us such great consolation.*[vii]

In 1846 the Dominican sisters, Mary Vincent Martin and Mary Magdalen O'Farrell,[viii] set out for Caen in France with two Deaf students Agnes Beedom and Mary Anne Dogherty. How wonderful to know their names! While the girls would have some communication with one another in their own native or *home* signs, it would not be long before they learned and picked up the French Sign Language – most likely more quickly than Sisters Vincent and Magdalen. The task of the Sisters was to learn the system of signs with the signed alphabet and other signs, then to learn the skills of teaching Deaf children. A formidable task was ahead of them. This intense period of training for eight months was all for the benefit of the Deaf children at the new St Mary's School for Deaf Girls back in Cabra, Dublin, on the Liffey River.

When the Sisters returned from France they immediately began to teach at St Mary's with fifteen children. Although they were well-qualified and educated women in their own right, teaching Deaf children was another story. As older Deaf students learned and developed, further skill and more complex linguistic patterns were required in order to communicate and to teach subjects in greater depth. While Abbe Furon's help was significant, it was not enough – they needed more.

The Vincentian priest, Father John Burke, was seconded to assist because of his fluency in the French spoken language. He studied the French *Dictionary of Signs* and the Sign language program, adapting the system to the Irish environment and developing the educational component. Acknowledged as having significantly contributed to the development of Deaf education in Ireland, Father Burke became proficient in Irish Sign Language, well loved by the Deaf community and highly respected.

By 1848 the school had grown and a new wing was opened. The Sisters established a vocational department for ex-students, who were given work and accommodation – this was the model adopted at Waratah too. They had specialised training in spinning, dyeing, embroidery, dressmaking and tailoring.[ix]

Suffering from a lack of understanding by the wider society, Deaf people were marginalised, as in other countries, and often classed as *stupid*, and in some cases considered mentally ill;[x] they were known as or called *Dummy* or *dummies*,[xi] and often excluded by family and members of the public. The work and accommodation model was vital since if the girls returned to their rural homes, they were often deprived of good communication and became lonely for their school friends who had become family and who had formed a community. This happened for girls at Waratah too. The Sisters in Cabra stood by Deaf people and remained their friends for life – as did the Sisters in Waratah.

As the Cabra school continued to grow and develop, a number of selected ex-students were trained as teachers. They were significant Deaf role models and took a strong parental role in the lives of the smaller children. In 1887 the number of students increased to two hundred and eleven.[xii] Even then it seems that the wider Irish community did not recognise the Irish sisters for their commitment and innovative work.

* * *

I discovered that while the school for girls had been established in Ireland in 1846, the time was ripe in 1857 for a school to be set up for Deaf boys. The Diocesan committee approached the Christian Brothers with the request that they take responsibility and staff the newly built, elaborate St Joseph's School for Deaf Boys. Having entered the same driveway at St Joseph's as hundreds of boys had done before me, I thought about the enormity of the task the Brothers had shouldered. Seven years later, it was enlarged with a new wing to accommodate the requirements of the growing numbers of boys from various parts of Ireland. While the Brothers learned Irish Sign Language and teaching methods for Deaf children from the Sisters and Deaf teachers at St Mary's across the road, they developed a particular style with their preferences. One notable difference was its significant emphasis on fingerspelling of words in their communication.

A few days later I found myself in another part of Ireland – fingerspelling. Somehow I was lost and unsure of where to find my car. *What a nuisance!* Some young people were sitting outside a pub. I asked what street I was in and in which direction was the street I wanted. They were from out of town and had no idea.

With typical Irish humour, they jokingly pointed to an older man dressed in a well-worn coat and an old hat. Downtrodden and having had plenty of the Guinness in his day, he was often teased and the butt of jokes. He looked older than he was. *Dummy will tell you what direction you need to walk, one of the boys yelled.* Before I saw the man, I recognised the guttural tone of a profoundly Deaf person. I swung around, looked at his face to make contact with him and I fingerspelt and signed to him *Are you deaf?* His face broadened into the biggest smile. We had a conversation in his Irish Sign Language and established a magic moment of dignity, communication and respect for one another. He asked, *Where from? Australia* I signed. He told me he was an ex-student of St Joseph's and he was pleased when I told him I had been there. He now stood taller and looked younger. The young men, who sat at the table outside the pub, looked on in amazement. *She can talk with him!* He was called *Dummy*, but he had a name that was his – *Mick*, he fingerspelt. I was glad of that moment and my heart was uplifted as was his. As I walked away I wondered if my father and perhaps how many others had been treated playfully in ignorance.

Another enlightening encounter reaffirmed the global inclusivity of the Deaf community, and took me by surprise again. When I arrived in a regional city in Ireland, I left my contact number for the chaplain of the Deaf community, an elderly priest who was always hatted in black. A humble man whose pastoral outreach uplifted many hearts, he lived as a free spirit with his heart and mind in the community – with not an ounce of paternalism. Later that night when he returned home he phoned me. It was dark that evening but he immediately offered to come and take me out – to meet with a Deaf family. And we did – with a family where I felt so much at home. Next day he arranged for me to meet the community there. He knew the people and they knew him – I had met a good shepherd.

On a short train journey two days later, I found myself in the company of one of the Deaf women I had met the day before. Surprised and pleased to see me, she sat opposite so we could see one another to communicate in Irish Sign. Both joys and sorrows were shared. In her desire she signed, *Can't we continue this journey? With someone who understands my language, I want to discuss more – I have more life questions to unravel.* We communicated our good-bye in Irish Sign Language and I felt a life-giving burning passion as I realised our ease in communication and the strong Deaf link with Australia.

Another Irish keystone of my journey was my meeting in Dublin with the Catholic Irish Deaf community in their own Centre. I could not help but be fully focused on the Sign language that was so familiar to me in its essence. In the chapel during their Signed Mass, I was transfixed by the glass window, which was designed with the image of one hand predominantly outlined. Here the language was respected and given dignity in artistic form. As I sat with the elderly Deaf people at their aged care facility, I observed how much I felt at home when we shared stories and laughed together. They were so surprised to know how their language was the basis for the Sign language taught in the Catholic school system in Australia from 1875 to 1953. They wanted to know more. *Who was the Irish teacher who took the Irish Sign Language to Australia?* There was more to discover.

* * *

The story of Ellen Hogan was also enlightening for me. Born in 1842 in Dublin she was a vivacious and intelligent child who could hear her parents' voices, and the wind as it blew and the rain as it fell. Advanced for her age and with her keen mind she learnt to read and write English like other children. Her family were well-educated people, well established and actively involved in Irish politics with a good understanding of the social issues of the day.

Then, at the age of seven, Ellen contracted scarlet fever, which left her totally deaf. She no longer heard familiar sounds and with her diminishing ease of communication with others, she could not manage her schooling without a specialised education system for Deaf children. It was not long before her parents made the decision for Ellen to attend the recently established Deaf school – St Mary's, with the Dominican sisters.

I had heard the familiar story of Deaf people who lose their hearing as children through illness or disease. They have told me of their shock and not knowing what had happened to them. Initially, the sick little girl, Ellen, would have been mystified and frightened. Fear would have gripped her when she could no longer hear familiar sounds – her mother's voice, music and children playing. She no longer heard her own voice as she read aloud. Deaf people had told me how they were frustrated and angry and had found it hard to manage at first. Their loving parents felt guilty and disappointed yet so relieved that their child could walk and run, laugh and read. Ellen's parents would have found ways to communicate with her. They would have made sure they talked to her face-to-face, rather than behind her head. They would have mouthed words and gesticulated to her, as they pointed to things – they would have written messages on paper when she did not understand.

At St Mary's Ellen learnt the Irish Sign Language – her new mode of communication and learning. She took solace in reading prolifically. At thirteen she was skilled in the language and began to teach other children. She was a natural educator. Father Burke, who by this time specialised in the linguistics of Deaf Sign, tutored Ellen to further her education. Drawn to the inspirational life and work of the Dominican sisters, she felt the attraction to prayer. She wanted to dedicate herself to the work of God as she developed the enthusiasm, zest and determination to educate Deaf girls.

Ellen completed her preparation and was accepted as a member of the Dominican order. Given the new name of Sister Mary Gabriel, she continued her work in education with vitality and love. She developed friends among the Sisters and wrote encouraging and informative letters to those who had left their homeland and worked in missionary lands in Portugal and Africa.[xiii]

While well-read and well informed on the complex issues of Deaf language and education, Sister Gabriel understood the different views that were held by those in the Deaf community. She knew about *Oralism*. Her experience told her that for profoundly Deaf people to learn speech and lip-reading required intensive speech therapy. In her view, it was labour intensive and progress came slowly. She noticed that more hours of tuition were given to speech, rather than to education. She also saw that, in the long term, speech therapy was not always adequate for clear speech, especially when the Deaf child became an adult and no longer had a speech therapist each day or week. She also believed that those children who would benefit from speech lessons should be given the opportunity to practise in the course of their schoolwork. But the emphasis should be on their education and not on speech lessons. This made so much sense to me – I understood clearly because of my experience of being with the adult Deaf community as they shared their stories. She believed they also needed to be taught appropriate general behaviour.

As I reluctantly left Ireland, I was in awe when I thought about the history of St Mary's and St Joseph's and how the same model had been developed on a smaller scale in Australia. I acknowledged their work in educating many fine women and men and opening up the development of Deaf language and culture in Ireland to also include Australia. In Ireland I had felt close to the earth identifying with my roots more firmly – roots both of family and of Deaf heritage.

* * *

During the nineteenth century, a strong Ireland-Australian link was formed as the missionary spirit of many Irish religious sisters, priests and brothers saw them travel to Australia where they established schools, hospitals and welfare institutions. Their arrival in Australia coincided with many factors – British colonisation and the eviction of local indigenous peoples from their lands, convict settlement, the famines in Ireland, the gold rush and the opening up of land opportunities in *the new colony.*

But what I learned from my Irish pilgrimage was how the first Dominican Sisters came to Australia. In 1864 the Irish Bishop James Murray invited the Dominican sisters from Kingstown to teach in Maitland in his diocese in Australia. The first group of eight Sisters arrived with Bishop Murray's cousin, Sister Agnes Bourke, as the Prioress. Their mission was to teach not only the less fortunate, but to educate young women who would have the financial backing and social standing to become the first generation of Catholic teachers for the people in that diocese.[xiv]

How coincidental was it that on their journey to Australia, they actually met a Deaf person on board the sailing ship, the *Martha Birnie*. An Irishman, whose name has not been recorded, was a steerage passenger – travelling in the crowded conditions below the deck. After 7.00pm in the evenings he was permitted to come up *on the poop.*[xv] Sisters Teresa Molloy and Augustine Fagan in particular took delight in the opportunity to join him by moonlight[xvi] and for him to teach them basic Irish Sign Language. Moonlight was essential because without light they could not see to communicate. Each morning the Sisters eagerly practised as they signed to one another, showing new signs they had learned the previous evening. The Sisters were kind to him but he generally looked for Sister Agnes. She was slim and graceful with a manner that combined elegance with warm friendliness.[xvii]

Added to this information I found that Sisters Augustine and Hyacinth Donnellan had been educated at the Dominican school close to St Mary's so would have been aware of Deaf people and Sign language. Presumably, the unnamed Irish passenger was the first person and first Deaf person, who used Irish Sign Language on Australian soil. He disappears from Australian history – no one has identified him.

* * *

As I continued to thus unravel the history of the link between Ireland and Australia in the education of Deaf people and the arrival of Australian-Irish Sign Language, I found that in 1872, Bishop Murray initiated negotiations with the Dominican sisters at Cabra for an educational institute for Deaf children in Australia. He asked specifically for Sister Gabriel as a teacher, because he had previously seen her and noticed her vivaciousness and talent in education. While surprised and amazed at the request, she immediately accepted to become a missionary – not in Portugal or Africa like her missionary friends, but in Australia. Due to sickness she was unable to travel straight away and had to wait another three years.

On 3 July 1875, Sister Gabriel began the journey at the age of thirty-three, thirty years after St Mary's was established. She boarded the boat named the *Mirzapore* with the party of travellers who all came to serve in Australia – ten Sisters of Mercy, a Jesuit priest and five more Dominican sisters from the Kingstown group – a different group from Cabra where Sister Gabriel was from.

While the journey took seven weeks as far as Ceylon,[1] Sister Gabriel filled in the time reading books that she brought with her, as well as books given to her by others on the boat. Being a reader from her childhood, she had learned the value of reading. This I recognised as one of the legacies she passed on to her students – including my parents' teacher, Miss Hanney.

---

[1] Ceylon became Sri Lanka.

I learned that at this early stage Sister Gabriel was a woman with many interests. She also had the resilience to involve herself in activities, as well as to engage significantly with others. From Ceylon on the *Golconda*, they sailed across the Indian Ocean and the Great Australian Bight to Melbourne where she first stood on Australian soil. I wondered what was it like for her. *How did she describe it when she wrote back to the Sisters in Ireland or to her missionary friends?*

On the *Ellora*, she continued along the east coastline and arrived in Sydney. The journey had not yet finished for her. After two nights on land they set out on wild waters through the Sydney heads on the *Coonanbarra*, a paddle steamer that chugged along magnificent white beaches before it entered the Hunter River at Newcastle.

At this stage of my pilgrim enlightenment, I wanted to proclaim: *Australia, here she comes, the small Irish woman with a big heart! Meet the skilled educator of Deaf Children. See the Irish Sign Language in all its beauty.* And yes, subsequently, see that this language is the basis for the Australian-Irish Sign Language taught through the Catholic education system in Australia.

* * *

Back in Australia I had more questions! While it was forty-five years after Sister Gabriel arrived in Australia that a School for Deaf Boys was established in Sydney in 1922, I wanted to know how that happened and who was involved – on the Australian scene and in Ireland.

The Christian Brothers had already built and staffed many Catholic schools throughout Australia and New Zealand. By this time fewer Irish Brothers were coming to Australia.

In 1920, when Archbishop Michael Kelly was in Dublin, he invited the Christian Brothers to begin a school for Deaf boys in Sydney. The Melbourne Archbishop Mannix was in London – he had been refused entry to his Irish homeland due to his support for the Irish Independence movement. *Did the Archbishop Kelly on a visit to Archbishop Mannix happen to mention that the generous Brother P.J. Hennessy, the Christian Brothers' General, offered to provide Brothers from St Joseph's for the proposed Deaf boys' school in Sydney?* They would be well educated, qualified and skilled, as well as specialised in Deaf education.

My parents were both second and third generation Irish emigrants to Australia and I realised my father's teachers and mentors came directly from Ireland. I asked the question: *who were the well-trained Brothers who came to teach at the new St Gabriel's School for Deaf Boys in Australia?* In other words, who influenced my father, Don during his adolescent years? Sifting through research material revealed further information for me.

I discovered that Brother Jerome Barron, the Provincial in Australia, was already in Australia when he was first introduced to the Deaf world during negotiations for the new school. He committed himself to the new and different venture and became a constant presence at St Gabriel's for public events. Born in Tipperary he entered the novitiate the same year that Sister Gabriel Hogan left Dublin for Australia. Never did he dream that seventeen years later he, too, would take the long journey to Australia – and make decisions about Deaf education!

The first significant Brothers who came specifically to teach Deaf boys were Brothers Joseph O'Farrell, Damian Allen, and Henry Esmonde, who all received extensive training and mentoring. *But who were they? Tell me about their families. How did they get into Deaf education?*

Brother Joseph O'Farrell

Brother Joseph O'Farrell was from County Waterford and from a family of eleven children – he was born in 1877. My research revealed that while he began his education in the national school at Ballygunner, he later transferred to Mt Sion and Waterpark College where he was a sportsman and captain of the local cricket club and gained distinction in his studies. Ah! He was a sportsman *and* a good student! An obvious leader, he then made the decision to join the Brothers. By the time he was a young nineteen year old, he began his active work with the Deaf boys at St Joseph's School. Witty and argumentative in nature, his educational gifts were recognised and he then taught in hearing schools in both Ireland and England for fourteen years. At that stage he was asked at the age of forty-five in the Irish autumn of 1921 to go to Australia and set up St Gabriel's, even though he had not taught in Deaf education for many years.

I also learned he was sensitive and anguished over the political issues of his beloved Ireland. A forthright defender of the rights of the Irish to self-govern as a nation, he conveyed his strong beliefs to the senior Deaf boys through vivid storytelling and forceful descriptions in sign as he educated St Gabriel's boys – many of whom had Irish heritage.

In further research I found that the interesting and industrious Brother Damian Allen was chosen at the age of thirty to travel with Brother O'Farrell to establish St Gabriel's. He was born into a Wexford faith-filled family of ten children. With simple devoted parents, he enjoyed work on the farm as a young adolescent, often diverting from his studies to do so. Yes, his background

Brother Damian Allen

made him well suited to pioneer the farm life at St Gabriel's. Brother Allen, small and wiry, loved Ireland.

In 1898, at the age of seven, the same year as the centenary celebrations in Wexford of the Irish rebellion of 1798, his patriotic family and friends named him '98', a name he was proud of and which indicated his strong adherence in the struggle for Irish freedom. How poignant for him when he arrived at St Gabriel's and discovered that many Irish convicts including representatives of Wexford men of the 1798 uprising were sent to the Castle Hill penal settlement. He would have remembered his earlier family nickname of '98'.

How interesting to learn that his siblings served as missionaries – three of his sisters were religious who joined the Sisters of Charity in USA, two of his brothers were Christian Brothers, another brother, William, followed the Jesuit tradition and taught in colleges in Melbourne and Sydney, and one was a priest with the Missionary Oblates of Mary Immaculate.

Being appointed to St Joseph's as a young man, he became skilled in Sign language. In a write-up of his life, I read the following: *In the conventional language of sign, he had few equals. With the greatest of ease he would deliver a homily to some three hundred past pupils of St Joseph's, assembled in the school at mission time and the attention of the spectators never flagged.*[xviii] He signed well, so his communication with the boys and Deaf people generally was of a high standard.

Brother Henry Esmonde

Next I learned about the young Brother Henry Esmonde, who was born in 1901 at Dun Lavin, County Wicklow, the third of a family of six children. From a loving home, he was tender hearted, kind, persuasive, courteous and of strong faith. When he was still young and in his late twenties he was a strict teacher and a disciplinarian, but as he grew in wisdom and experience and as he aged, he developed a humble nature and had a strong sense of humanity about him. He was thought of as warm and generous, gentle and a gentleman.

Brother Esmonde was considered a loss to the signing Deaf community in Australia when he returned to Ireland in 1938. He was soon appointed back to St Joseph's in Dublin at his own request, where he was superior for many years and became an icon, a person with a sense of humour and well loved by Deaf pupils, their parents and the Brothers. He filled the role of a father figure for generations of boys at St Joseph's.

Another Brother came to St Gabriel's in the initial stage, Brother Dominic O'Shea. He had come from County Cork and was already in Australia by 1922 and had previously taught at St Joseph's a number of years beforehand. It seemed to me to be common sense to call him to assist in the new mission at Castle Hill, but he only stayed for the first year until he returned years later in 1938-1943.[xix]

To make the contrast clear in my pilgrim mind, I asked the question – to no one in particular: when they came to Australia how did they sustain their equilibrium? In the heat of summer or the hard days in their work – did they look for greenness of countryside and soft, misty days like that of their homeland? When the rewards of their work were evident and they could see the boys develop into good young men – did they look to celebrate and sing?

My growing understanding helped me realise the depth of the relationship between Australia and Ireland. Little did the Sisters and Brothers realise the profound impact they made on the Australian Catholic Deaf education and the Deaf community with the Deaf language Australian-Irish Sign Language.

[i] Thomas MacNamara, *Claims of the uninstructed Deaf-mute to be admitted to the Sacraments*, 1809-1892, published 1878, held in National Library of Ireland

[ii] Ibid

[iii] These questions Father John Wallis asked at the time of the foundation of the Missionary Sisters of Service

[iv] Thomas MacNamara, *Claims of the uninstructed Deaf-mute to be admitted to the Sacraments*, 1809-1892, published 1878, held in National Library of Ireland

[v] Ibid

[vi] Nicholas Griffey OP, *From Silence to Speech – 50 years with the Deaf*, Dominican Publications 1994, p.15

[vii] Sarah Fitzgerald, *Open Minds Open Hearts*, CCOD Publication, Lidcombe NSW 1999, p.38

[viii] Nicholas Griffey OP, *From Silence to Speech – 50 years with the Deaf*, Dominican Publications 1994, p.16

[ix] Nicholas Griffey OP, *From Silence to Speech – 50 years with the Deaf*, Dominican Publications, Dublin 1994, p.16

[x] Ibid, p.20

[xi] Sarah Fitzgerald, *Open Minds Open Hearts*, CCOD Publication, Lidcombe NSW 1999, p.39

[xii] Nicholas Griffey OP, *From Silence to Speech – 50 years with the Deaf*, Dominican Publications Dublin1994, p.16

[xiii] Sarah Fitzgerald, *Open Minds Open Hearts*, CCOD Publication, Lidcombe NSW 1999, p.44

[xiv] Elizabeth Hellwig OP, *Up she Gets, for up she must!* Published by Dominican Sisters 2001, p.13

[xv] Ibid

[xvi] Ibid. p.65

[xvii] Ibid. p.18

[xviii] Necrology – Christian Brothers Educational Record, p.286

[xix] Johnston, Brian James, *Memories of St. Gabriel's 1922 – 1997*, Researched and published, 2000, p.77

CHAPTER 17

ON AUSTRALIAN WATERS
PADDLE-STEAMING UP THE HUNTER

On Australian soil in 2000, before I took the journey to other countries, I was on a small mini bus that was driven from Melbourne through the dry countryside along the familiar Hume Highway to our destination – Newcastle and Waratah for the One Hundred and Twenty Five Years of Catholic Deaf Community Life in Australia.

On the bus were people from the Melbourne Catholic Deaf community, who in reels of laughter were spearing text messages to one another and in all directions – still a novelty! With access to mobile phones newly available for ordinary people, my Deaf friends very quickly learned the new art and skill of text messaging. As they were highly motivated to be in direct contact with a person wherever they were and with as much immediacy as possible, their daily lives were changed. They did not need to depend on others to make phone calls for them – a text message, emailing a client or using Facebook did the job.

However, new visual signs were required for new technology, e.g. mobile phone and text message. Initially, signs were formed and were tentative until the community tested them so that eventually throughout Australia the Deaf community gradually accepted particular signs that became part of the official lexicon. Such words included computer, hard drive, Skype, mouse, I-pad, I-tunes, emails, Facebook and tweeting – they had to be adopted by the community.

With these evolving changes in language floating through my mind, I let my thoughts wander further back to our Australian Deaf history and asked the question: *What do we know of our earliest Deaf people and their language in Australia?*

The Aboriginal and Torres Strait Island peoples and Deaf people in their communities came to mind first. Of course, many Aboriginal cultures traditionally had a Sign language as a counterpart of their oral language. Different opinions exist about Aboriginal Deaf people. Some cultures included them into the mainstream Aboriginal community. For others they were isolated in their hearing communities but developed *home* signs within their extended family. In far north Queensland an Aboriginal and Torres Strait Islander dialect of Auslan presently exists.

Then I thought about Deaf people who came to Australia since colonisation. *What about them?*

I learned about Elizabeth Steel,[i] a convict on the *Lady Juliana* from England who died in Sydney in 1795. In 1825 a Scotsman, John Carmichael, who was educated at the Deaf residential school in Edinburgh[ii] using British Sign Language, arrived in Sydney, and with his amazing skills engraved drawings of Sydney scenery, his works being well recognised.[iii] He was a great storyteller too. I also learned that as early as 1836 the English Deaf man, Henry Hallett, who arrived in South Australia married a Deaf woman, Martha Pike.

I thought about the differences in Sign language – the British Sign Language and the Irish Sign Language, which were visually very different and two separate languages. Each had its own syntax and its own lexicon. Like any language it had its own grammatical rules. The British Sign Language included the two-hand fingerspelling alphabet. The Irish Sign Language was based on a one-hand fingerspelling alphabet. Both languages came into Australia, the dominant being the British Sign Language. Both languages changed and developed further in the Australian setting, north and south, east and west. The British Sign Language with its influences, including Australian-Irish Sign Language, became known as Auslan.

In 1860 Thomas Pattison who was educated at *The Edinburgh Deaf and Dumb Institution* in Scotland arrived in Australia and established a Deaf residential school in Sydney, *The Deaf and Dumb Institute*. At the same time Frederick Rose, who was educated at the Old Kent Road School in London, also set up a Deaf residential school, but in Melbourne. Pattison and Rose were both Deaf and communicated in British Sign Language. Because they attended different schools, some of their signs differed and formed two main dialects of the British based language in Australia. With the two residential schools established in Australia, a strong Deaf community developed that became part of the global Deaf community.

I was puzzled and sad when I found that both Pattison and Rose after a period of time in charge of the Deaf schools were dismissed as teachers of the Deaf. Hearing persons replaced them – seemingly more able to teach Deaf children. Deaf teachers were considered as less competent. The emphasis was soon placed on learning to lip read and speak rather than signing as a language in which they could be educated.

* * *

As we approached Newcastle, I thought about what happened in Melbourne just prior to the entry of Sister Gabriel into Australia, when active church discussions regarding the Catholic spiritual care of Deaf children arose in the public media. *So what was that all about?* In 1874 at the St Kilda *Victorian Institute for the Deaf and Dumb*, the evangelical protestant superintendent took Christian education on a regular basis as part of the curriculum. Catholic church leaders objected when

Catholic children were not being permitted to attend Mass and have Catholic instruction, especially given the increasing proportion of Catholic children at the school.

Approximately three hundred Deaf children were in attendance by the end of the nineteenth century. To resolve the unpleasant negotiations, the board of directors of the Victorian Deaf and Dumb Institution resolved to ask the parents what they wished for their children. They responded with a resounding *Yes* that the Catholic parents wished their children to attend Mass and have Catholic instruction[iv] at the local parish of St Mary's at Windsor. The Catholic parishioners treated the children generously and kindly with a Sunday dinner and food treats and transported them to and from the school.

* * *

Catherine Sullivan
Newcastle Waratah Archives,
circa 1878

I had never been to Newcastle and Waratah before yet I knew these names from early childhood from my mother Kathleen and her stories. When the bus finally arrived there for the celebrations I learned about Catherine Sullivan who was instrumental in Sister Gabriel's coming to Australia. *Why was that so?* I needed to follow her story. I stepped into the imaginary shoes of this young sparkling Deaf girl from Bathurst, who was indeed a spark for the intriguing development of Catholic education for Deaf children in Australia.

On 7 January 1859, Catherine Sullivan was born on a property at *Swallow Creek* near Bathurst on the Macquarie River in the central tablelands of NSW. In a rural setting, the little Deaf girl, Katie, as she was known at home, was the only daughter in the Irish Sullivan family. She had three brothers with whom she spent much of her time as a child. As a pioneer in the country, her father, Patrick, continued to acquire land out west and was often away from home. Her young mother, Sarah, unhappy in the marriage, left the home and the family when Catherine was five years old. The well-loved Mrs Coyle moved into the home as housekeeper, and became mother, teacher and friend to Catherine and the boys for the remainder of her life.

From 1866 to 1872, Catherine attended the residential school, the NSW Deaf and Dumb Institute in Sydney, until the age of thirteen. She was the only Catholic girl there, except for one person for one year in that period of seven years. Catherine's first Sign language was based on the British Sign Language with the

Sydney dialect. Towards the end of her time at the school, she did not seem to appreciate or understand her Catholic faith, because she had had no faith education. This was anathema to her Irish Catholic family. Accordingly, it is not surprising that they raised their concerns with their local Bishop in Bathurst.

Bishop Matthew Quinn of Bathurst was a cousin to Bishop James Murray of Maitland and also Sister Agnes Bourke, the warm, friendly Prioress of the Dominican Sisters. No doubt the three cousins discussed the possibility of Catherine attending the Dominican school and furthermore the possibility of establishing a Deaf school. Bishop Murray spoke with other Bishops about Catholic Deaf children *in the colony*, arguing that they should have the opportunity to receive a Catholic education,[v] knowing that in Ireland, schools existed for such children. *So why not in Australia?* He seized the idea and inspired others with his zeal and energy to bring this about in the burgeoning Irish Catholic community.

When Bishop Murray recruited more young Sisters and priests for Australia to serve the educational needs in the Catholic system and in parish life, he knew there would be no employment costs. The Sisters were dedicated women who lived on providence – whatever was given them, food or donations. He now wanted them to educate Deaf children.

In 1872 Bishop Quinn cared for Bishop Murray's diocese while he was away. This required him to travel by horse drawn coach to Sydney[1] and then by boat to Maitland. Catherine travelled with him to attend the Dominican school with hearing students. *Did the Sisters tell her about the Deaf man they met on the boat when they travelled to Australia in 1867?* Attuned to Deaf visual language, it gave them a head start in their communication with Catherine

Bishop J. Murray, Maitland 1866-1909, NSW

even though her Sign language was based on the British system. Catherine learned the Irish alphabet to assist in their basic communication. I mused, how strange! *Would she ever have thought that her life would be valued so much by people like myself because of what it meant for my parents and our family?* In a strange way, the articulate and refined Catherine was the catalyst for Sister Gabriel to come to Australia. Because of her being deaf she drew attention to the need in Australia for the care and education of the Catholic children who were deaf. *Did they not have souls too?* This was the consistent cry.

* * *

---

[1] The train station at Bathurst opened in 1876.

In the meantime with Catherine, Sister Agnes saw to the inauguration of work with Deaf children in Maitland.[vi] I learned that from here the focus of Deaf involvement transferred to Newcastle with Sister Gabriel's arrival in 1875.

When Sister Gabriel did eventually arrive, she was taken up the steep hill to the Dominican convent with its three hundred and sixty degree view of all the activity on the waterfront in one direction, and the small town and background bush in the other. Down the hill in the middle of the grounds stood the small building, *The Cottage*, where Catherine, sixteen years of age, waited expectantly for her. She was Sister Gabriel's first student in Australia. Elizabeth Rowald aged ten also arrived. David Rice, a sixteen-year old, was the third student and first boy. Mary Meehan aged five soon arrived and they all lived in *The Cottage* with Sister Gabriel.

In her engagement with Catherine, Sister Gabriel became familiar with British Sign Language in Australia with the two-hand fingerspelling alphabet, as Catherine became competent with the one-hand Irish alphabet. Sister Gabriel preferred the greater ease of the one-hand signed alphabet, especially in teaching, because she could write on the blackboard with one hand and still sign with the other hand. One-hand signing people had a sense of glee and a tinge of triumphalism when they claimed that the one-hand sign was superior or easier. You could sign while the other hand held the steering wheel or the baby! If one hand was incapacitated with a burn or a broken arm, the other could still sign.

Up until 1883, the competent Sister Gabriel had ten students and the school was doing well in spite of great difficulties. Catherine, when she finished her schooling, returned to the family property at Bathurst, and became a significant person of hospitality in the family and in the Irish milieu in which she lived.[vii]

School for Deaf Children, Waratah 1888
University of Newcastle Archives

Driving five miles west of Newcastle to Waratah, I read the inscription on the front of the now tired building and learned that the opening of the new Holy Rosary Convent, *The Institute for the Deaf and Dumb*, took place on Sunday, 3 October 1886. The newly arrived Irish Archbishop of Sydney, Patrick Francis Moran, laid the foundation stone with great ceremony before a crowd gathered at the front of the two wings of the building that faced the Pacific Ocean. Bishop Murray and the priests were congratulated at the time on the huge task of completing the project.

Waratah, an imposing structure on the landscape, occupied *an elevated position, commanding a fine view of the ocean and the district around Waratah and its neighbourhood.*[viii] The main entrance was approached by a series of large stone steps, with stone balustrades. In the front rooms were stained glass windows that caught the sunlight and cast slivers of colours around the large room. The land and building cost £10,000.

Waratah was called a *Cabra* at Newcastle, NSW,[ix] after St Mary's School for Deaf Girls in Ireland. It was thought desirable that a transplanted *Cabra* would be useful in a central spot to several Catholic Australian populations.[x] Modelled on St Mary's, including the system of teaching Deaf children, the Dominican sisters managed and cared for the Institute. *How close is that link to Ireland!*

Above the front doors appeared the Dominican motto, *Veritas, Laudare-Benedicere-Praedicare: Truth, to praise, to bless, to preach.* The students were encouraged to sign the motto with pride – and they did in beautiful sign. They were encouraged to desire to know Truth, to give praise for the goodness of life, to be a blessing in people's lives and by their own lives to give witness to God's love wherever they were situated.

Sister Gabriel Hogan,
circa 1910

What a difference for Sister Gabriel and her Deaf students when from their cramped *Cottage* in the centre of Newcastle they moved to Waratah, the building especially designed for them and for future Deaf children as a home and school for care and education. Seeing Sister Gabriel at work, Bishop Murray remarked that there must be *several Deaf people in the colony* who should be in charge of Deaf institutions.[xi] He recognised they were capable of professional life, which was contrary to society's view at the time.

Explanations as to why such Deaf institutions should be established were published in many articles in *The Advocate*, the weekly Catholic newspaper in Victoria. Bishop Murray with the early members of the hierarchy of the Australian and New Zealand Catholic Church strongly supported the work of education for Deaf children. At their Plenary Council of Bishops they made a significant pledge: *The Fathers of the Australian Church, who assembled in the Plenary Council of Sydney (1886) promised patronage of the Institution for the Deaf education of children conducted by the Dominican Sisters. They took a personal interest in this work of the Church as a national charity.*[xii][2]

* * *

As I continued my learning, I took a closer look at the stance that Sister Gabriel took in her Deaf educational methods while various opinions and controversies stewed on the Australian and global scene.

At the time, Sister Gabriel was the only Deaf sister in her Dominican community at Waratah. While a most significant educator through the Irish Sign Language, she kept up-to-date with the discussions on education generally as well as on Deaf education.

Already in Australia, she was aware that in 1880, the famous international congress on Deaf education that had major global consequences was held in the city of Milan in Italy.[xiii] At this congress the decision was made to eliminate Sign language altogether for Deaf children. A hard line was taken that no longer would Deaf children learn or be educated through Sign language. Families and Deaf children were discouraged in their use of Sign at home or anywhere.

Teachers universally began to teach children to lip-read, to articulate words, and not to sign. This approach was called *Oralism*. While eight resolutions were passed at the Congress, the significant decisions have affected the education of Deaf children and their language up until today.[xiv]

As did educators in Deaf education before her, Sister Gabriel believed that in the long term, *Oralism* was rarely successful, fulfilling or satisfying for Deaf people, unless the option for Sign language was also present. Many Deaf people who were taught through *Oralism* took up signing after they left school when they met with signing Deaf people outside of their school environment. To their detriment, Sign language was not their first language, although as children it may have been their natural visual language.

---

[2] The early work of advocacy in the second half of the 19th century and into the twentieth century was predominantly activated through the influence of a number of Bishops and their significant contacts in Church circles. They were:
- Bishop Murray of Maitland diocese, and his cousins, Bishop Matthew Quinn of Bathurst diocese and his brother, Bishop James Quinn of Brisbane diocese;
- Bishop Vince Dwyer of Maitland, who was appointed initially as Bishop Murray's coadjutor, and his brother, Bishop Joseph Dwyer of the diocese of Wagga Wagga;
- Archbishop Michael Kelly of the Archdiocese of Sydney;
- Archbishop Daniel Mannix of the Archdiocese of Melbourne; and
- Bishop Francis Redwood of Wellington Archdiocese, New Zealand.

In her possession, Sister Gabriel had a well-worn hand-written copy of the 1886 booklet by the German, Professor Heidsick: *On the Results of the German Method.* The research was published six years after the Congress of Milan. The thesis argued that the Oral method was a failure. Sister Gabriel obviously had studied the document and treasured it. *Who knows how she had this document in Australia?*

It was essential that educators of Deaf children were well versed in understanding Deaf language, culture and history when making decisions about their education. In 1889 Rev. William Blomefield Sleight, whose father was the head master of the Brighton Institute for the Deaf in Britain, shifted in his thinking and reluctantly signed a document that showed the 1880 Milan decision was not working satisfactorily. Published in *The Times* the document's contention was that the Oral system broke down after school life, and that its pupils not infrequently resorted to writing and the Signed alphabet. The document therefore advocated the *Combined Method* (signed education by means of the fingerspelling alphabet and signs, with articulation and lip reading) being taught as accomplishments to those who showed aptitude for receiving such instruction (October 1889).

In the Waratah Report of 1888 Sister Gabriel expressed her opinion clearly: *We are not convinced of the advisability, or of the advantage, of devoting the limited time allowed for the education of the Deaf and Dumb to the slow and in most cases, the unsatisfactory process of teaching them to articulate a certain number of words or sentences. These must serve them for all the purposes through life. For the accomplishment of this very doubtful feat then to neglect to cultivate their minds with the vast amount of useful information they might acquire, by reading and explanation, in their natural language of sign.*[xv]

It was not long after this in 1892 that Sister Gabriel was sorely tested on the issue. She was informed that a Sister who was trained in the Oral method in England would come to Australia and revamp the educational method at the Waratah School. Sister Gabriel's superiors' were influenced, but by whom, this is a mystery. The plan was that the School would become an Oral school following the worldwide trend. This would mean that the children at Waratah would not be permitted to use their hands to communicate. Various disciplinary methods would be used to stop them.

As I heard of the proposal, I cringed with sadness as I imagined the confusion of the children and the methods of discipline used to stop their innate expression in communication and from the fear of using their hands or having their hands restrained behind their backs – as happened in many parts of the world at that time. However, for whatever reason, this did not eventuate at Waratah at that time, but such restriction was to come sixty years later. Both Kathleen and Don were spared from this – they were educated earlier.

Then I found an important event that happened as recently as the year my mother died in 2010. When I read the statement issued in July of that year at the twenty-first International Congress on Deaf Education in Vancouver Canada, my heart was uplifted. The Chair, Claire Andersen, presented the statement that regretted and rejected the eight resolutions passed at the Milan congress in 1880. It took almost one hundred and thirty years for this formal rejection. The Congress expressed sadness for those who suffered under the *Oralism* method and did not live to see it rejected.

The Congress further stated that globally many Deaf children encountered the general population's perception of being Deaf as one of disability: *The disability mindset contributes directly towards the exclusion and devaluation of all people who are considered different including those who are Deaf. As a result, Deaf citizens in many countries are still hindered and excluded from participation in the larger society. Many are prevented from equal access to decision-making, employment opportunities, and quality education.*[xvi]

So it is that Deaf citizens contribute positively to societies that embrace diversity and creativity. They improve their lot with education, economic activity, politics, arts and literature. The Congress declared that for Deaf people it was an inalienable right that they be acknowledged as a linguistic and cultural minority integral to every society.[xvii]

Sister Gabriel, with her strong conviction that Deaf people had the right to possess their own Deaf language and recognise their own culture, introduced such attitudes into Waratah. She passed on her beliefs to those she trained and mentored, including the Deaf teachers. She was a messenger of glad tidings[xviii] and a pillar of light and strength,[xix] and all her thoughts and interests in life were for her children, who sought her counsel and guidance long after their years of school life. Her great work of hidden worth continued until her death.[xx] She remained the mistress of studies until she died at the age of seventy-three. On her death, the Deaf community deeply lamented, and the *haze of grief* stayed with the family of the Deaf.

During my visit to Waratah I found myself at the Sandgate cemetery as the sun shone and sparkled on the gravestones. At her grave I stood in stillness – it indicated she died on 25 November 1915 – a hundred years ago. I recalled how she came to Australia to work in education for Deaf children beginning in a humble way in *The Cottage* in the convent grounds and then progressing to the grand building of Waratah.

* * *

Not far away was the grave marked Sister Columba Dwyer, who together with Miss Marianne Hanney, was trained as a teacher of Deaf children by Sister Gabriel. Besides being a faithful friend to Sister Gabriel, Sister Columba held great sway and was significant in the development of Waratah and Deaf education. However, I also came to realise the importance of her parents and family and their influence in the early Australian Church – in education and the early Catholic Deaf educational story in particular.

I discovered that William, who was Sister Columba's father, began his teaching career in Albury on the Murray River soon after he and his wife Anastasia arrived from Kilkenny, Ireland, in 1856. As an educator, principal of schools and inspector of the public schools in NSW, William was committed to the Catholic Church and a great advocate for the Dominican sisters. During the period when he and his family lived in Maitland and Newcastle, he saw the Sisters at work and assisted by making the latest in educational development available to them. He developed a high regard for the quality of their education and was well aware of the school for Deaf children. He, indeed, influenced his daughter in education. With his family he remained a strong and active advocate for Waratah.

Dwyer family, circa 1900
Centre: Sister Columba (Kathleen Dwyer)

Sister Columba, born as Kathleen Dwyer in Albury in 1860, was seven years old when the family moved to Maitland and when the Dominican sisters first arrived there from Ireland. The family moved to Newcastle and within three years, the Dominican Sisters established a school there. Living across the street from the convent in Newcastle,[xxi] young Kathleen Dwyer surely came to know Sister Gabriel, Catherine Sullivan and the Deaf students after they arrived in *The Cottage* in 1875. I wonder, as others wondered, did that influence her later involvement in Deaf teaching?[xxii]

By 1878 the Dwyer family had moved a number of times and then settled in Goulburn. Kathleen Dwyer's family knew she could contribute and make her mark in any walk of life, whether it was music, art or literature.[xxiii] In 1881 and at the age of twenty-one, Kathleen, coming from a family of educators, joined the Dominican sisters and was given the name Sister Mary Columba. Interestingly, one of William's granddaughters was Sister Francesca (Kathleen) Dwyer – presumably named Kathleen after her aunt. She joined the Presentation Sisters in Wagga Wagga.

This surprised me on my pilgrim way. I was at school in Wagga Wagga and she taught me – and my sisters![3] And it was her aunt, Sister Columba, who taught my father when he first arrived at Waratah.

Bishop P.V. Dwyer
Maitland NSW

Father Vince Dwyer, Sister Columba's brother, was involved in education very early in his priesthood and became inspector of Catholic schools in the diocese of Maitland. The Deaf students warmed to him as a father when he became a regular visitor as the inspector and when in 1909 he became the first Australian-born bishop in Australia and appointed as Bishop of the Maitland diocese. Later, with Archbishop Daniel Mannix, he further raised awareness that Waratah was a national institute and that bishops were all responsible for raising funds for the school and for ensuring that Deaf children from their dioceses were sent to the school.

Another brother of Sister Columba's, Father Joseph Dwyer, was also involved in education. In 1917, he became the first bishop of the newly established diocese of Wagga Wagga on the Murrumbidgee River. Learning to sign, he too had a fondness for the Deaf students and visited them, as well as his sister at Waratah. In 1939 Agnes Lynch, a Deaf teacher at Waratah wrote that they were *delighted to see their dear friend of many years, Dr J.W. Dwyer of Wagga Wagga, as he entered their schoolroom. He spoke to them in Sign language and seemed very much pleased to see them all.*[xxiv]

It seemed Sister Columba encouraged her family to become fluent in Sign language or did they begin to sign as small children when they lived across the road from *The Cottage* at Newcastle? After she was trained and coached by Sister Gabriel, she was appointed to teach Deaf children who loved her dearly. She became a significant figure in the education and the development at Waratah. In 1895 she was appointed superior at Waratah and directress of the school. With her rare gifts of heart and mind, she was a wise administrator and the motivating influence behind all that was accomplished in Deaf education during her life at Waratah. While she was gentle, she was also strong and filled with enthusiasm. She worked tirelessly and she made known the requirements of Deaf education far and wide, and thus she invited the interest and sympathy of the hierarchy and clergy throughout Australasia.[xxv]

---

[3] Mother M. Francesca Dwyer was well known to Don and Kathleen Wallis, when their three daughters attended the Presentation school, Mt Erin High School, Wagga Wagga in the 1950s and 1960s, but they did not know the connection. The eldest daughter, Carmel Mary, joined the Presentation Sisters in 1960.

At the Educational Congress in Sydney in 1921, Sister Columba as educational directress at Waratah, wrote an article *From Darkness to Light* that was read on her behalf at the Congress. She explained the training of Deaf children and re-enforced that the two most important organs of sense, the hand and the eye, must be used to gain entrance to the mind, so from the hand to the head, and thence to the heart, and these three must work together.[xxvi] She expressed her strong belief that language was the key to the mental and emotional life of Deaf children, as of all human beings.[xxvii] She knew the importance of well-trained teachers of the Deaf.

When Sister Columba died in 1924, the *boys fell on their knees on receiving the sad news, because from their early childhood they had looked upon her as a mother, who reared, educated and trained them before they were handed to the care of the Brothers* – the loss of a mother who could not be replaced. *The gloom of death* was said to pass over St Gabriel's school at the news. The Brothers wrote: *Better or smarter children could not be found in any school for the Deaf. They are a magnificent proof of the splendid education given at Waratah.*[xxviii]

* * *

Miss Marianne Hanney

Miss Marianne Hanney was the other special teacher trained by Sister Gabriel at the same time as Sister Columba. While still walking around the Sandgate cemetery, I followed a group of Deaf adults to Marianne's grave, where they prayed the Hail Mary in Australian-Irish Sign, the prayer she prayed so often with both my father and mother when they were children. I had seen the prayer signed so often.

So who was Marianne and how did she land on the steps at Waratah? On 1 August 1869 Marianne Hanney was born to Irish parents. With her brother and sister her family lived in impoverished circumstances in Paddington NSW. Marianne was three years old when her mother was left with three children to care for after her abusive father died. There was no welfare system in place to support them. After her baby sister died of scarlet fever, and later her mother, Marianne was taken into care in crowded conditions of the Catholic orphanage in Parramatta managed by the Good Samaritan Sisters. Infectious diseases were common. At the age of seven Marianne also contracted scarlet fever and her sickness left her profoundly deaf. Sister Gabriel accepted her at Waratah in 1876 as her sixth student. How she must surely have thought about her own story, when Marianne having already acquired spoken language was just like her at that same age. She knew the experience and the possibility open to Marianne who became a fluent signer in Irish Sign Language.

Marianne was both intelligent and empathic. She was a close friend to Sister Gabriel – they communicated with ease and naturalness, their conversations broad, rich and meaningful. She made sure she read the newspaper each day so she kept abreast of political and social events and personalities and was happy to discuss Australian and international affairs at length.[xxix] They passed on the importance of such discussion to the students in their care and insisted that it helped them mentally and socially.

Trained by Sister Gabriel as the first Deaf lay teacher, Miss Hanney was ever gentle and kind. A very good educator and teaching for fifty years at Waratah, she shared the responsibility in education without a title being given to her, except *Miss Hanney*. She exerted her influence among the students and ex-students of Waratah, the place she called home. While the Sydney Catholic Adult Deaf Association had been established in 1914, Bishop Vince Dwyer wrote to her in 1925 to express his pleasure on the occasion of her election as Vice-President – at a time the organisation was re-energising itself with the support of the Brothers.

In 1938 she suddenly became ill and died within the year, having lived in a Deaf environment all her life. The Dominican Sister Marcella described her as loved, appreciated, respected and revered. In a real sense Miss Marianne Hanney became the *Mother Prioress* of Waratah after Sister Columba's death. She was *so calm, so holy, so dignified...*[xxx]

Miss Hanney, Sisters Gabriel and Columba formed the pioneering trio of teachers of the Deaf in the early story of Catholic Deaf education in Australia. Their spirit leaves an indelible mark on the Waratah that my parents Kathleen and Don knew, a place focused on an education of mind, heart and spirit of Deaf children.

[i] Jan Branson & Don Miller, *The Story of Betty Steele: deaf convict and pioneer*, published Deafness Resources Australia, Petersham NSW, 1995

[ii] Dr Adam Schembri Retrieved 25/09/08: http://www.deafau.org.au/info/info.php

[iii] *http://deafhistoryaustralia.com/2014/08/26/john-carmichaels-works-artworks-for-publications/*

[iv] The Advocate, *Catholics in the Deaf and Dumb Institute*, 11July 1874, p.8

[v] The Advocate, *A Cabra at Newcastle, N.S.W.*, 31 May 1884, p.16

[vi] Elizabeth Hellwig OP, *Up she Gets, for up she must!* published by Dominican Sisters, 2001, p.117

[vii] *Diary of Catherine Sullivan*, held in the University of Newcastle Archives Newcastle

[viii] The Maitland Mercury, *The Deaf and Dumb Institution at Waratah*, 14 August 1888

[ix] The Advocate, *A Cabra at Newcastle, N.S.W.,* 31 May 1884, p.24

[x] Ibid

[xi] The Advocate, *A Cabra at Newcastle, NSW*, 31 May 1884, p.16

[xii] The Advocate, *Diocese of Maitland*, 15 November 1890, p.17

[xiii] *https://en.wikipedia.org/wiki/Second International Congress on Education of the Deaf*
1880 Milan Congress – Resolutions:
1. The Convention, considering the incontestable superiority of articulation over signs in restoring the deaf-mute to society and giving him a fuller knowledge of language, declares that the oral method should be preferred to that of signs in the education and instruction of deaf-mutes.
2. The Convention, considering that the simultaneous use of articulation and signs has the disadvantage of injuring articulation and lip-reading and the precision of ideas, declares that the pure oral method should be preferred.
    Other resolutions passed dealt instructing impoverished Deaf students, how to instruct them orally, organising instructional books for Deaf oral teachers, what the long-term benefits of oral instruction would be expected, the best ages for oral instruction and length of time for instruction, and the plan to phase out signing students.

[xiv] Sinclair, Wayne, *We Did It! The Rejection of Milan Resolutions,* Deaf History International Newsletter 6, Summer & Fall 2010, Nos. 42 & 43 Canada

[xv] *http://www.opeast.org.au/discover-our-story/fx-obituaries.cfm?id=246&loadref=13*

[xvi] Twenty-first International Congress on Deaf Education, Vancouver, Canada
http://wfdeaf.org/news/21st-international-congress-on-the-education-of-the-deaf-iced-in-july-2010-in-vancouver-canada

[xvii] Ibid

[xviii] Ibid

[xix] Ibid

[xx] From the Euology of Sister Gabriel Hogan – Dominican Archives, Strathfield, 1915

[xxi] Sarah Fitzgerald, *Open Minds Open Hearts*, CCOD Publication, Lidcombe NSW 1999 p.77

[xxii] Ibid

[xxiii] Sarah Fitzgerald, *Open Minds Open Hearts*, CCOD publication, Lidcombe, NSW 1999, p.77

[xxiv] From *The Dominican, 1939:75* held in the Dominican Archives, Strathfield

[xxv] Dr. M J O'Reilly Requiem Mass for Sister Gabriel Hogan, Dominican Archives, Strathfield

[xxvi] Article *From Darkness to Light* by Mother Columba Dwyer, Dominican Archives, Strathfield

[xxvii] Ibid

[xxviii] The Annals of St Gabriel's, p.39

[xxix] Sarah Fitzgerald, *Open Minds Open Hearts*, CCOD Publication, Lidcombe NSW 1999, p.102

[xxx] Ibid, p.119

Tribute to Ellen who became Gabriel

You, little Ellen, became deaf,
You embraced Irish Sign Language,
To converse and communicate
Express yourself exquisitely
In lilting signs and patterns.

A woman with zeal and passion
You shared your skill and knowledge
With those who became your Deaf friends
And grasped with deepened awareness
A life committed to Deaf education with the Sisters.

Sister Gabriel, did you ever dream
Of teaching Deaf children
Downunder in Australia?
In 1875, you brought your language with you
Into the Catholic School system in Australia.

Teaching, training and raising children
With a natural flow and flair
That released the energies of love and hope
In the walls and on the steps
Of Newcastle and Waratah.

Little did you know
The importance of your place in my life
As I inherited your Irish Sign Language
In the Australian setting
As my first language.

Less did you know
Of your major contribution
And the significance of your life
In Australian Catholic,
Deaf culture and history.
Thank you.

Bernadette T. Wallis 2015
for the centenary of Sister Gabriel's death.

CHAPTER 18

ON AUSTRALIAN SOIL
WEST OF SYDNEY TOWARD THE HILLS

The Sisters at Waratah knew the importance of extending the education of their Deaf children, both boys and girls, into vocational training. Their own background and experience enabled them to do this for the girls, but they continually worried about the provision of vocational education for boys at Waratah.

It may be that even from the very early days of Waratah the Sisters had concerns about whether they were best placed to fulfil the needs of Deaf boys. Interestingly, I found myself sitting in the Dominican Sisters' archives workroom entranced with an old exercise book that had some pages half torn or torn out. In it was a list of names of the Waratah students – it was a school Register. I was very moved to see my mother's name, Kathleen Walsh, with a little information regarding arrival date, her parents' names and address – but no record of the year she left school.

And where were the boys' names? I was shown pages at the back of the book as if hidden – and yes, silent. My father's name was there without any information as to his age, his parents' names or their address. This was the same for all the boys. Why was that so? Was it that they were not supposed to have boys at Waratah?[i] What was the background to this? Was this an expectation that belonged to St Mary's in Ireland – they only had girls? Was it that the Sisters only ever saw themselves as temporary custodians of the boys – I don't know and may never know! I wonder, if an original register was lost in time, or was it ever created?

Sister Columba had persisted in her efforts for a more appropriate education in a system or school for her Deaf boys. She wrote a letter to her brother, Bishop Vince Dwyer,[ii] expressing her concerns that were of great torment and worry to her. She continued to make her plea to Archbishop Kelly and any church dignitary who visited Waratah. In the end she wanted Cardinal Patrick Moran in Sydney to find trained Christian Brothers from Cabra in Ireland to teach the boys, or at least the bigger boys. Cardinal Moran in turn suggested in 1904 that the Sisters organise a special branch of their establishment as a temporary institution[iii] for the boys and that an experienced man be employed in immediate charge. This did not happen – possibly because the Sisters knew it would not work.

However, in 1909 an arrangement was made for two of the boys to transfer to the vocational training section at St Vincent's Westmead Boy's Home in western Sydney. This arrangement was a joint venture with the St Vincent de Paul Society and the Marist Brothers. Following negotiations with the *Institution for the Deaf, Dumb and Blind* it was then agreed that a special teacher for the Deaf boys would be employed at St Vincent's Home so the boys could complete a trade. As more Deaf boys transferred to St Vincent's Home the project appeared to be successful to the extent that a new extension was built for them. But without staff who were specialised in Deaf education and who had an understanding of Deaf language and culture, it did not work in the long term.

The Waratah Institute Report of 1920 noted that the superiors of the Marist Brothers visited Waratah, presumably to discuss the issues relating to their experience at Westmead. A few days later, the Australian Christian Brothers' provincial, Brother Jerome Barron, came to Waratah – presumably to discuss the setting up a school specifically for Deaf boys. Accompanying him was Brother Dominic O'Shea who was already in Australia from Ireland and understood the issues of Deaf education.

Archbishop M Kelly
Sydney NSW

Soon Archbishop Kelly returned to Sydney from Ireland and then made known the decision that a school for Deaf boys would be built. At the same time he established a committee to find a suitable location for such a school.[iv] He also organised advertisements and articles in *The Freeman's Journal* in Sydney and *The Advocate in Melbourne* appealing for funds.

In November 1921, in the name of the Catholic Church in Sydney, Archbishop Kelly together with the Vicar General, Patrick Coonan, Father Thomas Phelan and Brother Barron signed off as joint tenants, for the purchase of thirty-five acres of land with the *Southleigh* mansion, which became the temporary *St Gabriel's School for Deaf Boys*. Also included were a few acres from neighbouring land for access to future street frontage. The sale price of the property was £7,450. It became the land on which the anticipated new *St Gabriel's School for Deaf Boys* was built.

I found that while the main debt for Waratah was cleared by 1921, they still required funding for the support of the children, for renovations at the mansion and for the new building. Stirring descriptions in the Catholic paper about the Deaf children called on the faith and generosity of everyday people. Obviously a chord touched their hearts. They responded generously through donations. Deaf children were *silently and unconsciously appealing to us to unveil for them the mysteries of their own existence, the world around them and of the world to come, claiming at our hands the light and knowledge of Christianity.*[v]

* * *

Further into my discoveries, I visited Castle Hill and was driven through the gates and down the tree-lined driveway of St Gabriel's. I imagined the young boys and the big boys all signing to each other while involved in sports, including my father, Don. I could see him going in the chook house or in the piggery, riding the faithful horse or working in the trades' room. *But what had happened on this land and around Castle Hill prior to the arrival of the boys?*

Cumberland Argus and Fruitgrowers Advocate (Parramatta, NSW): 26 Feb. 1921

ON THE RICH FRUITFUL HILLS. ORCHARD (Citrus) of 20 acres, and good five-roomed COTTAGE. Citrus, 1•7 acres; summer fruit, 1 acre; trees from 7 yrs. up; perm. water supply; £500 crop on now: 3/4 hour's run from Parramatta. Packing-shed, stables, cart-shed, sulky-shed; stock & plant, 2 horses, cart, dray, plough, spray pump, chaffcutter, sets harness, harrows, hoes, spades. Terms... £2000

[1]

White settlement in the Castle Hill district took place as early as 1791. The boys may or may not have known its colonial history, including the Battle of Vinegar Hill in 1804 where Irish convicts were killed and many captured by troops in the rebellion. Two escaped convicts from the Castle Hill Government Farm forced entry into the mansion at *Southleigh* and were executed for assault on the occupants.

---

[1] *http://www.thehills.nsw.gov.au/Library/Library-e-Resources/Local-Studies-Family-History/Historical-Subdivision-Plans-of-The-Hills-Shire/Castle-Hill-and-Glenhaven-Subdivision-Plans*

A few years beforehand, on 11 November 1799, Governor Philip had granted 100 acres of land that became *Southleigh* to James Thomas John Bean, a free settler from England. But he was not a good farmer. While the land titles showed that a number of different people were subsequently in possession of the *Southleigh* property, a section of about thirty acres was sold off with the *Southleigh* mansion which was owned by Mr Rhule from 1919 – 1921 just prior to being bought for St Gabriel's. According to the *Annals of St Gabriel's*, he had lost his wealth due to the living of the high life by his wife and family.[vi]

* * *

The new building of St Gabriel's was designed as a replica of St Joseph's School for Deaf Boys at Cabra, back in Ireland. Brother Barron appeared at St Gabriel's functions and reported on the financial progress at regular intervals. At the official opening on 6 May 1923 – Don was there as an eleven year old – donations were expected to significantly reduce all of the debts. Although over £16,000 was contributed, a debt of £10,000 was still upon them. The building program continued to accommodate the increasing number of Deaf boys, but more workspaces were required for teaching the various trades which were offered at the school.

The Bishops not only took on the responsibility with authority and knowledge, they were forthright advocates. They gave encouragement and spoke of the value of the work. They each wrote letters to the priests in their dioceses requesting that firstly, appeals be made in their parishes for funds for both building and the care of the children, and secondly, that they search for any Deaf children in their parishes and encourage the parents to send them to the Catholic Deaf schools for their education.

Research took me into the tedious work of examining Catholic newspaper archival material. I found that in Victoria, Archbishop Daniel Mannix of Melbourne wrote a public letter to the priests in February 1923 when St Gabriel's School was just established and prior to some of the boys still to be transferred from Waratah:

Dear Rev Father,

The Irish Christian Brothers have come to supply a long-felt need for the Catholics of Australia. Under the immediate patronage of the Archbishop of Sydney, they have established at St Gabriel's Castle Hill, Sydney, a home for the education of the Catholic Deaf and Dumb boys of the Commonwealth. Hitherto, the Dominican Sisters at Waratah have been doing whatever was possible for the boys as well as for the girls. But the Sisters have long been anxiously looking for the coming of the Brothers to relieve them of the charge of the boys, especially the more grown boys.

The Brothers have been for many years successfully engaged in this work in Ireland. I am confident that the results will be equally satisfactory here. In spite of their hard lot and their great patience, the deaf…children are tractable and intelligent as a rule; they can receive and profit by a full course of religious training; and they can fit themselves for most of the trades or occupations to which other boys and girls turn for a living. Left in their own homes, the plight of these poor children is truly deplorable…but in the institutions conducted by the Sisters and Brothers, the welfare of the children in this world and in the other will be in safe and devoted hands…

I believe the initial expense of setting up this home will run into something close on £20,000 and, of course, the annual upkeep will also be considerable. But all the Bishops of Australia have promised to help and to ask their generous-hearted people to help, so the burden will be comparatively light…

It was the intention of the Brothers to depute one of their number to call on the people in their homes and to take subscriptions. But that would be a slow and laborious process. I have thought it better to appoint Sunday 25th February, for a collection in all the churches for St. Gabriel's Deaf Mute Institution. Brother O'Connell who is in charge of this appeal will supply in due time to the different pastors special envelopes for taking up the subscriptions. You will kindly request one or more of the parish societies to undertake the work of distributing these collection envelopes at the Church on Sunday February 28th. Commending this most urgent and charitable work to you and hoping that you will kindly commend it to your people…[vii]

…The obligation upon us here in Melbourne to contribute towards the new institution was recently brought home to me. I visited St. Gabriel's and found that among the boys already under the care of the Brothers in their new home, the majority of boys are from the diocese of Melbourne. And I may say too that happier, or more intelligent, or better-trained boys one could not hope to meet and I am sure that we have in this diocese other boys waiting for the completion of St. Gabriel's, to place themselves under the care of the Brothers. We, therefore, must do our share to help the Brothers in this new institution…Commending this most urgent and charitable work to you, and hoping that you will commend it to your people…[viii]

Don was one of the boys of whom the Archbishop spoke. My grandparents, Abe and Emma, read the Catholic paper, *The Advocate*, in their parish of Yea. Yes, they were glad of Archbishop Mannix's comments. They knew he was acutely aware a number of the Deaf children came from Victoria. In 1927, there were eleven girls at Waratah and twelve boys at St Gabriel's. The total number of students for Waratah was sixty-one and for St Gabriel's it was fifty-one.[ix]

In August 1926 the Irish Brothers at St Gabriel's took the opportunity to educate the general Catholic population through the Catholic media. They were keen to remind them of the history of the Catholic Deaf education in Europe and Ireland with the title, *The Establishment of Deaf Mute Schools*. The article began:

How they (Deaf Mute Schools) came to be established is an interesting story, and one which should be known to every Catholic lay man and woman in an era like ours, when so many thinking people outside the fold are keen to find out the part the Catholic Church has taken in every movement for the betterment of humanity.

Prior to the 18th century the education of the Deaf was looked upon as almost impossible; but in 1712 was born at Versailles, in France, Charles Michel de L'Epee, who became illustrious prelate of the church, the originator of the Sign Language practically as it is used today, and the founder of the first school for the Deaf – the National Institute for the Deaf and Dumb at Paris.

The methods thus originated and taught in the famous Paris school, were subsequently introduced into Normandy by the Sisters of Le Bon Pasteur. To their school for deaf-mutes at Caen were sent two of the Dominican nuns from Cabra, Dublin to study the system. On the return of these Irish nuns in 1846, the Cabra Institution for Deaf mutes was launched – the first Catholic one of its kind in the United Kingdom.[x]

Understanding the background of St Gabriel's, people were encouraged to financially support the venture. This extended to many ordinary generous people. In Sydney in 1926, Archbishop Kelly presided at St Gabriel's annual meeting of friends and subscribers, which was attended by three thousand people. The director, Brother O'Farrell, read the balance sheet, which indicated the net liability as £3,118/14/2. The collection amounted to £800.[xi]

In 1927 at St Gabriel's everyone benefitted by a new kitchen! *How wonderful!* The Brothers publicised the debt incurred with both the education of the boys and the plans for more new buildings.[xii] In 1928 student numbers increased. Funding for their care was a priority, so building developments were delayed. The buildings included in the original plans were only half erected due to funds still being required for the steady increase in the number of boarders and *due to the impossibility of carrying out the building work in a manner suitable to the peculiar circumstances found in schools for Deaf children. Thus the present buildings proved quite inadequate.*[xiii]

* * *

Anger fired easily among the Irish hierarchy, especially where there was injustice by the Australian government in the nineteenth century and into the twentieth century. The lack of government financial support for the good works the church undertook was evident. *Not one penny was given for the work of the Christian Brothers and the Dominican Sisters*[xiv] in the education and maintenance of Deaf children until the mid-twentieth century.

How interesting then when I find that in England at the same time, the local government paid from £56 to £64 for the support of a Deaf child to all schools, whether it was a Catholic school or not. In Ireland, North and South, local councils contributed £20 per child towards their maintenance. In America, the payment was £77 per head to support Deaf children in their various schools.[2] How unjust and how foolish a Federal Government policy in Australia! *The Brothers and the Sisters save these children from being a burden later on in mental asylums and state hospitals.*[xv] No salary was asked by the Brothers for their welfare – all donations went to the boys' welfare or the building project.[xvi] It was the same for the Sisters – they did not receive a salary.

* * *

Archbishop Kelly, an outspoken advocate, became a great friend to the Deaf community and was a significant influence in St Gabriel's continuing growth. He insisted on visits to St Gabriel's regularly to encourage the Deaf boys and their teachers, even in his declining years. He remembered that in the joy of the foundation, accolades were made that honoured those who had selected the site, which was described *as a soul-stirring abode to inspire the Deaf boys with all that was noble and elevating.* He added that *the beauties of nature in this locality, enchanting the human mind, fascinated youth and caused the boys to yearn in later years for something better than worldly life.*[xvii]

When the Dominican sisters celebrated the golden jubilee of Catholic Deaf education in Australia in 1925, they were acknowledged for their zealous work of years of painstaking effort: *Consider what a noble work has been done. Over 300 Catholic boys and girls had settled down comfortably in life. The children benefitted greatly as they were enabled to communicate...to hear with the eye and to speak with their hands by means of gestures and the written language.*[xviii]

The Dominican sisters with the school at Waratah set the scene for St Gabriel's, which had now begun their journey of the education of Deaf boys in Australia. Both these schools provided the setting and cultural experience for the education of both my father and mother in the 1920s. *Where to from here?*

---

[2] In Africa, where the Dominican nuns had taught since 1862, the African Government by 1935 paid for half the loans raised for buildings and half of the cost of equipment.

[i] Johnston, B.J., Memories of St Gabriel's 1922-1927, p.7

[ii] Sarah Fitzgerald, *Open Minds Open Hearts*, CCOD Publication, Lidcombe NSW 1999, p.93

[iii] Sarah Fitzgerald, *Open Minds Open Hearts, Letter from Cardinal Moran to Bishop Dwyer 4 May 1904*, CCOD Publication, Lidcombe NSW 1999, p.93

[iv] The Advocate, 14 April 1921

[v] The Advocate, 'For the Deaf and Dumb – St Gabriel's New School, Castle Hill', 11 June 1925, p.7

[vi] Annals of St Gabriel's 1922, p.9

[vii] The Advocate, *God's Silent Ones – The Archbishop Urges Supporting of Appeal*, 16 February 1923, p.27

[viii] The Advocate, *God's Silent Ones – The Archbishop Urges*, 2 February 1923, p.27

[ix] The Advocate, 'Ephpheta Sunday – Patronal Feast of the Catholic Deaf and Dumb', 11 August 1927, p.17

[x] The Advocate, Australian Catholic Institutions for Deaf-Mutes', 1 August 1927, p.2
Regular articles on Waratah and St Gabriel's appeared in The Advocate:
In 1921, when the land was bought for St Gabriel's School an article was headed, *Deaf and Dumb Institutes – His Grace's Appreciation*, which expressed Archbishop Michael Kelly's plans as coming to fruition. On 2 February 1923, when Don was eleven and Kathleen was seven, the heading of an article stated, *God's Silent Ones – the Archbishop Urges*, which implored parents that their Deaf children attend the Catholic Deaf Schools. In 1926 the heading stood as *Catholic Institutions for Mutes – a Word to Parents of Deaf Children* and *The Patronal Feast of the Deaf – Aid the Afflicted in our Catholic Institutions*. All the articles followed similar themes. In the following year were headings, *A Grand Work for Charity – St Gabriel's School for Deaf Boys* and *Deaf and Dumb Institutes*. A further heading read, *Our Catholic Deaf and Dumb Children – An Institution that Cares for and Trains them*. In 1929 the article title was *Deaf and Dumb Collection, Deaf and Dumb Institutions – Appeal supported by His Grace, Aid the Afflicted in our Catholic Institutions, Deaf and Dumb Institutes, Our Catholic Deaf and Dumb Children – An Institution that Cares for and Trains Them.*

[xi] The Advocate, 4 September 1926

[xii] The Advocate, '*Australian Catholic Institutions for Deaf-Mutes*', 11 August 1927, p.17

[xiii] The Advocate, '*St Gabriel's School for Deaf Boys*', 2 February 1928, p.31

[xiv] The Advocate, *A Work of National Importance – The Training of Australian Deaf and Dumb Children*, 4 February 1925, p.1

[xv] Ibid, p.4

[xvi] The Advocate, Waratah Deaf and Dumb Institute, 1 November 1934, p.10

[xvii] The Christian Brothers' Educational Record, 1923 p.208

[xviii] The Advocate, 'The Patronal Feast of the Deaf', 29 July 1926, p.17

CHAPTER 19

IN VICTORIA
THE CATHOLIC DEAF COMMUNITY

I had always known that Deaf people gathered easily for companionship and conversation through story-telling. After my discoveries overseas and in Australia, I was particularly interested in the adult Catholic Deaf story in Victoria and especially where my parents and their friends were involved.

In Sydney there has always been a greater population of Australian-Irish Signing Deaf people than in Melbourne, because of the proximity to Waratah and St Gabriel's. Some searching on the Australian scene showed me that in 1914, the first Catholic Deaf Association in Australia was established in Sydney with Deaf leaders in the community, Arthur Powell, Marianne Hanney and Esther Hutchison. Arthur was an ex-student from Waratah, whose love for Waratah never wavered. After his schooling at Waratah, he was one of the students who went to Westmead to do a trade. Marianne Hanney established the alumni connections from Waratah and was faithful in her networking and contact with ex-students. Esther Hutchison, another Deaf teacher and later Agnes Lynch and others, were mentors who exerted a profound effect on the ex-students and continued to contact them by letter.

The Sisters and Brothers were key people as they continued to develop a strong network in the adult Catholic Deaf community. They kept contact with ex-students and extended an outreach to them to care for them spiritually. They encouraged them and gave them current news of Waratah and St Gabriel's. They gathered them together for annual retreats and reunions. These events were important social occasions at Waratah and Sydney. Later, the Dominican sisters sent out the magazine *Veritas*, edited by Sister Madeleine Egan in her retirement.

* * *

I wanted to find out more of the story in Victoria and how the Catholic Deaf community kept their spirits alive. *How did they care for one another — and celebrate?* So I found myself wandering the highways and byways of my mind as I sat in libraries and archive rooms, trawling the Internet. Then I had fascinating discussions with various people over coffee and picked up snippets of information that added to my understanding of my Deaf heritage.

Deaf societies and clubs and where groups of Deaf people gathered were most valuable and significant, because they contributed to the exchange of sign and understanding of signs – the development of Sign language in Australia. In these spaces for Deaf people as a community they were informed on various issues, and they shared news and views. They met socially to develop friendships and find future life partners. As they formed friendships, interest groups emerged whether for Deaf sports, mothers' clubs or family holidays together.

In Victoria the Waratah and St Gabriel's ex-students retained strong links with their school. In 1918 after Sister Gabriel died and before Sister Columba's death in 1924, fourteen women and men who were ex-Waratah students from Victoria returned to Waratah for a spiritual retreat given by Redemptorist priest Father John Treacy.[i] They were all Australian-Irish language signers. They formed a solid sub-cultural group, who identified as Catholic, Deaf and as the unique Australian-Irish Sign language group in Victoria.

In 1922 St Gabriel's School for Deaf Boys opened. After the first twelve months Brother Dominic O'Shea, who was one of the first Brothers at the school, moved to Melbourne where he taught at St Kilda. Together with the ex-student of Waratah, Annie Holcroft, he seems to have been initially responsible for bringing the Catholic Deaf community together in an organised way in Melbourne. Annie was a leader in the community and committed to supporting the ex-students' wellbeing.

In the Annals of St Gabriel's in 1924, I found that the first formal Catholic Deaf Association in Victoria was established at a meeting held at St Vincent Boys' Orphanage, South Melbourne, where Brother O'Shea lived. On his arrival in Melbourne he had immediately made contact with Deaf people and he continued his interest in the Deaf community. This notation refers to Christmas 1923:

At Christmas time the Victorian Deaf held their first meeting in the South Melbourne orphanage. Bro. D. O'Shea was elected President, Miss A. Holcroft, Secretary, and a strong committee of ladies and gentlemen. It was arranged that monthly meetings were to be held.[ii]

A year later the first retreat for the Catholic Deaf community was organised and held in Melbourne between Christmas 1924 and New Year at St Vincent's. The Carmelite priest, Father Robert Power, gave the three-day retreat, with his sermons being interpreted by the Brothers,[iii] Brothers Allen and Esmonde from St Gabriel's. It meant that the retreat was in Australian-Irish Sign Language, which further indicated that the retreat was primarily and exclusively for the ex-students of both Waratah and St Gabriel's who understood the language.

The retreat was conducted over a full weekend from Friday night until Sunday afternoon. Archbishop Mannix came to give them a blessing and encouraged the adult Deaf to love their own association and to make the retreat well. He promised them that the needs of the Catholic Deaf community would be attended to as soon as possible – the main issue being a place of their own where they could meet. The Deaf adults were overjoyed and thanked him for his *fatherly solicitude*. A telling report[iv] was recorded:

First Retreat: The members of the Australian Catholic Deaf Association assembled in great numbers at the beautiful oratory at St. Vincent de Paul's Boys Orphanage to make the Triduum, which was conducted by Very Rev. Prior Power, O.C.C. All the sermons were interpreted in the Sign language of the deaf by a Christian Brother from St Gabriel's School, Castle Hill, near Sydney. They were followed by the silent ones with rapt attention, and the proof of the usefulness of a retreat for the deaf was evident by the retreatants all approaching the Holy Sacraments and the Blessed Eucharist. The final lecture was delivered at 3.00 o'clock when all the members renewed their Baptismal vows and resolved to be faithful to the rules of the Catholic Deaf Association. This was followed by the crowning blessing of Jesus of the Blessed Sacrament. They concluded with such a happy reunion for the retreat, the first given in the beautiful Sign language which is the best of all mediums of communication of the deaf. The adult deaf wish to express their best thanks to the Very Rev. Prior Power for attending to their spiritual wants with such fatherly care. To the Rev. Brother O'Neill, superior of the orphanage, they are also deeply indebted for allowing them the use of the oratory during the retreat, and for the use of the schoolroom for the monthly meetings of the association. Now that the Christian brothers have done a long-needed good work for the Catholic deaf in organizing them into one association, it remains for some of the generous Catholic laity of Melbourne to provide a suitable clubroom for the children of silence so that they may meet often for conversation and recreation. There can be no more noble work than to safeguard the helpless deaf who are so much cut off from society through the loss of hearing and speech.

Deaf Retreat in Melbourne December1924: Brothers Allen and Esmonde at each end of back row. Father Robert Power centre front row; 4th from right is Annie Holcroft; left in front row is Dorrie Campbell (aged 23). Dorrie's brother who was a professional photographer is credited with the photo.

I was particularly interested that Dorrie Campbell[v] at this first retreat in Victoria and her later husband Herbert Wilson, parents of Michael and Geraldine, were friends of my parents and visited our farm in Berrigan. Dorrie looked to Annie Holcroft as a mentor and they both knew my aunt, Marie, being closer in age to her. How interesting too, as I discovered in the next article with a photo of the new committee of the Catholic Deaf Association that Dorrie's father, who was not Deaf, was elected as secretary and Annie Holcroft remained on the committee.

Brother Allen stayed in Melbourne for the holidays visiting Deaf people and their families. He was present later in January when the Catholic Deaf Association gathered for their monthly meeting, which was reported in *The Advocate* 8 January 1925 in an article titled, *Our Melbourne Catholic Deaf*. It seems that his presence gave a unifying momentum. He then returned on the train to St Gabriel's with the boys returning to begin the school year:

The members of the Catholic Deaf Association assembled in great numbers at St Vincent de Paul's Orphanage to farewell the Christian Brothers who came from New South Wales to give the adult deaf a retreat and to organize them into a society of their own for their mutual comfort and benefit. They were addressed by Rev. Brother Allen on the need and advantages of being united as one body for the promotion of their spiritual and temporal welfare.

The better to secure this grand object, a secretary, a treasurer, and a committee of four members were elected by the adult deaf themselves. It will be their duty to assist every Catholic deaf mute they know of, and also to arrange for monthly meetings, socials, etc. for the members. Rev. Brother O'Shea of St Kilda Brothers' College, will conduct the monthly instructions at Middle Park Hall on the last Sunday of each month at 3 o'clock.

The secretary elected was Mr J. Campbell, with Mr Bryan as treasurer, and Mr P.J. Bourke, Mr O'Driscoll, Mrs. Muir and Miss Holcroft on the committee. The members paid a high tribute to Mr P. Bourke and Miss Holcroft for their noble work for the association during the past year.

A special vote of thanks was passed to the Brothers from St Gabriel's School for their fruitful work amongst the Catholic deaf of Melbourne, and for their self-sacrifice in attending to the needs of members.

It was resolved to make every effort to have a Catholic club opened for the Melbourne deaf as soon as possible. It is hoped some generous benefactor will come to their aid in providing for this pressing need. Thrice blest shall be he who thus helps to safeguard the helpless children of silence in the faith of their childhood.[vi]

At this meeting, the second elected committee for the Catholic Deaf Association took place and the venue for instructions in the future was announced as Middle Park hall. Meetings took place at 3.00pm on Sundays each month – the custom was established. The Association became operational.

Catholic Deaf and Dumb Association Committee elected in January 1925:
Left to Right: Mr W. O'Bryan Hon. Treasurer; Mr J.A. Campbell, Hon. Secretary; Mr J. Bourke, Mr D. Driscoll.
Sitting: Miss Annie Holcroft, Brother Allen, Mrs Adam Muir

* * *

The Archbishop's personal encounters with Deaf people gave him an acute awareness of the need to advocate for them in Melbourne and on the national scene.

In 1934, three years after he left school, Don attended his first spiritual retreat in Melbourne at the time of the Eucharistic Congress. He attended with ex-students of Waratah and St Gabriel's, many of whom were his friends and part of his Deaf family. At the St Vincent de Paul Orphanage in South Melbourne,

Retreat by Father Dominic Phillips held at St Vincent De Paul Orphanage. December 1934.
Don: Back row, fourth from right

Vincentian priest, Father Dominic Phillips, presented the retreat. He was an Australian-Irish Sign Language signer, whose sister was deaf. Father Phillips became chaplain for the Deaf community in Sydney in 1936 and was much loved by the community.

In September 1936 Father Dominic Phillips conducted another retreat, this time at St Vincent's South Melbourne. Don and Marie, his sister, were there. Charlie, Don's brother, was still at school but joined his siblings for retreats in later years. During the 1930s and 1940s retreats took place at various Catholic centres including the Jesuit centre at Loyola in Watsonia, the Carmelite centre at Middle Park and in Essendon, sometimes as separate retreats for Deaf men, and similarly for Deaf women. At some stage during this period of time, retreats and talks were interpreted into Australian-British Sign Language, not yet called Auslan – the language that was more inclusive of all Deaf people and not only those who attended Waratah and St Gabriel's. From the 1940s this was the situation for all interpreting for Church services in Victoria. However, it did exclude those who only had Australian-Irish Sign Language, including my mother Kathleen, possibly one of the reasons she did not attend these earlier retreats.

At the retreats, presentations were given on various life topics for information and to encourage good behaviour as Catholics living in the world. They included topics on gossip[vii], sex and marriage. Don endured the signed talks and while he did not always comprehend the theological content, the moral content was clear to him: Don't talk badly about one another. Don't have sex before marriage. Marry a Catholic and be responsible for your family. While the signed talks were often a chore, he did respond with enthusiasm to the spiritual and devotional aspects of the days when they knelt in the chapel or church for Benediction as a prayer of blessing. Don appreciated the beauty in churches with their timber and artwork, and with the many candles and abundance of incense, which involved the senses both of sight and smell.

Don enjoyed the social and community aspects, too, as they ate food together and conversed with one another about their lives and interests, whether it was sport, work, politics, the developments in Sign language or news of the Church, Australia and the world. They went to great lengths to renew contacts and maintain friendships – and express concern for one another in times of difficulty.

* * *

In Melbourne, those who attended Waratah and St Gabriel's and the Catholic ex-students from the local Victorian School for Deaf children integrated gradually. The cross-fertilisation of language was evident especially from the 1930s and 1940s, although ex-students from Waratah and St Gabriel's were especially attracted to one another because of being a sub-cultural distinct minority group with their own language – their comfort zone for communication.

With two different Deaf languages side by side in Australia, tension sometimes existed between the two groups. The Australian-Irish language group being the minority was expected to learn the dominant language after leaving school, even though often among themselves they still signed their *one-handed* Sign language for two main reasons – to feel quite at home in their language of origin or to have a private conversation. Sometimes in the community and in their own families, the language was referred to as a *secret language* and used as a private language. Sometimes non-users were envious and could not join in the conversation or know what was being conveyed. Others resented the use of the language in the visual company of those who did not understand it. Sometimes it was labelled as an inferior language, which was hurtful to those who belonged to the language group. There were no qualified Australian-Irish Sign Language interpreters in Australia and few who could interpret accurately in such situations.

* * *

As a young woman in the 1930s and 1940s, Marie Wallis took a significant role in the Catholic Deaf Association. As indicated earlier, her mentor in Melbourne was Annie Holcroft, who had been the first secretary of the Catholic Deaf Association and who was very involved in the Catholic community.

Marie with her sure, simple and intelligent faith and with her thoughtful and forever open mind entered into conversations with the educated local priests. When Father O'Connor, her parish priest in Seymour, came to *Wallis' Café,* he enjoyed Marie's cooking – eating a pie and tomato sauce. But he was challenged by the young woman's intelligent questions on her foolscap paged writing pad.[viii] With a priest-friend, he visited her old school at Waratah. He reported to Marie's friends that he knew Marie as well

Marie Wallis, circa 1940

as his right hand and spoke very highly of her as a *good exemplary Catholic girl.*[ix] She not only attended Mass on Sundays and refrained from meat on Fridays, as was the Catholic tradition, but was also interested in, and wanted to know more about her faith.

Father Johnny Pierce was one at the receiving end of Marie's questions. Marie's brother, Jack, who attended Assumption College at Kilmore and was ordained as a priest in 1932, brought his contemporary school mate, Johnny Pierce, to meet the family in the Café at Seymour, where Marie had conversations with him too with pen and paper. She had many pages of conversations with him, including her questions of faith.

Out of her commitment to the Catholic Church and her insights into the Deaf community, Marie asked Father Johnny: *Why doesn't the Catholic Church give us our own priest as a chaplain?* He had no answer. She summed up his skills for the job. He was open, patient, understanding, expressive, sociable and compassionate, and ready to learn from others, including people who were different.

Father John Pierce
First appointed Chaplain for the
Deaf community in Victoria.
Photo: The Pierce Family

When Father Phillips from Sydney visited in Melbourne, she sat with him for two hours at St Joseph's presbytery in Malvern and discussed the issue of a chaplain for Victoria. Not afraid of the hierarchy, she wrote to Archbishop Mannix.

Could they not have a priest dedicated to the Deaf community? She requested that a priest chaplain for the Catholic Deaf of Victoria be appointed and suggested that the person be Father John Pierce – and so it came to pass. The request was granted in 1936. With Father Phillips present, the first meeting with Father Pierce and the Deaf community took place at St Francis Hall, Elizabeth Street in the city.

Marie taught him much about the Deaf way of life and showed him the basics in the *two-hand* fingerspelling and some basics in sign. He was never able to sign the Australian-Irish Sign Language.

The Deaf community appreciated him as their spiritual director and valued the continuity of a chaplain, as well as his capacity to learn to communicate and be among Deaf people. With other Deaf men in Melbourne, Don played golf with him – an informal way for Father Pierce to enter the Deaf community, learn the language and culture and to be accepted by the community. At this point Don became treasurer of the Catholic Deaf Association so had significant encounters with Father Pierce.

Before Father Pierce enlisted to serve the country between 1940 and 1945 as a military chaplain during World War II, he celebrated *Ephpheta Sunday*[x] with the Catholic Deaf Association. He then spent time in Singapore and Malaysia, where he was noted for his courage and his prized common sense. His injuries affected him considerably and resulted in the amputation of a leg. On his return the Deaf community honoured him as *their* War hero.

February 5, 6, and 7 in 1944 Retreat at *Loyola*, Watsonia conducted by Father Templeton CM:
Standing: J. Murphy, G. Kemple, Harold Fulton, Don Wallis, Charles Wallis, A. Lauretig, J. Thompson, M. Clarke, A. Wighton and N. Fiorini.
Sitting: W. Bukcley, V. Wilson, W. O'Bryan, H. Wilson, Father Templeton CM, Father O'Collins SJ, Father Fennessy, A. Anderson, N. Durston and G. Boyce.
Front: Child Fiorini

So what was *Ephpheta Sunday*? *Ephpheta!* I had known this Aramaic word since I was a child – not that I realised it was Aramaic. Nor did I then know the origins or meaning of *Ephpheta – Be Open.*

The word *Ephpheta* is used in the gospel story of Jesus encountering and healing the Deaf man.[xi] The passage has many layers of meaning – and many pages of exegetical studies have been written on it. Jesus says, *Ephpheta,* and puts his finger into the ear of the Deaf man. Touching the Deaf man so intimately – how is he communicating and relating to him? Besides opening the ear of the Deaf man, I asked myself, what else Jesus was really saying to those who were with him. Here was a Deaf man ostracised from society, cut off from the life of the community. Surely Jesus was also saying, *Be Open! See! Do not cut off, do not reject – anyone.* In the Deaf community they understood it to mean *open your minds and hearts* – to all of life and to one another. Jesus also offers, *I have come that they may have life, life in all its fullness.*[xii] Celebrate!

I discovered that Pope Pius X, who served as Pope from 1903 to 1914, approved and encouraged the celebration day for the Deaf to be the eleventh Sunday after the feast of Pentecost each year. This usually fell in August. The occasion provided a special opportunity to raise awareness in society of the richness of Deaf people's lives and to highlight their presence at a global level. That is how the annual Deaf celebration day became known as *Ephpheta Sunday.* Their sign for *Ephpheta* was formed with the letter 'E' from the Australian-Irish alphabet, with the hand facing outwards making a circle at chest level. On this day throughout the world, Catholic Deaf people and the community celebrate their language, culture and faith – their story.

It was an important day for my parents – the day in the year when they planned and made every effort to attend the Deaf celebration, however difficult their circumstances – even travelling from the country after doing the milk round.

In Melbourne, *Ephpheta Sunday* was a day Archbishop Mannix could see the Deaf community in action. Each year he arrived dressed in his flowing robes to give a blessing to each individual person present, including the children and babies. I remember as a five-year-old standing in anticipation in the long queue for my turn for acknowledgement and for the Archbishop's blessing. I remember the blessing – I remember each person kissing the ring on his finger and giving a polite bow of thank you. Blessings over, everyone followed their faith leader in procession to St Francis Church next door for Benediction with flowers, candles and incense. No interpreter was present and while there was music, it was a silent but sensory faith celebration.

And as my knowledge has expanded through my closer involvement with the Deaf community, *Ephpheta* has become increasingly important to me. On this day Deaf people quenched their thirst for communication, filled their minds with new thoughts and nourished their spirits with hope on the journey of sustaining life friendships. I saw it as a child and knew it as an adult – opening to life around them. They celebrated well.

Archbishop Mannix, who did not sign, had taken a spiritual fatherly interest in the Victorian boys and their families after he visited St Gabriel's School at Castle Hill back in the 1920s. He was very pleased now to see a community of faith-based people, who had a conscious or unconscious yearning for God and who reached out to one another in genuine friendship, as goodness and love impelled them to do?[xiii] He confirmed generations of children in Deaf families and remembered them. He knew Marie, Don and Charlie from childhood. He had come to know all of the Wallis family in different contexts. He saw in the community the fruits of a wholesome Deaf education, where Deaf people had become independent and lived full lives as they contributed to society. He observed those who became leaders in the Melbourne Catholic Deaf community.

Victorian Catholic Deaf Community, circa winter of 1945:
Back: __, Kevin Leonard, Chas Hennessy, Tony Lavtig, __
Second row: __, Harold Fulton and daughter Mary, Norm Begg, Jim Hennessy, __, Max Clarke, Ron McKay, Neil Durston, __, John O'Keefe, __, __
Third row: 5th from left Bill O'Bryan and 5th from right Marie Fulton (Wallis)
Sitting front: Alex Anderson, Eileen O'Bryan, Brother Adrian Dean, Father John Pierce, Father Bridgewater, Emma Wallis (Don's mother), Olive Anderson and Gertie Hennessy

Victorian Catholic Deaf Community, circa 1940:
Back: ——, Thompson, ——, Ray Kemble, ——, Bill O'Bryan, Dick Chaundry, —— Jack Brundell, ——, ——, ——, ——, ——, Max Clarke, John O'Keefe
Middle: Kevin Leonard, Dorothea McKay (Eileen O'Hagen), —— fifth from right: Marie Wallis, third from right: Annie Holcroft? Second from right: Ron McKay
Front: Neil Durston, Child, Kath O'Gorman, Bryan (O'Gorman), ——, Alan Wilson, Brother Esmonde, Father John Pierce, Archbishop Mannix,
Father Bridgewater, Brother O'Farrell, Alex Anderson, Gertie Hennessy, Don Wallis and unknown child

What about leadership in the community? I wondered. Leadership was always a juggling process in the community – a fine balance was required. Sometimes leaders were hearing people, often a relative or someone skilled in Sign language. Often they were Deaf people who had a little hearing and speech – it was considered easier for them to liaise with hearing people. Rarely did a profoundly Deaf person emerge to take leadership – either deferring to those who had some speech and hearing, or they were not perceived as capable of leadership – a cause of tension and a reminder that Deaf people could and wanted to manage their own affairs.

Don had taken the role of treasurer as early as 1936 when Alex Anderson was secretary of the *Australian Catholic Deaf and Dumb Association Victorian Branch*. In 1939 the office bearers for the Association were: President Father J. Pierce, Vice-President Brother P.J. O'Farrell, honorary secretary Mr Alex Anderson and the honorary treasurer was Mr D. Wallis, Don, with other members of the committee, Mrs E. O'Bryan, Miss G. Kinsella, Mr V. Wilson, Mr H. Wilson and Mr N. Durston. Soon after this period Mr Alex Anderson became President as a Deaf person. Then I discovered that from 1949 – 1952 Don was elected as president and his brother Charlie was treasurer. My sister, Carmel, remembered Don sitting at the redwood dining table preparing for meetings and presentations that he was to make.

Alex Anderson, an important leader in the Deaf community, was a childhood friend of Father Pierce, who lived in the same neighbourhood in Coburg. Their mothers, Mrs Pierce and Mrs Anderson, were good friends. Archbishop Mannix was well aware of Alex, whose persistent and trusting aunt had written to him in 1916 to plead for his prayers for her nephew. Alex was then a very ill seven-year-old boy, suffering meningitis.[xiv] Alex, left with a little hearing and speech, attended a hearing school for most of his school life. He did, however, spend a period at St Gabriel's with Don when he was about nine and ten – and met the Archbishop. His schooling at St Gabriel's gave him an experience of community in the Deaf world. He attended the retreats in Melbourne, and as a man of faith he became a long-time leader in the community.

With his brother in Coburg they managed Anderson's Hosiery Mill and employed a number of Deaf people, who were good workers because of their capacity for concentration on their work. Many Deaf people came to him for assistance. Father Pierce was the celebrant when Alex married Olive Minton, an ex-student of Waratah. Olive taught him to improve and upgrade his signing. They had eight children. *Were they Deaf or hearing?* That was the usual question asked of Deaf parents. Yes, they were all hearing!

Used with permission – Marianne Bridge (Anderson)

> Raheen,
> Kew Victoria
> 5 Mar
>
> My dear Miss Holzer
> I have received your letter. I shall gladly comply with your request and I pray God to
> hear your petition.
> I am sincerely yours
>
> +D Mannix

As Olive was a school friend of Kathleen's, and Alex and Don were friends, they visited one another. Later the Anderson family regularly came to the farm. In 1975 Alex received an honour from Cardinal Knox of Melbourne in recognition of forty years of dedicated service to the Catholic Deaf of Victoria.

In Geelong, Charles Hennessy and Gertrude Kinsella, Chas and Gertie, were leaders too, and mentored many younger Deaf people. Chas was educated at the Victorian School for the Deaf and Gertie, also a friend of Kathleen's, was educated at Waratah. Appreciating the faith they shared, Gertie and Chas became life-long and cherished friends of my parents. They had four children, Anthona, Frank, Monica and Kevin who all signed with an emphasis on two-hand fingerspelling. The Australian-Irish signing, the one-hand fingerspelling, in their family was the prerogative of the parents. They, too, regularly came to the farm at Berrigan.

Don's younger Deaf friend, Stan Batson from Geelong and originally from Colac, viewed him as a trusted mentor. After discovering Stan was deaf, his parents talked with the parish priest who had been at the seminary with my uncle Jack and knew about the Deaf members of the Wallis family at Seymour. Mr and Mrs Batson drove to Wallis' Café in Seymour and had a long conversation with my grandparents, Emma and Abe, about their son, Stan. The outcome was that Stan at the age of five went to St Gabriel's for two years signing in Australian-Irish Sign Language. When the War broke out he returned to Victoria where he attended the Victorian School for Deaf Children. There he was taught in the *Oralism* method and also learned the Australian-British Sign Language, still not yet called Auslan. Signing was his comfort zone and later he became an avid advocate for signing.

On leaving school, he travelled and lived in England where he fell in love with the young English girl Myra Daly from Liverpool, who was educated in the *Oralism* method. After their wedding in Geelong, they took their caravan on their honeymoon. Myra, a beautiful twenty-one-year-old, knew no one in Australia and wrestled with loneliness, after coming from a close-knit family. One stop was our farm in Berrigan where Stan wanted Myra to meet Kathleen. He saw in her the possibility of support and guidance for Myra, as well as friendship in the early years of their marriage.

Stan also introduced Myra to two other significant women who were mentors too – Olive Anderson and Gertie Hennessy – friends of Kathleen. Myra always knew she could trust these women to keep her confidences. Stan and Myra had four children, Carmel, Anne, Andrew and David – all hearing too. Their method of communication in the family combined both signing, fingerspelling and mouthing of words particularly for their mother for clearer communication, although she had learned to sign. Carmel became very involved in the Deaf community in Victoria and later in other rural centres.

Gertie and Chas, Stan and Myra were long-term leaders in the Deaf community in Geelong and in the Catholic Deaf community in Victoria, as were others.

In the 1970s when a national Catholic association was established, *Catholic Association of Deaf and Hearing Impaired People in Australia (CADHIPA)*,[1] Stan was a key figure in its initial direction under the guidance of Father Peter Robinson, the chaplain in Melbourne at the time. Stan was well informed and attended international Deaf conferences, as well as Deaf conferences in Australia on all

---

[1] CADHIPA closed in 1998.

related issues. In this way he kept pace with accelerating change in the Deaf community, the Church and the world. Learning from being part of many Deaf organisations, including in leadership, he shared his experiences with Deaf people, formally and informally, educating them in the process by outlining the many issues that affected Deaf people.

Storytelling and laughter was always part of life in the Deaf community. In 1990 at the national *CADHIPA* Conference in Melbourne, Frank Hennessy, Chas and Gertie's elder son was asked to make a presentation on his experience of being a hearing child with Deaf parents. Gertie was very proud of her son and sat in his view in the centre towards the front. Frank, a Christian Brother and teacher, told a story from his childhood. In their family they prayed the Rosary on Sunday evenings at the time of their favourite radio serial. Initially unbeknown to Chas and Gertie, they prayed while the children also listened to the wireless at the same time. Gertie, one evening, saw the light bulb on in the wireless and realised the radio was on – she was very upset with her children and let them know. The next week she saw that there was no light on in the wireless – good! And they prayed the Rosary. She did not know that Frank had taken the light bulb out of the wireless. This continued – praying the Rosary at the same time as listening to their favourite radio program! Everyone at the conference laughed – Gertie's face fell. She did not know until this moment that the radio had been on during all those Rosaries. She signed to Frank as he looked at her with a glint in his eye, *Bad Boy!*

Frank was on the Board of the John Pierce Centre for many years from the 1980s and a voluntary manager for a period of time. He received the John Pierce Centre Directors' Award in 2012 and an Order of Australia in 2016. How proud Gertie would be! Kevin became a priest of the Passionist Order. Anthona and Monica have children and grandchildren. One of Gertie's grandchildren, Therese, is a professional Auslan interpreter.

* * *

As a social and cultural group, Deaf people gathered whenever an opportunity arose for conversation, gleaning information and sharing from a deep place of understanding with a common language and history. Face-to-face gatherings were the only way to make arrangements and find out the news or the gossip. So a meeting place was always important.

St Francis' Hall where the Deaf community met for a period of time, Melbourne CBD.

Their hope for a permanent Catholic club did not eventuate in the 1930s, 1940s and 1950s. They used various venues. In 1934 they met in the *Catholic Federation Rooms* at *The Block* in Elizabeth Street. Then in the 1940s they gathered in St Francis' Hall, the old olive green rooms of the Christian Brothers' first school building in Victoria. It was situated down the laneway off Little Lonsdale Street, behind St Francis Church. The kitchen facilities were extremely limited and there were no toilets, except the public ones on Elizabeth Street. Outside and inside were dark, dreary, dull and not at all inviting but it was a venue, where the generous Catholic Women's Social Guild also met and often hosted the Deaf functions with afternoon tea as one of their charities.

In the evenings when all was done, and as Don and his friends closed up the club-house or meeting place after the activities, they walked from street lamp to street lamp and continued their lively discussions in sign in the half-light before they took their leave and rode their bikes in the dark, or travelled home by tram or train. Their minds had been re-fuelled for further thought and reflection.

In the 1960s and 1970s they continued to meet in different places often according to whether the priest chaplain had contacts for places to meet. The Victorian Deaf Society chapel in Jolimont was used for a number of years for Mass on the third Sunday of the month. Mr Ernest Reynolds from the Adult Deaf Society and later Mr John Flynn often interpreted at weddings and funerals. Parents of the younger Deaf people frequently assisted with events during these years.

Finally in 1980, while Father Robinson was the chaplain, a permanent venue was obtained for the next fourteen years through the financial support of Dr Pierre Gorman. The Archdiocese owned the former site of Holy Redeemer School at Ripponlea. Formally established and named the John Pierce Centre in honour of Father John Pierce, it became the Catholic centre for the Deaf community with many types of activities. Led by parents of Deaf people, dedicated friends of the community and Deaf people, a board of directors was appointed for the newly established legal entity, Bryan Ahearn being the committed long term Chair. Stan Batson was also a director.

When Stan called on Don and Kathleen in rural Victoria and stayed the night, Kathleen would clear away the dishes following a home-cooked dinner. They would sit around the oval table until the early hours of the morning, as they discussed what was happening in the Church and the world and the changes that were taking place, especially following Vatican II which was held earlier from 1962 to 1965. From the sacramental life to the liturgy, from attitudes to marriage, family life and ecumenism, from attitudes to developing countries and global responsibilities, including world economics and the environment, the world was changing. And the Deaf community was changing.

Don's much younger brother and good friend, Charlie, married Valerie Hayes who was educated at Waratah. In their family they used Australian-Irish Sign as the first language for their eight children – they visited Don and Kathleen regularly. Charlie was hardworking, honest, gregarious and open in character. His humorous antics drew smiles and laughter from any human face he engaged with. His hugs were genuine and spontaneous. Charlie reinforced his feelings of the moment with anyone he met with the sign *good* or *bad*.

Visiting Don and Kath's farm at Berrigan – Charlie and Valerie Wallis (Hayes) with six of their eight children 1964: Bernard, Gerard, Christopher, Gabrielle, Pauline, Karen

Charlie was dearly loved in the Catholic Deaf community in Melbourne. A skilled carpenter and builder working on various projects in Melbourne, he later became involved in the maintenance jobs at the John Pierce Centre.

The annual bush day for the Deaf community was held at Don's brother Chester's farm at Broadford. It was another event for Deaf people and a time of gathering, as was the annual New Year camping event at Porepunkah in the north-east of Victoria organised by Father Peter Robinson. Such outings supported the flow of communication in a casual setting.

* * *

In 1987, at about the time when the dominant Sign language in Australia was officially recognised and referred to as Auslan and a time of much ferment and discussion in the Deaf community, Father Greg Bourke was appointed to the parish of St Francis Xavier's at Prahran and then as chaplain for the Deaf community. Further education around the meaning of *Ephpheta Sunday* was given with its celebration of the Deaf way of life – its history, culture, language and faith.

1991 at Port Arlington, Victoria Deaf friends gather:
Kath Johnson, Ron McKay, Stan Batson, Gertie Hennessy (Kinsella), Myra Batson,
Eileen McKay (O'Hagen) and Kathleen Wallis (Walsh)

Nellie and Mary Elligate and Kathleen Wallis
with Father Greg Bourke. Wodonga, circa 1993

Father Bourke encouraged the Deaf community to attend the regular parish Sunday Mass at St Francis Xavier's at Prahran and generally to become more integrated into mainstream parish life. The Mass was deaf-friendly, enabling both Deaf and hearing people to participate together. A Deaf St Vincent de Paul conference was established locally. The Villa Maria Institute for blind people was situated opposite the Church, so that the Church became a place where Deaf people, blind people and able-bodied people were able to minister to one another as equals. It was during this time that I began my work at the John Pierce Centre at Ripponlea. So the pathway for me in my understanding of my Deaf heritage took a more defined direction.

By 1994 before he was appointed elsewhere, Father Greg Bourke initiated the change of venue for the John Pierce Centre to St Francis Xavier parish school and hall next to the Church. The new location was closer to public transport and closer to the precincts of Deaf history in Victoria. The change also presented the opportunity for greater involvement in parish and diocesan life. During Father Bourke's chaplaincy, Deaf participation in diocesan pastoral formation courses began being interpreted in Auslan.

In 1997 St Francis Xavier parish, Prahran, was absorbed into the neighbouring parish in South Yarra. The John Pierce Centre continued on in the hall for its activities – and Mass was celebrated once a month and on special feasts in the church.

The Redemptorist community became involved again in the Deaf community when Father John Hill became chaplain at the John Pierce Centre in 2000 after being introduced into the Deaf community some years earlier when he was a Scriptural advisor in the translation into Auslan of the Book of Ruth.

In 2003 at the Redemptorist monastery in Kew, I was introduced to Brother Albert Jouaneau who was known to have a phenomenal memory at the age of ninety-three. During my conversation with him, I discovered that he remembered Don, the young tailor from St Gabriel's who used to come to Pennant Hills to make the habits for the new students – and teach them Sign language in the process. For me this confirmed the earlier stories.

In 2008 the John Pierce Centre moved its permanent premises into the renovated St Francis Xavier Church next door. This provided offices for pastoral staff and an inviting space for many types of gatherings of the Deaf community, including their regular third Sunday Mass in Auslan. This was mainly due to the persistent work and support of a friend of the Deaf community, John Davies, and of other people on the board of the John Pierce Centre, who viewed the necessary improvements as a matter of justice to the community. Archbishop Mannix's initial hope for a dedicated space for the Deaf community was finally realised.

The permanence of the Catholic centre for the Deaf was symbolised through placing a memorial altar in a quiet garden behind the centre where families placed plaques to remember loved ones from the Deaf community who had died. How amazed the early Catholic Deaf community would be to see this permanent reminder of their presence in Victoria! What a journey for the Victorian Catholic Deaf community!

---

[i] The Advocate, *Mission for Catholic Deaf Mutes*, 18 May 1918

[ii] Annals of St Gabriel's, 3 February 1924, p.41

[iii] The Advocate, 1 January 1925

[iv] Ibid

[v] *Gathered together by Brothers Allen and Esmonde of St Gabriel's, Melbourne's adult Deaf had their first retreat. Father Robert Power's sermon was translated into Australian-Irish Sign Language by one of the Brothers. Photo by Mr J. Campbell.* Reported in The Advocate 8 January 1925

[vi] The Advocate, *Our Melbourne Catholic Deaf*, 29 January 1925 p.25

[vii] Notes held in Deaf Catholic Archives

[viii] Ibid

[ix] *Diary of Agnes Lynch*, Waratah section of the University of Newcastle. Entry 16 October 1931

[x] The Advocate, 28 July 1940

[xi] Mark 7.31-37

[xii] John 10.10

[xiii] Bourke, Gregory, Thesis *The History of the Catholic Deaf Community of Melbourne, 1997*

[xiv] Interview in 2015 with the daughter of Alex and Olive Anderson, Marianne Bridge, who was a senior interpreter of Auslan

CHAPTER 20

NEGOTIATING DEAF LANGUAGE
AND DEAF EDUCATION

As my remarkable pilgrimage – discovering my Deaf heritage – was coming to a close, I found myself reflecting back on some of the key changes in Deaf education since my mother and father left school. I needed to understand why my Australia-Irish Sign Language ceased being taught and how it had so quickly become one of the languages that could disappear without a trace in Australia.

After my parents completed their schooling, teachers at both Waratah and St Gabriel's, became active participants in the broader professional discourse about Deaf education. For example, the two Catholic Deaf schools contributed two significant papers to the Australian Conference of Teachers of the Deaf held at the Institute for Deaf Children in Melbourne in 1935.[i]

In presenting his paper entitled *The Development of a Sound Mind in a Sound Body*, Brother Esmonde spoke of the need for physical development in education. He called for teachers of the Deaf to have a good anatomical knowledge and especially to have a good understanding of the psychological development of children from birth to the age of seventeen. He claimed that physical and mental training was needed to produce well-educated men and women. He said that to secure mental alertness, the response and co-ordination of the sensory and motor nerves must be stimulated. The boys must be challenged in their physical training, which demanded self-discipline. With his experience he pointed out that organised games were of value both to Deaf children and to other children, even more for their effect on character than on physique.[ii]

Mr Peter Gallagher, from the State Education Department, presented the second talk on behalf of an anonymous Dominican sister from Waratah. At the time the Dominican sisters were a cloistered order – there were rules that required the nuns to live according to a monastic lifestyle, which meant the Sister may not have been permitted to leave her convent to travel to Melbourne. The paper was entitled *Spiritual Drought of Deafness*. The Sister insisted on the importance of soul culture – the knowledge of right and wrong as a mark of true refinement. What was emphasised was a thorough religious and moral training. She pointed out the need to have the habit of reading and the importance of training in the right use of leisure. This was a flow on from earlier approaches – my parents had learned this. They had taken this on board in their lives.

The author was convinced that great progress was possible for Deaf children in both work and play. She closed with a tribute to the virtues of Deaf children and a statement that the teacher who opened the *imprisoned* souls to light and joy was repaid by a tender love on the part of the children – that all who came in contact with the children could testify to the delightful *gaiety and cheerfulness*. Such *afflicted* people displayed this at all times. I was pleased to read that the conference audience showed the highest appreciation of both the papers given; they were especially impressed by the beauty of language and thought, as well as by the erudition of the anonymous sister...[iii]

In this same year, October 1935, Kathleen attended the retreat and reunion at Waratah where her future mother-in-law, Emma spied her. Emma had returned home to tell her son to act out of his Christian duty to visit this isolated girl over the Murray River in rural NSW. Of course he did and was caught by her loveliness and her shared language of communication.

* * *

I then noticed that ominous shifts in thinking started to take place from this time onwards in the Catholic system. With audiology equipment developing in the 1930s and other influences, significant changes were made in the orientation of education for Deaf children.

As I studied the history that I have recorded, I found it was affecting my pilgrimage of the heart. I found it difficult to remain emotionally detached and I found myself questioning how I could simply search for and tell the story without becoming agitated – I felt that I was walking on eggshells. When I centred myself, I recognised that everything in the Deaf world had become more complex as society itself had become more complex. But I also began to suspect that while everyone did what they thought to be right, some had simply been captivated by the increasingly rapid change in thought and by the new experimentation in the technical and medical sciences – without reflecting on possible long-term consequences for the individual and the community.

The visits to Australia of educational consultants from England, Canada and America, and Australian educationalists studying trends overseas, brought about change in the Australian Catholic education system – there seemed to be constant change in the policy and methods of teaching Deaf children. *Oralism*, the teaching through lip reading and speech training only, became the mandated approach to education for the Deaf children. The adoption of *Oralism* was followed by the emergence of new technology and an increase in medical interventions that changed national and international Deaf education beyond just the Catholic sector.

Upon reflection it seemed to me that educators lost sight of children who were pre-lingual and profoundly deaf and failed to appreciate the importance of a thorough visual approach to teaching of, and communication with, the profoundly Deaf children. To maintain such a way of thinking and acting was difficult. The teachers thoroughly trained by Sister Gabriel had died or moved on, except for Marianne, who was then in her sixties and networking with ex-students through personal visitation and letter-writing. Perhaps the easier road was taken and not the less travelled road.

* * *

At Waratah Sister Madeleine Egan had been teaching in Deaf education in 1931, the last year Kathleen was at school. By this time she had taught in hearing schools for at least fifteen years. She was a competent woman and a leader and was one of the first teachers of the Deaf who had not been directly influenced by Sister Gabriel and Sister Columba. In 1935 she became an honorary foundation fellow of the Australian Association of Teachers of the Deaf. She was possibly the anonymous sister who that same year had the paper presented at the conference. In 1938 she was at the conference to present her next paper in person: *The Residential Deaf Girl in the World of Sport and Leisure*. The rules of the Dominican sisters had changed and they were permitted to attend educational development opportunities.

In 1938, together with the Brothers at St Gabriel's, Sister Madeline invited Father L. Page, the principal of a large school for the Deaf in Montreal, Canada, to come to Australia for several weeks.[iv] He was to teach and demonstrate the latest *oral* techniques – speech, lip-reading and the use of modern equipment to amplify sound. I read that considerable debate emerged within the Dominican order in the 1930s and 1940s between those who advocated *Oralism* and those who favoured Sign language.[v]

In 1941 Archbishop Mannix wrote clearly about his thoughts on the matter having been greatly influenced. He described the recent developments, as follows:

At St. Gabriel's School and at the Rosary Convent, Waratah, the most modern methods are used in the education of the deaf children. Less than two years ago the Rev. Fr. Page, C.S.V., of Montreal, who has an international reputation as an educator of the deaf, gave a course of lectures in each of these schools in which he outlined to the teachers the most recent developments in Europe and America in the methods of teaching the deaf. He had previously inspected more than sixty schools for the deaf in North America and Europe and so he was well qualified to speak on the subject. He gave a good deal of his time to the methods of teaching speech and lip reading and his methods are now being practised at Waratah and Castle Hill with very good results.

The instrument known as the Multitone Group Hearing Aid is in use at both schools. The idea underlying, it is that children who are practically deafened and who, as a result, are unable to hear ordinary sounds, will be able to hear these sounds when amplified to a greater or lesser degree. It gives them access again to that world of sound from which they have been cut off. This idea of sound amplification for the deaf has naturally been suggested by the common employment of the system at meetings, etc. It has been introduced into Australian schools for the deaf in recent years...[vi]

* * *

Another person of great power and influence was Dr Alexander Ewing, the Professor of Education of the Deaf in the University of Manchester in the U.K. and Director of the Deaf from 1944 until 1964. He strongly advocated and publicised that Deaf children not be exposed to Sign language and that they be trained in the *Oralism* method. In 1946, St Mary's at Cabra in Ireland became an Oral school.

In 1945 a Report of activities of Waratah for the previous two years was published. It stated that the *Combined Method* of teaching was still followed at Waratah. Speech and lip reading were systematically taught to all who were found capable of profiting by them.[vii]

In the Report of Waratah activities, there was also an article entitled *Lip Reading.*[viii] Although there was no indication of the author, it was obviously written by a Sister who did not approve of the changes in the educational approach. The article made a strong criticism of the claimed disadvantages of lip reading although still upholding it as an essential requirement *in the life of every deaf and deafened person.*

The article continued: *But lip reading can never be completely satisfactory in itself. It is 50 per cent guess work, a perpetual mental strain and concentration. Except in the case of commonplace remarks the purport of what is spoken is not fully grasped and much depends upon the intelligence and ability to make sense from the words of each sentence, which have been understood. The result is sometimes ludicrous and often embarrassing...With the exception of close intimate relatives and friends, conversation remains very elementary...* The article continues: *The exaggerated claims frequently made that the deaf and deafened can lip read successfully at the cinema and even follow a sermon in church...are hardly worth repudiating. The pity is such claims arouse hopes of success doomed to failure...*[ix]

I found a further strong warning at the end of the Report which made me realise the extent of the conflict that existed in Deaf educational circles: *We cannot warn Catholic parents too often that much deception is practised by unscrupulous... promoters of the cause of the Deaf, who assert that children born deaf can be educated by means of Speech training and Lip reading. Let them remember that such accomplishments are of rare occurrence, and so much valuable school time has to be devoted to oral teaching that cultivation of the intellect and religious training have to be crowded out. It is quite a different case where children have some remnant of hearing... The natural language of the deaf, the Sign language, is too often looked upon with disfavour, its use even forbidden.*[x]

How quickly things changed! The new approaches seemed so appealing and so right. In 1948 the Dominican sisters established the school at Delgany in rural Victoria, an alternative to sending the children to faraway Waratah. In May that year, a contingent of four Dominican Sisters, including Sister Madeleine and a Brother from St Gabriel's, visited New Zealand where by law all schools for the Deaf used *Oralism*.

There was consternation at St Gabriel's on their return when Irish-born Brother Dunstan Cahill, a dedicated teacher who came to Castle Hill in 1937 after having trained at St Joseph's in Cabra at the same time as Brother Dominic O'Shea, wrote to the Provincial Brother Leonard Mackey in July 1948. He expressed his concern after seeing a Report that stated: *We have come to the conclusion that the oral system of education of the deaf has advantages which we cannot afford to neglect and therefore it should hold first place in our schools.*

In his letter to the provincial, he told of the headmistress of St Mary's in Cabra going to England and Scotland to investigate the question of *Oralism*. Her *splendid* report with an accompanying letter indicated that they should and must use signs because of the uncertainty of lip-reading. She added that she would not dream of abandoning the Sign language and that mental development would suffer from pure *Oralism*. She stated that thirty per cent of Deaf people were *oral failures* because there was no effort to contact their minds in any other way. In her conclusion she stated that they could not accept such a position and that they were bound to the Sign language. At the end of the letter to his Provincial superior Brother Cahill reinforced that no revolutionary methods were required but a judicious and sane use of methods that had proved themselves.

Brother Dunstan Cahill

Later in the same year, Brother Cahill wrote again to Brother Mackey about another but sketchier report by the Brothers at St Joseph's in Cabra during a tour of inspection in England and Scotland in October 1948. He quoted: *By finger spelling, methodical signs and writing, the Deaf can be educated better and faster than by the oral method. In Britain clergymen in charge of the adult Deaf are in favour of the sign and manual method, while parents, on the contrary, prefer their children to speak a few words however indistinctly, rather than have them well educated through the medium of signs. But, after leaving school, all the Deaf whether partially or totally, turn to signs as we saw in the various clubs we visited. Signs seem to be their natural means of giving expression to their ideas.* In the conclusion to the report the Brothers in

Ireland stated that they would continue the system that had produced fine results in the past and that they would tailor the methods used to the pupil. Speech and lip-reading would be taught to those who could benefit from it.

Brother Cahill added that his local superior had found new enthusiasm for *Oralism* after his New Zealand trip and would not be pleased with such a report from Ireland and that this local superior was out to convince the members of the education committee that *Oralism* was the El Dorado of Deaf education. Brother Cahill forewarned Brother Mackey, the Provincial superior, to be prepared to deal with it.[xi]

In 1985, Brother Reginald Shepherd, a former *Oralism* teacher, who in his latter life signed in Australian-Irish Sign Language and who was a wonderful pastoral and well-respected person for the Deaf community, chronicled Brother Cahill's life stating that Brother Cahill was deeply concerned to see a new system gradually replacing one that was second nature to him.[xii] Brother Cahill had been at St Gabriel's for almost thirty years and continued his involvement with the adult Deaf community for the rest of his life. The Deaf people knew he was deeply interested in them, their families and how they were getting on in their working lives. With the controversies that were going on, no wonder he worried about their language and advocated on their behalf – but to no avail.

* * *

Waratah soon became an Oral school too. Approximately eighteen ex-students[xiii] who had been engaged and worked at Waratah all their lives as Deaf teachers and Deaf role models were no longer required as staff. It was the beginning of entire generations of young Deaf people isolated from a Deaf culture, a community and a visual Sign language.

In 1950 the oral supporters, Sir Alexander Ewing and his wife Lady Irene Ewing, who was partly deaf, visited Australia and travelled extensively to various Deaf educational centres, including Delgany, explaining the *Oralism* approach to Deaf education.

With a number of outside influences the Sisters made significant changes in Deaf education within the Dominican schools. In 1952 the children arrived for school at Delgany to discover they were not permitted to sign any more. They were confused. Australian-Irish Sign Language ceased to be taught or used in the school, except when the children, although forbidden, signed to one another behind the shelter sheds outside or when one of the older Sisters objected to new methods and secretly signed to them in the classroom. Parents were encouraged to send their children as early as two and three years of age so they could begin the task of speaking and lip-reading.

At a later stage Sister Madeleine Egan, who had been an advocate for change to *Oralism*, using lip reading and speech only, had a change of heart and eventually concluded that *Oralism* by itself was insufficient and suggested behind the scenes that Sisters should also be trained in Sign language.[xiv]

* * *

The influence of the initial Irish Brothers had waned by the 1940s and certainly by the 1950s when some returned to Ireland. Accordingly, and in the face of the move towards *Oralism* in Australia, changes at St Gabriel's were inevitable and a decision was taken to change the educational approach from the *Combined Method* of teaching to a pure oral method with all its supports supplied through the beginnings of a more developed technology and increased medical intervention.

So from 1953 St Gabriel's no longer taught Australian-Irish Sign Language, except secretly in the classroom when Brother Cahill defied the new system and still taught in Sign language much to the delight and pleasure of the boys. And though some significant Brothers from St Gabriel's dedicated their lives to the interests of Deaf people, visiting them and encouraging them even after the Brothers themselves had retired, the Australian-Irish Sign Language began its path towards an endangered language.

Also in 1953 a significant conference was held in Sydney – *The Fifth Triennial Conference of the Australian Association of the Teachers of the Deaf.* All the teachers who attended were hearing. The participants at the conference formally resolved that in Australia, Sign language would not be used as a means of education and that Deaf children would be taught the oral method. Both fingerspelling and gestures were considered outmoded. The following year, after a psychologist travelled to England to acquire skills and establish the courses, the professional training of teachers in support of this resolution began in Australia.[xv]

In 1957 St Joseph's in Cabra also became an Oral school. While all this change was going on, the adults who were deaf steadfastly held to their belief that signing was part of a Deaf person's language, culture and identity. They believed they had every right to the mastery of a language. Sustained Sign language disappeared from the Catholic education system in Australia and along with it the strong corporate knowledge of education through Sign language.

The influence of Sister Gabriel, Sister Columba and Miss Hanney and the first Irish Brothers, Brother O'Shea, Brother O'Farrell, Brother Allen and Brother Esmonde, no longer held its charisma. Their values and aims in Deaf educational methods were seen as either no longer relevant or as being achievable in new ways.

An added dimension to the change in educational policy was the fact that Archbishop Mannix wrote to the Sisters requesting them to listen to the ideas and take advice from Mr and Mrs Gorman. They had a son called Pierre who was deaf. Pierre was educated at Melbourne Grammar School and visited France regularly with his well-educated mother for tuition in the Oral method. After further studies at University, he did research on the Oral method at the University of Manchester where Dr Ewing was based and then transferred to Cambridge. He gained a Bachelor of Agriculture, a Diploma of Education with Honours and a Doctorate of Philosophy. He worked for twelve years at the Royal National Institute for the Deaf in London returning home to lecture at Monash University. He was an extraordinarily gifted person.

A great friend of the Dominican sisters, he and his parents regularly visited the school for the Deaf children at Portsea assisting with advice and material goods.[xvi] Pierre also visited St Gabriel's and gave a speech to a large group of teachers and parents of the Deaf children advocating the *Oralism* system of teaching.

Archbishop Mannix, the friend and advocate for the Deaf community, knew that Mr and Mrs Gorman offered considerable finance to the Catholic Deaf entities as indicated in the Dominican magazine: *Indeed the progress made by the Delgany school, educationally, socially and financially was due in a large measure to Mr Eugene Gorman (now Sir Eugene) and to Madame Gorman and also to Pierre.*[xvii] The death of Sir Eugene in 1973 was a great loss to the school at Portsea: *Sir Eugene…a friend of and an intercessor for the Deaf of Melbourne and particularly for our school at Portsea. As soon as the establishment of a school for deaf children was decided upon, Sir Eugene…Madame Gorman and their son Pierre, became deeply interested… To them chiefly, the Sisters were indebted for the firm establishment of the school, its resources, its status in Government Departments and its finance… No wonder then that the Dominican sisters, especially those of St. Mary's, Portsea and their pupils mourn the loss of one of their greatest benefactors and well-wishers.*[xviii]

Pierre was an oral communicator and did not sign. Unfortunately, later in his life when I first met him, I could not understand his speech so our conversation was stilted and stunted whenever we met. Not finding it easy to communicate with hearing people, he also did not communicate easily with Deaf people.

* * *

When thinking about Deaf language in education, I remembered that in 1967 when I undertook social welfare studies and for an assignment on organisations responding to the issue of difference and disability, I wrote to a number of places, including St Gabriel's School for Deaf children. I received an enthusiastic response from one of the Brothers who had been to America to study a new method to supplement the Oral approach. It was called *Cued Speech*, which was invented in 1966 by Dr R Orin Cornett at Gallaudet College. In 1969 Dr Cornett visited Australia.

According to the National Cued Speech Association, *Cued Speech* is described as a visual mode of communication using hand shapes and placements in combination with the mouth movements and speech to distinguish one spoken word from another. However, it was not a language and was designed to assist with a pre-existing language, e.g. English.[xix] For a while it was adopted in the Catholic education system at Waratah, St Gabriel's and Delgany at Portsea. Deaf people did not tend to use it in their adult life with one another, although some used it with their parents who had learned it when their children were very young. I was mystified and thought at that time, why they did not just learn Sign language.

In 1968 two American Sisters from St Joseph's Institute for the Deaf in St Louis, Missouri, spent six weeks in Australia imparting their up-to-date expertise on the Oral method in education.

Don's sister, Marie Fulton was critical of the new developments in the education of Deaf children. She still felt strongly about the issue for the younger generations of Deaf people. In earlier times, she wrote regularly to her loved priest-brother, Jack, in Tasmania, and lamented sadly that the younger generation lacked a full education. They could not read nor write fluently or they could not have proper conversations in Sign language with her, she regretted. She was not afraid to convey her thoughts and she often asked the uncomfortable question. How very proud she was to propose the toast at the *Ephpheta* celebration the year before she died in 1986.

Marie Fulton (Wallis) 1954

Whatever the situation Jack, Father John Wallis, appreciated the role the Dominican sisters played in the education of Deaf children – he had known of them since his siblings went away to school at Waratah. He always retained his professional relationship with the sisters and valued their gift of quality education in the Church in Australia. In 1959 he invited them to staff the new parish primary school at St John's in Glenorchy in Tasmania. He remained in contact with some of the Sisters all his life.

* * *

Another major change was the demise of big residential schools in Australia. New options opened up to parents for the education of their Deaf children. Deaf units attached to schools and the provision of teachers for the Deaf and interpreters in integrated schools were provided. By 1983 the Deaf school *Delgany* at Portsea was relocated to Melbourne with eight students and became St Mary's at Wantirna, where it was a partner school to the hearing school, St John's Regional College at Dandenong. Families chose whether the children would be day students or boarders. Boarders would be accommodated in small group housing. This gave more opportunity for some Deaf children to remain in home settings.

As these orally formed children became adults, some joined the Deaf community where they found themselves comfortable and at home; others did not or could not. The reality was that many Deaf children came through the oral education system without ever being part of a Deaf community. Often they only discovered the community after they left school. Many of them learned Sign language as a second language. Their hearing parents had simply not seen the necessity to identify a Deaf community to which their children could belong. Indeed, it is likely that some parents were so focussed on integrating their children into the hearing world that they steered their children away from engagement with the Deaf community.

* * *

The Oral approach and the developing preference to treat deafness as a health issue led to the increased involvement of health professionals. Hearing aids were improved and cochlea implantation was initiated. Medical involvement became the norm for Deaf children. I read with further discomfort: *Deaf schools were becoming virtual medical clinics with education becoming little more than audiometry and speech therapy.*[xx] *...Deafness was a symptom to be treated, ameliorated, and denied, though never quite cured... By means of oralist education, taught...by an increasingly professionalised body of hearing teachers, deafness and a deaf identity were being defined as pathological conditions to be denied and overcome... The goal was to transform a deaf child into a hearing adult.*[xxi]

At this point I was grateful that my parents did not have to go through the confusing years of the change of methods of education or being treated medically because they were deaf – and there were no medical bills for them or for the Government, except when my mother was a child and was experimented upon with a shock treatment of sorts in the 1920s.

An educated Deaf woman who spent her childhood at Portsea told me that she thought on leaving school after an Oral education that she would be like hearing people and they would all be the same as her. She was baffled and disillusioned when time and time again on encountering a person and speaking to them, they looked blankly at her for a moment and with an apology asked her to speak again. Soon she realised that her voice and her speech were not like that of others. While her immediate family and friends understood what she meant, she was not understood in other contexts. So she then learned and studied through Sign language – with much success and satisfaction.

An ex-student of St Gabriel's from the same era in the 1960s said he too expected that on leaving school he would be like anyone else and he would develop hearing friendships easily. It was a shock and he felt depressed when his expectations were dashed and the reality that he was different was realised. Between his schooling and his work life, he undertook sessions that prepared him for employment in the world. He also learnt Sign language.

Adult children of families with parents who came through an oral system or a signing system – or both – find their own way of communicating with their parents whether it is with finger spelling, signing or mouthing of words for lip-reading. As each family develops their own linguistic method, each is to be respected and acknowledged for their capacity for such highly skilled communication in their family units.

During the late 1990s I had felt compelled to do a course in Auslan linguistics at La Trobe University, Melbourne. It was an unintended journey for me. It showed me how Deaf languages had their own intrinsic linguistic properties – properties that, without realising, I had used all my life, properties that were important to, and intrinsic to, communication for my uncle Charlie. He loved his language and believed it enabled him to express well whatever it was that he wanted to convey. I recalled how he was distressed when he was interpreted differently. If he meant to communicate *joy* he did not want it interpreted as *happy*. He understood the finesse of meanings and he wanted his signing interpreted as he meant it. The Irish sign for *joy* uses the Irish alphabet 'j' with the little finger on both hands that form circles on the chest. Charlie still belonged to the era of strong fingerspelling. He emphasised with his spelling on one hand *j-o-y*. He was fearful that his erudite, visual and specific language would be lost.

* * *

Further advances in technology, from hearing aids to improved cochlea implants to Teletypewriters, use of fax machines, mobiles and computers, were introduced into the lives of Deaf people and into their educational curriculum and environment. Medical intervention and advances in medical technology gave Deaf children the opportunity to hear and distinguish between sounds, although their hearing was sometimes distorted. These advances included the experimentation of cochlea implants from the 1970s in Australia and the gradual improvement of this technology for Deaf children and Deaf adults, including adults who lost their hearing and became deaf later in life.

Parents were required to numerous decisions about their Deaf babies – one of these was in regard to cochlea implantation. The criteria as to who can benefit from the cochlea implant have changed considerably since the introduction of these medical devices. Other decisions parents had to make was whether the child would be educated through Sign language or would their child take up an oral approach with the parents' belief that the child would hear well through the medical intervention path. Parents came under even greater pressure when medical technology enabled the ability to screen in utero to discover if the baby was deaf or not.

Technological innovations allowed for integration of Deaf children into schools of the parents' choice. With the cochlea implant, most parents did not see it necessary that their children acquire a Sign language. It was also believed that learning Sign language could interfere with the process of learning to listen and hear through the new medical devices, so parents were not encouraged to sign to their children. Something different was required for the new era. Who could have imagined the incredible accelerated advances and the inevitable rapid changes that took place up until today?

However, while changes affected the general Deaf community with seemingly fewer younger members as part of the community, including in the Catholic Deaf community, there were still Deaf people who came through the *Combined Method* system with all the advantages – a Sign language, speech and lip reading where appropriate, and with all the technological supports in place as well. With social media now available to young and old, Deaf people were now part of society in a new way not available to them in the previous eras.

* * *

By the 1980s with the emphasis that had been placed on an Oral education, I found it surprising to see that at a global level, Deaf people and the Deaf community stood firm and took action to retain Sign language and to assert their rights and celebrate their language and culture with confidence.

It happened earlier in Australia with Australian Sign Language than in other parts of the world. In 1986 the Australian Association of the Deaf claimed Auslan as an official language – Australian Sign Language based on British Sign Language with its various influences over one hundred and fifty years. One of its influences was that of Australian-Irish Sign Language.

Within a short time it was finally written into the Government's Australian Language and Literary Policy that signing Deaf people were recognised as a constituted group like any other non-English speaking language group in Australia, a distinct sub-culture recognised by a shared history, social life and sense of identity, united and symbolised by fluency in Auslan, the principal means of communication within the Australian Deaf Community.[xxii]

The Deaf community had lobbied consistently for the language to be recognised as a language of a distinct linguistic minority group, which had access to regulations set down for the rights of such groups,[xxiii] such as interpreting. Trevor Johnston, whose parents were deaf, worked with others in the field of Deaf linguistics and coined the name *Auslan*, which was accepted by the Deaf community who greatly rejoiced and celebrated when the declaration was made.

With approximately 30,000 Auslan users with total deafness[1] and following the recognition of Auslan, more qualified professional interpreters were needed for such situations as medical and legal matters for an increasingly educated Deaf community. A greater vocabulary with new signs and new concepts was also required.[xxiv] Auslan expanded through the younger generation of Deaf people who chose to learn signing and who had improved access to education through the provision of interpreters at both secondary and tertiary levels.

Deaf people became active in campaigns for matters relating to their lives. Into his eighties, Stan Batson was one of those people taking responsibility on various Boards of management. While a leader in the Catholic and wider community he received a number of awards, including one in 2014 from the Deafness Foundation in Victoria for outstanding contributions as an ambassador for the Deaf, promoting understanding and inclusion. Stan and Myra's daughter, Carmel, became an interpreter and advocate in the Deaf community, as well as President of Children of Deaf Adults International. In 2007 she won the Distinguished Service Award for her work in the association that connects codas from around the world.

How much more education is needed to place equal access at the forefront of society's consciousness? Children of Deaf parents tire of explaining the need for an interpreter not to mention the legal requirements for this. They become exhausted and disheartened.

Our senior Deaf man, Stan Batson, after his extended years of advocacy entered a capital city hospital for unexpected major surgery in the year 2016 – this day and age, thirty-five years after the International Year of the Disabled legislated changes in Australia. In the six critical days in the hospital, his family was told that *no interpreter was available, that the hospital could not afford it, and that they needed twenty-four hours to obtain the services of an interpreter.* Medical staff were frustrated by the lack of support for their patient's care. The family knew there were highly qualified interpreters who were at home and on standby, waiting for the call from hospital officialdom. The interpreters were not called. How familiar this experience is to Deaf people and their families! The badly flawed system let Stan and his family

---

[1] Deaf Australia is the national peak advocacy and information organisation in Australia for Deaf people who are bilingual – using both English and Auslan (Australian Sign Language).

down – and the Deaf community. Just five weeks later Stan's life came to an end – he lives on leaving a legacy of his unfailing belief in Deaf people and their right to inclusion and equality.

Since 90 per cent of those Deaf people who have children give birth to hearing children, it is usual that a Deaf generation will be followed by a hearing generation. *If this hearing generation does not pass on sign to the subsequent deaf generations then the language will be lost from that family.*[xxv] It follows that hearing people may well be the very people who ensure the survival of the signing Deaf community.

Daughters of Stan and Myra, Alex and Olive, and Don and Kathleen
Carmel Batson, Marianne Bridge (Anderson) and Bernadette Wallis at the
XIII World Congress of the Federation of the Deaf, Brisbane 1999

* * *

However, although Sign languages were officially suppressed from 1880 at the time of the Conference of Milan throughout Europe and many parts of the world, not all institutions complied. As well, adult Deaf communities had kept the Sign languages alive and passed them on to the younger Deaf people who turned to signing after leaving school. Children of Deaf adults also contributed by becoming interpreters or using the language in their professions. They lead others to appreciate the need to learn the language. Globally, movements towards recognition of Deaf Sign languages began to make their mark in at least some countries. In this way the thread of languages continued.

In 1988 the European Parliament resolved to ask all member countries to adopt their national Sign languages as official languages of the Deaf.[xxvi] In 1998 another resolution was issued with the same content.[xxvii]

In 1995 Uganda's national Sign language was recognised in the country's new constitution, making it one of the few constitutionally recognised Sign languages in the world[xxviii] and by 1996 a 27 year-old Deaf signing man, Alex Ndeezi, had been elected to the Ugandan Parliament.

In 2003 the Parliament of French-speaking Belgium recognised French-Belgian Sign Language in a decree that recognised it as a unique culture and recommended the foundation of a commission to advise the Government of the French Community in all matters related to Sign language.[xxix]

In that same year, 2003, the British Government recognised British Sign Language as a language in its own right, quoting an estimated 70,000 people whose preferred language it was.[xxx]

In 2006 the New Zealand Parliament declared New Zealand Sign Language as an official language.[xxxi]

In 2007 the Spanish Parliament recognised three Sign languages claimed by Deaf organisations in Spain: Spanish Sign Language, Catalan Sign Language and Valencian Sign Language.

The situation in the United States of America was different in that many individual states had laws recognising American Sign Language as a foreign language and some recognised it as a language for instruction in a school. A number of universities accepted Sign language for credit to fulfil foreign language requirements.[xxxii]

What of Ireland? In Northern Ireland, Sign Language was recognised as a language. In the Republic of Ireland the Irish Sign Language has never had official recognition as a language; it has no official status in Irish legislation. For many years there has been a strong campaign to ensure equality for Deaf people in Irish Society. Because of the suppression of Irish Sign Language during the latter part of the last century, not all teachers of the Deaf are fluent or qualified in Irish Sign Language, so no Deaf child can fully learn Irish Sign Language. In the Education Act of 1998, Irish Sign Language was considered a support service, rather than a language in its own right.[xxxiii]

* * *

I found a parallel with the Australian Indigenous languages and Australian-Irish Sign Language. While the Australian Indigenous languages developed along the rivers and in the deserts of Australia and within diverse Aboriginal cultures and nations, the Aboriginals lost their languages, partly due to repression by Governmental policies. The first Commonwealth policy to significantly address indigenous language was the *National Policy on Languages* of 1987.[xxxiv] At the time of colonisation in Australia there were two hundred and fifty languages used which were whittled down to only eighteen languages that were *strong in the sense of being spoken by significant numbers of people across all age groups.*[xxxv] What a loss of a rich heritage, identity and culture, where social structures had broken down! In 2009 the Commonwealth Government announced a national Indigenous languages policy in response to a report in 2005, which found that the situation was grave and that like Australian-Irish Sign Language, Australian Indigenous languages were critically endangered as a language.

Australian-Irish Sign Language was never recognised as an official language with its own complex linguistic structure, rules and features – a visual and spatial language that had its own distinct grammar and a language using hands, facial expression and body movement. It was never recognised as belonging to a distinct linguistic minority sub-group within Australia with its unique character and identity.

However, it existed and there are still remnant signs of its existence in Australia. I attended an eightieth birthday party in 2015 where I joined with thirty people – more than two-thirds were Australian-Irish signers educated at Waratah, St Gabriel's or Delgany at Portsea. I was the only one present who was a child of parents who had attended Waratah and/or St Gabriel's. What an amazing experience as we sat around three round tables close together in a secluded nook of the restaurant, with conversations taking place predominantly in Australian-Irish Sign, but also in Auslan. Throughout the party people regularly swapped languages across the tables with ease, and with consideration for the few there who did not know Australian-Irish Sign. The image stays with me as a reminder of the richness of the language. I wonder, whether with so few custodians of the language remaining, numbers may not be sufficient to prevent its disappearance. What a sad loss – the loss to the world of another treasure, a rich heritage, identity and culture!

* * *

With all the historical information presented in this book – facts sometimes seemingly isolated – I can see my father exclaiming, *How fascinating!* Even with all of this, *what more can I learn – can we learn together? Bring everything and everyone to the table of conversation for understanding. Include the main stakeholders in all decisions relating to them in all matters now – Deaf people and the Deaf community as a whole – around kitchen tables and all sorts of tables.* He was always open to the new – curious and seeing the new horizon that was emerging in the complexity of life.

My pilgrimage led me on a journey to painful and joyous understandings of human activity in relation to Deaf people and Deaf communities. I discovered the Deaf world I had come to know through my family opened to a much wider world that literally spanned seas and continents. In this wider world context, I discovered the stories that linked my family to a tale of liberation that extended over one hundred and fifty years. These are stories of ardent, insightful and inspired individuals, hearing and deaf, who committed themselves to the dignity of Deaf people. It was like seeing a river with a sunrise unfold – night into day – that taught me how I was so intimately and unknowingly connected to the rich heritage of the Deaf world – a silent book of story.

As the life force of Australian-Irish Sign Language slowly draws to an end in this Great Southern Land, I feel the urgency of preserving it in some way. I imagine fragments of this treasured Australian-Irish Sign Language, the language of my heart, being carefully gathered and placed onto websites so that future generations will see and understand. I feel the urgency of this project.

---

[i] Ibid. p.38

[ii] Letters from Brother T.D. Cahill to the Provincial Superior dated 1 July 1948 and 29 November 1948 held at the Archives, Christian Brothers, Sydney

[iii] Chronicle of the life of Brother Dunstan Cahill by Brother Reginald Shepherd held at the Christian Brothers' Archives, Sydney

[iv] History of Catholic Deaf Education in Australia 1875-1975 p.33

[v] This article was published in *Australian Dictionary of Biography Vol.14, (MUP), 1996*

[vi] The Advocate, *Archbishop's Letter*, 1941

[vii] *Veritas, Institute for the Deaf and Dumb, Waratah*, March 1943 – March 1945 p.2

[viii] Ibid p.12-14

[ix] Ibid

[x] Ibid. p.38

[xi] Letters from Brother T.D. Cahill to the Provincial Superior dated 1 July 1948 and 29 November 1948 held at the Archives, Christian Brothers, Sydney

[xii] Chronicle of the life of Brother Dunstan Cahill by Brother Reginald Shepherd held at the Christian Brothers' Archives, Sydney

[xiii] *Veritas, Institute for the Deaf and Dumb, Waratah*, March 1943 – 1945, Photo: Ex-pupils Engaged in the Institution, p.33

[xiv] This article was published in *Australian Dictionary of Biography Vol.14, (MUP), 1996*

[xv] Ibid

[xvi] *Veritas*, Christmas 1970

[xvii] Ibid

[xviii] *Veritas*, Vol. 30, August 1973

[xix] *en.wikipedia.org/wiki/Cued_speech*

[xx] *Damned for Their Difference: the cultural construction of deaf people as disabled – A Sociological History of Discrimination* by Jan Branson and Don Miller, Gallaudet University Press, Washington 2002, p.206

[xxi] Ibid

[xxii] Dawkins, J (1991). *Australia's Language: The Australian Language and Literacy Policy.* Australian Government Printing Service: Canberra, p.20

[xxiii] *http://www.deafau.org.au/info/policy_auslan.php*

[xxiv] Johnston, T. (Ed.). (1998). *Signs of Australia: A New Dictionary of Auslan.* North Rocks, NSW: North Rocks Press. (First published as Johnston, T. (1989). *Auslan Dictionary: A Dictionary of the Sign Language of the Australian Deaf Community.* Sydney: Deafness Resources Australia.)

[xxv] Austen, Sally & Crocker, Susan, Editors *Deafness in Mind – Working Psychologically with Deaf People Across the Lifespan*, Whurr Publishers Ltd. London & Philadelphia 2004, p.15

[xxvi] European Parliament Resolution on Sign Languages 1988 *http://www.policy.hu/flora/ressign2.htm*

[xxvii] Official Journal C 187, 18/07/1988 P. 0236

[xxviii] World Federation of the Deaf News, April 1996

[xxix] In *Décret relatif à la reconnaissance de la langue des signes* Decree on the recognition of French – Belgian Sign Language

[xxx] British Deaf News, 2003, April 5-7

[xxxi] New Zealand Sign Language Bill, Part 2 cl 6

[xxxii] *https://en.wikipedia.org/wiki/Legal_recognition_of_sign_languages#United_States_of_America*

[xxxiii] *https://www.irishdeafsociety.ie/irish-sign-language/irish-sign-language-recognition-campaign/*

[xxxiv] *www.aph.gov.au/parliamentary_business/committees/house_of_representatives_committees*

[xxxv] *www.aph.gov.au/parliamentary_business/committees/house_of_representatives_committees*

ACKNOWLEDGEMENTS

I had not dared to say I was writing a book for some months before I was into the process and I thank the people who gave me the courage to say so. They gave me confidence that the subject of the book was important to document and to trust it would be well received.

Editors, readers and proof-readers each have their role. I am indebted to them for their various parts in the book and to varying degrees – for their interest, commitment and professionalism especially to Margaret Peoples, Fiona Regan, Michael Rebbechi, Patrick Leech, Jillian Smith, Sue Black, Gerard Wallis and Frances Cardigan.

I also acknowledge other professionals I consulted, some of whom are my friends and/or peers – in Deaf linguistics, Deaf education, Deaf cultural history, and Deaf pastoral ministry, as well as those who have studied the sub-cultural group of Coda's – Children of Deaf Adults – as a group of people with a unique background of experience.

My thanks go to many people I met and spoke with especially the Dominican Sisters and Christian Brothers. I acknowledge historian Brian Johnston in the Deaf community in Sydney for his in-depth work on the history of St Gabriel's School for Deaf Boys. I thank those associated with the University of Newcastle library, Latrobe University, the Myer archives at Baillieu Library, University of Melbourne, the Missionary Sisters of Service archives in North Hobart and the Historical Society of Berrigan.

For their support, I thank my Deaf friends who are native Australian-Irish signers or who know the language. Your conversations with me are precious. Thank you to friends in the Deaf community for standing by me as I wrote this book, including staff at the John Pierce Centre in Melbourne and the Ephpheta Centre in Sydney. Thank you to the Deaf people and their families – those with whom I have had contact during my lifetime, especially in Victoria.

To the Missionary Sisters of Service, thank you for encouragement and support. Special thanks are due to Stancea Vichie MSS and Corrie van den Bosch MSS on the Governing body of the Missionary Sisters of Service, who encouraged me specifically to take the time to write, as well as Cecilia Bailey MSS who read most versions of the manuscript.

Thank you to my myriad of encouragers – for listening patiently to my discoveries and where I was up to in the work. I was enlisting encouragement when I doubted myself!

I thank my cousins who had Deaf parents and who shared closely in our family story – Mary, John, Jane, Frances, Kathleen and Anne; Chris, Bernard, Gabrielle, Gerard, Pauline, Karen, David and Loretta. My other cousins on my father's side and my mother's side, I also thank them – they also supported and shared in the Deaf world in a unique way – Gerard RIP, Moira, Marie, Peter and Brian Wallis; Laurene, Bernadette, Graeme, Gerard, Marlene, Karen and Donna; Terry, Kaylene and Majella, Des, Mary RIP and John; Ray, Kerry and Damian; John, Mary and Adrian RIP; Mark, Phillip and Cathryn. I also pay special tribute to my mother's brother, Uncle Jim, as the only surviving sibling of my parents.

Lastly, thank you to my family – my brother-in-law David, niece and nephews Mark, Michelle and Joseph. My special thanks to my sisters Carmel and Margaret, who dared to allow me to publish this story.

BIBLIOGRAPHY

Books

Adams, John W:
You and Your Deaf Child
Clerc Books, An imprint of Gallaudet University Press, Washington, DC 20002.
Copyright 1997 by Gallaudet University, Published 1997, Printed in the USA.

Austen, Sally & Crocker, Susan, Eds:
Deafness in Mind – Working Psychologically with Deaf People Across the Lifespan
Whurr Publishers Ltd., London & Philadelphia 2004.

Blanks, Harvey:
The Story of Yea – A 150 Year History of the Shire
First published 1973 by Harvey Blanks, Melbourne. Reprinted 2001 by Goulburn River Printers Seymour Pty. Ltd., 21 Alfred Street, Seymour 3660.

Dominican Sisters:
History of Catholic Deaf Education in Australia 1875 – 1975
Private publication.

Dominican Sisters:
Pictorial Centenary Souvenir – Companion to History of Catholic Deaf Education in Australia 1875 – 1975
Designed and printed by Newey & Beath Pty. Ltd. Photos and cuttings provided by Sister M. Madeleine Egan, OP.

Dooley, Annette:
To Be Fully Alive – A Monograph on Australian Dominican Education of Hearing Impaired Children
Privately type-set collection.

Eriksson, Per:
The History of Deaf People
Translated from the Swedish by James Schmale. The Swedish original, Dovas Historia, en faktasmaling.
Del 1, was published by SIH Laromedel, the Learning Materials Division of the National Swedish Agency for Special Education in 1993. TRYCKMAKARNA I Orebro AB, 1998.

Fitzgerald, Sarah, Ed:
Open Minds Open Hearts: Stories of the Australian Catholic Deaf Community
A CCOD publication, Lidcombe, NSW, Australia 1999.

Gordon, H.C:
Yea – Its Discovery and Development 1825 – 1920
Murrindindi, Yea.
Reprinted with amended copy (by Donald Drysdale) Tom Dignam 1997.

Griffey Nicholas OP:
From Silence to Speech – 50 Years with the Deaf
Dominican Publications, 1994.

Hellwig OP:
Elizabeth Up She Gets, for Up She Must!
Published by Dominican Sisters 2001.

Johnston, Brian James:
**Memories of St Gabriel's 75th Anniversary Commemorative Book –
St Gabriel's School for the Deaf, Castle Hill, NSW 1922 – 1997**
Printed by NSW Government Printing Service, 2000.

Lane, Harlan:
When the Mind Hears – a History of the Deaf
Published by Penguin Books, first published in the USA by Random House Inc. and
simultaneously in Canada by Random House of Canada Ltd 1984. Copyright Harlan
Lane 1984.

MacGinley, M.R:
**Ancient Tradition New World – Dominican Sisters in Eastern Australia 1867 –
1958**

Mowbray, Patricia, Ed:
We Have a Story
A collection of stories from people with disability, their families and faith
communities participating fully in the life of the Church in Australia. Published
Australia, Australian Catholic Bishops Conference, Canberra ACT, 2006.

O'Brien, Dorothy:
The Cochlear Implant – Parents Tell Their Story
Published by Full Moon Press 2002, Australia.

Preston, Paul:
Mother Father Deaf – Living Between Sound and Silence
Harvard University Press, Cambridge, Massachusetts, and London, England.
Copyright 1994 by President and Fellows of Harvard College, Second Printing 1995.

Sacks, Oliver:
Seeing Voices
Published by Pan Books,
First published 1989 by University of California Press, Berkeley and Los Angeles.
First published in Great Britain in Picador by Pa Books 1990.
Copyright The Regents of the University of California 1989.

Tonya M. Stremlau Ed:
The Deaf Way II Anthology – A Literary Collection by Deaf and Hard of Hearing Writers
Published by Gallaudet University Press Washington, D.C., published 2002.

Symington, Brian and Carberry, John:
British and Irish Sign Language
First published 2006 by The Linen Hall Library, Belfast.

Walker, Lou Ann:
A Loss for Words – The Story of Deafness in a Family
Published Fontana Paperbacks UK, 1987, Reprinted 1989. Made and printed in Australia by The Book Printer, Victoria.

Dominican Sisters and Christian Brothers:
History of Catholic Deaf Education in Australia 1875 – 1975
Private printing 1975.

St Gabriel's School for Hearing Impaired Children:
St Gabriel's 75th Anniversary 1922-1997 – Celebrating 75 Years of Educating Children Who Are Deaf
NSW Government Printing Service.

St Gabriel's School for the Deaf:
St Gabriel's School for the Deaf Golden Jubilee 1922 – 1972
Printed by Macarthur Press Parramatta, Australia, 1972.

St Gabriel's Publications:

Silver Jubilee Review 1922-1947 by St Gabriel's School for Deaf Boys Castle Hill NSW

Annual Report and Balance Sheet 1933-1934 St Gabriel's School for Deaf Boys NSW

Fourteenth Annual Report of St Gabriel's Castle Hill 1935 – 1936

Seventeenth Annual Report of St Gabriel's Castle Hill 1938 – 1939

Eighteenth Annual Report of St Gabriel's Castle Hill 1939 – 1940

Nineteenth Annual Report of St Gabriel's Castle Hill 1940 – 1941

Twentieth Annual Report of St Gabriel's Castle Hill 1941 – 1943

St Gabriel's Review 1948 – 1949

Web Sites

Aboriginal History:
Yarrawonga Mulwala Visitor Information Centre:
http://www.yarrawongamulwala.com.au/about/history.html

Berke, Jamie:
Milan 1880 – An Event Has a Major Impact on Deaf Education:
http://deafness.about.com/cs/featurearticles/a/milan1880.htm

TIMELINE – HISTORICAL

1560 – 1620	Dom Juan Pablo Martin Bonet
1567 – 1622	Saint Francis de Sales
1570	Juan Fernandez Navarette – *Work of Art Nativity or Adoring Shepherds*
1620 – 1684	Pedro Ponce de Leon
1712 – 1789	Abbe Charles Michel de L'Epee
1771	First Public School for Deaf in France – Abbe Charles de L'Epee
1742 – 1822	Abbe Roch Ambroise Cucurren Sicard
1785 – 1869	Louis Laurent Marie Clerc
1787 – 1851	Thomas Gallaudet
1795	Elizabeth Steele, Deaf woman and convict dies in Sydney
1825	John Carmichael, first known British Signing Deaf person arrives in Australia
1836	Henry Hallet arrives in South Australia and marries Deaf woman, Martha Pike
1846	St Mary's School for Deaf Girls in Cabra, Ireland began
1857	St Joseph's School for Deaf Boys in Cabra, Ireland began
1859	Catherine Sullivan at Swallow Creek, near Bathurst is born deaf. She attends the Deaf school in Sydney 1866 – 1872
1860	Thomas Pattison, a Deaf man, begins the school for the Deaf in Sydney
1860	Frederick Rose, a Deaf man, begins school for the Deaf in Melbourne
1861	Abbe Pierre-Francois Jamet with the Sisters of Bon Sauver founded Le Bon Institute for Deaf
1867	From Kingstown, Ireland, the first Dominican Sisters in Australia arrive in teach in Maitland NSW
1872	Bishop James Murray from Maitland negotiates with Dominican sisters in Cabra regarding Deaf education in Australia
1873	Catherine Sullivan attends the Dominican boarding school in Maitland for a Catholic education
1875	From Cabra, Ireland, Sister Gabriel Hogan arrives in Newcastle and begins Deaf education in the Catholic System in Australia William and Anastasia Dwyer arrive in Australia. William begins teaching in the Government system in Albury. NSW
1880	Conference of Milan
1884	Foundation stone laid at the new school at Waratah on feast of the Rosary, 7 October

1887	Sister Columba Dwyer and Miss Marianne Hanney train with Sister Gabriel as teachers of the Deaf
1895	Sister Columba Dwyer is appointed Superior of the Convent at Waratah
1903 – 1914	Pius X is Pope
1909 – 1931	Patrick Vincent Dwyer, Bishop of Maitland
1914	Catholic Deaf Association is established in Sydney
1914	Sister Gabriel Hogan dies
	Marie Wallis starts school at Waratah Over 30 Ex-pupils men and women from Victoria attend the Retreat at Waratah
1918	Don Wallis starts school at Waratah
1920	Archbishop Michael Kelly negotiates with Christian Brothers in Cabra regarding staffing a school for Deaf boys in Australia
1922	St Gabriel's School for Deaf Boys is established in Castle Hill Christian Brothers, Joseph O'Farrell and Damian Allan arrive from Cabra to teach
1923	Don Wallis and other Deaf boys are transferred from Waratah to St Gabriel's
1924	Sister Columba Dwyer dies
1924	Catholic Deaf Association in Victoria is established Deaf Retreat and Reunion at Waratah
1927	Kathleen Walsh starts school at Waratah
1931	Don Wallis leaves school at St Gabriel's Kathleen Walsh leaves school at Waratah
1936	Father John Pierce appointed as chaplain to the Deaf community in Victoria
1935	Reunion in Waratah – Kathleen attends
1948	*Delgany*, Portsea Victoria: A school for Deaf children opens and becomes an Oral school
1953	St Gabriel's School, Castle Hill NSW ceases to teach Australian-Irish Sign language and becomes an Oral school

TIMELINE – FAMILY

1908	Abraham Wallis and Emma Corcoran marry in Carlton and live at Strath Creek
1908	Marie Wallis is born in Yea
1909	Richard Walsh and Mary Adeline Walsh marry at Sts. Michael's and John's Church, Horsham
1912	Donald Corcoran Wallis is born in Kilmore (living in Pyalong)
1916	Kathleen Agnes Walsh is born at Hamilton
1916	Marie Corcoran Wallis begins school at Waratah School for Deaf Children
1918	Don begins school at Waratah
1923	Don moves to St Gabriel's School for Deaf Boys
1926	Marie Wallis leaves school at Waratah
1926	Kathleen's family moves from Nhill in the Wimmera to Mt Gwynne near Barooga/Mulwala
1927	Don's mother, Emma, sets up Wallis' Café in Seymour and Marie works with her
1927	Kathleen goes to school at Waratah
1930	Charles Patrick Wallis begins school at St Gabriel's
1931	Don leaves school at St Gabriel's and Kathleen leaves school at Waratah
1932	Don's brother, John Wallis is ordained at Kilmore after his seminary days at Springwood and Manly, NSW
1940	Kathleen Walsh and Don Wallis announce their engagement
1941	Kathleen Walsh and Don Wallis marry at St Joseph's Church Barooga NSW and set up their home at Hughesdale, Melbourne, Victoria
1942	Carmel Mary Wallis born in Melbourne
1943	Kathleen's father, Richard Walsh, dies
1945	Bernadette Therese Wallis is born in Bethlehem Hospital, Melbourne
1945	Don's father, Abraham Wallis, dies
1947	Don and Kathleen move to Sydney Road, Fawkner, Melbourne
	Don's brother, Brian Wallis, is ordained a priest at Kilmore after seminary training at Werribee, Victoria
1950	Margaret Anne Wallis is born at Sacred Heart Hospital, Moreland Victoria
1952	Don and Kathleen move to *Forest Vale*, Berrigan
1955	Don's mother, Emma Wallis, dies

1960	Don and Kathleen move to the property next door, *Rosedale*, Berrigan
	Carmel joins the Presentation Sisters in Wagga Wagga, NSW
1965	Bernadette joins the Missionary Sisters of Service in Hobart, Tasmania
1967	Don and Kathleen sell the farm and buy a home in O'Leary Street, Wangaratta
1969	Margaret begins nursing at the Mercy Hospital, Albury NSW
1973	Kathleen's mother, Mary Adeline Walsh, dies
1975	Kathleen and Don's daughter, Margaret marries David Percy in St Patrick's, Wangaratta
1985	Don Corcoran Wallis dies and is buried in Wangaratta
1986	Kathleen sells the house at Wangaratta and moves to Albury
1991	Bernadette begins work in the Deaf community through the John Pierce Centre
2006	Kathleen moves out of her home and moves to Wagga Wagga for residential care
2008	Kathleen and Don's grandchild, Mark marries Jennifer Ewing in Denver, USA
2010	Kathleen Wallis dies and is buried in Wangaratta Hudson Jacob Percy is born in Denver, USA
2016	Kathleen and Don's grandchild, Joseph marries Emily Sinclair in Albury, NSW

Although the content of this book is a result of extensive research, any contributions towards identifying unnamed people in the photographs will be gratefully accepted

Please contact the author via Missionary Sisters of Service:

mssadmin@missionarysisters.org.au

or

info@johnwallisfoundation.org.au

Bernadette Therese Wallis was born to profoundly Deaf parents and although a hearing child, her first language of communication was Australian-Irish Sign Language. Her parents, Kathleen and Donald, initially lived in Melbourne where her father was a tailor. Then, with their three children, her parents moved to the rural town of Berrigan NSW where they operated a successful farming and dairy supply business.

Bernadette enjoyed a Catholic upbringing with predominantly Irish heritage and as an adult, joined an Australian Catholic religious order founded by Donald's brother, Father John Wallis; the Missionary Sisters of Service in Tasmania. She worked pastorally in rural and outback parish settings of Tasmania and western NSW before moving back to Melbourne. Here, she worked with a Catholic Deaf organisation, The John Pierce Centre, and provided advocacy, counselling and spirituality in the Deaf community. Bernadette loves the Australian bush and continues to maintain strong friendships and connections with the Deaf community.

Besides holding leadership positions in her congregation, Bernadette is a director of The John Wallis Foundation, which has been established to work in today's world while upholding the spirit of the Missionary Sisters of Service and its founder.